THE REST IS SMALL POTATOES

BY

JAMES GANNONE

The Rest Is Small Potatoes

© 2017 by James Gannone

Book design by SeaGrove Press
Edited by Ronald Thomas Rollet
Copy Edited by Koren Cowgill

ISBN: 978-0-9993218-0-5
Library of Congress Control Number: 2017952452

Printed in the United States of America

SeaGrove Press
638 Sunset Blvd
Cape May, New Jersey 08204
seagrovepress@gmail.com

DEDICATION

This book is dedicated to Christine, Michael and Lillian whose tolerance enabled me.

ACKNOWLEDGMENTS

The encouragement of my friend Jack Walters, who was a writer, poet and gentlemen, planted the seed to write this story.

The members of the Writer's Workshop founded and directed by Ron Rollet—I thank them one and all. My story would not have been written without their patience.

TABLE OF CONTENTS

TABLE OF CONTENTS

Preface

The original plan for this book was a story of my four years in the Democratic Republic of the Congo as a pilot for the cabinet and generals of the Joseph Kabila regime. I thought Christine Cote, my wife of forty plus years, was going to write it from the diary I kept and the emails we exchanged while I was in Congo from 2002 to 2006.

All of those notions changed when I was exposed to and—after a qualifying evening—invited to join the Writer's Workshop founded and directed by Ron Rollet. I thought it was the subject matter that piqued his interest enough to give me a try and found out later that was not true. As he explained (more than once, but I have a fairly hard head when it comes to praise for whatever I do or have done), Ron was convinced I could actually write my own story because of the way I used language in the telling of it—or, as he put it, I had a "voice" of my own. Later, Ron admitted that it is rare to find a non-writer who nevertheless has developed a knack for expressing himself in a unique way. He said that good writers spend their whole career developing this thing called voice. Who would have guessed I possessed this elusive talent? Not me.

The acceptance into the Workshop came in the form of a challenge. I had to write the story because it was mine, period. However, self-examination and self-revelation were going to be required in order to make sense of my life's ups and downs (all puns intended). Who runs off to fly a dictator's henchmen around in one of the most dangerous countries in the world when he has a family that loves him, a dog, a thirty-foot sailboat and a house on the Jersey Cape near the water? There was something wrong with the picture.

Ron wanted to make sure I was aware of the commitment such an undertaking required. Did I know I would have to come across with my personal flaws? Perfect is boring, he said. If you want more than your family to read it you will have to make it worth reading.

I thought I would be the last one to write any book. I dodged college preparatory English in high school because I was afraid of the term paper requirement. Like any training, learning to write is a painful process and I don't see myself emerging from behind its learning curve anytime soon. I'm not sure there is an end to it. I do know, without encouragement from Ron and others in the group I would have withered in this process. The seventy years of living that were already banked had to be exposed and put into a readable form.

At the weekly Workshop meeting, we read and respond to each other's work. These group sessions lasting three to four hours can be difficult, even eviscerating at times. As the least experienced participant, this inner humbling occurred more than once. My growth process as a writer began the first night. The group helped me improve every page. I do read for enjoyment but writing my own story was quite new territory for me. This five-year exercise has taught me whatever I know about writing. The patience of the group in listening to my many rewrites suggests canonization is in order for all. None of them more than the director of the group.

Sharing personal information with a half dozen others, whom I barely knew, was an obstacle and the decision to publish remains a question with deeper roots. Why reveal personal, compromising stories to the public and be subject to criticism, which I felt would surely come? Leaving those parts out would make an incomplete package. However, I realized that most of the people who would be hurt or disappointed by my life choices have passed away.

The Marine Corps and Vietnam were formative to who I became and am, though I never considered them a wrong turn, save for a few moments at Parris Island. There are regrets, though. The experiences I missed by wrong decisions cannot be recovered. I went to Europe by myself in the summer of 1970 and chose going to Stockholm from Paris instead of to Pamplona. I am sorry to this day not having taken part in the bull running when I was able and full of myself. There were other forks in the road I could have taken but many would have altered or thwarted the path to the Congo. Without having flown for some scurrilous operators and without the Corps, I wouldn't have been mentally prepared for Africa.

Justification of my behavior in the sixties and seventies as a product of the times is an easy out. Many strayed then. I like to think of those errors as youthful indiscretions, though they speak to my propensity toward enjoying risk in work and play. Cathartic as the writing has been for me, perhaps sharing my journey may stoke some memories in others who negotiated their way through those turbulent times.

The foolish behavior that put me in jail hinders my self-esteem but does not define my life. I have done more good than bad—of that I am sure. Just look at my children. Then as now I remain lucky in the big things. I went to war and didn't suffer like so many, I've been married to the same fine woman for forty-two years, have two great kids and all are healthy. The rest is small potatoes.

The following words tell my story.

Chapter 1
Arriving in Kinshasa

The journey from Philadelphia to Kinshasa, the capital of the Democratic Republic of the Congo (DRC), takes twenty-four hours. The N'djili airport has a single, three-mile-long runway that is an alternate landing site for the space shuttle. Stepping out into the warm night air, I begin to crack a sweat immediately. It is the humidity, the closeness, that one feels first. I am four degrees south of the equator in this city of nine million founded in 1861 by Henry Stanley.

The nice fellow portrayed by Spencer Tracy in "Stanley and Livingstone," has almost no resemblance to the real Stanley. In Hollywood's version of history, he wasn't laying to the backs of native Congolese with a hippo-hided chicotte. It and worse were de rigueur in the Congo Free State when it was King Leopold's garden. Colonization under the Belgians was brutal here.

This country is the size of the United States east of the Mississippi. The DRC is located south of the Sahara desert regions that stretch across most of the northern part of the continent. It is a country of thick jungles and grass savannas. There is a narrow boundary on the west coast with the South Atlantic Ocean, where the Congo River empties into the sea at the small town of Muanda. The DRC extends eastbound from the Atlantic all the way to Tanzania, which borders on the Indian Ocean.

Some consider the Democratic Republic of the Congo the most dangerous country in the world, but I am not getting that impression. This is my first visit to Africa and, at fifty-five, it is about time. I passed up on a chance to go to Kenya in the summer of 1970, when I traveled in Europe as a student.

The job that brings me here came about quite by chance. A fellow named Tim Roman posted a brief ad in an aviation trade paper that said, "Looking for a Sabreliner Captain to work in Africa." The Sabreliner is an eight-passenger executive jet. I just happened to be current in that airplane, with a fresh FAA Instrument Competency letter good for six months.

Roman has a contract to provide the President of DRC with transportation in a Gulfstream jet and members of the cabinet in a Sabreliner. This is to be VIP work African style. I am not coming here to suffer at the bottom of the food chain, either. I am, once again, chasing a buck and will be paid in cash USD with no paperwork. I don't feel scared yet—no reason to—but this is a dictatorship with the underlying tension that accompanies such absolute rule.

Nearly two hundred passengers file down the stairs that are pushed up against the exit—no air-conditioned passenger boarding bridge here. I can see a building with the name VIP lounge. There are some business jets parked in front of it, but I don't make the connection that I will be flying one of them. The floodlights of the airport ramp highlight the black foreheads of the great majority of passengers. There are only a handful of Caucasians aboard. We all move like a massive amoeba toward the reception doors of the terminal.

The reception area is crowded and checking our paperwork is a painfully slow process. After Visas, General Customs Declarations and health cards are examined, we head to the baggage claim area, which becomes a bit of a free-for-all scramble for positions next to the conveyor belt. There is a musty smell from the moldy concrete walls and floor. The humidity is so oppressive that I am reminded of Joseph Conrad's *Heart of Darkness*: "In the tropics one must before everything keep calm."

It seems like an hour before the first bags appear despite the fact that our plane is the only airliner on the ramp. Although there are a few tall people, for the most part I am a head above the rest, which isolates me somewhat from contact with the odors below in the melee. This humid climate and the Third World limits to personal hygiene are part of the package. The other passengers aren't constrained by any pressures to queue up, or so it seems.

There is no hint yet of anyone from Roman's company who could get me out of this turmoil before I lose the security that the crowd gives me. I don't want to be left here as bait for scavenging young men looking for an easy mark.

After more than an hour of the baggage drama, I pass through the terminal exit doors with my rollaway bag that—gratefully—made the transfer in Paris to the Kinshasa-bound flight. Outside in comparatively fresh, breathable air, I am surrounded by people trying to hustle me. My passport and money is in a wallet hanging around my neck and under my buttoned shirt so I consider myself somewhat safe from pickpockets, but remain vigilant always touching my bags, waiting for the diversionary bump.

Standing on a curb in a parking area, hoping someone was sent to pick up the new guy, doesn't seem to be getting me anywhere. I go back inside, where the crowd has thinned out a little. I find a corner, which provides a temporary sanctuary, to look through the paperwork that I brought for a contact phone number to call—something I wish I'd readied on the flight in case I needed it.

Fortunately, I had the forethought to bring small denomination dollars to get access to things like a phone or something to drink, without having to pony up a twenty and get no change. I find the phone number and a booth to make a call. Tim answers, which I take for a stroke of luck. He is surprised that I am here! This is not a good start. It doesn't indicate that he is running a tight ship. "Just stay there, I'll come and get you," he says.

I am wearing a white pilot's shirt with epaulets and tie in order to look professional. That shirt and ten dollars helps me get into the VIP lounge. The lounge is a rectangular room about twenty-five by fifty feet, with high ceilings and a few support columns that have gilded, ornamental trim at the top. There are numerous sets of cushioned furniture grouped on rugs around coffee tables. The walls are white with some African art hanging on them. A television is at one end of the room near the door that opens out onto the airport ramp. The other end is where the entrance and the security-screening machine greet the departing passengers. I take an empty seat and ask one of the waitresses for a beer. It is my first combat-sized bottle of beer (almost a liter) and makes me feel a little relaxed. The beer is cold and good. Down it goes and I start a second one.

A tall, stocky fellow named Bengilla comes with Frank, the pilot that I am relieving. I can see them from across the room and know immediately they are my ride. Frank looks familiar and then I remember meeting him at the Laredo International Airport in the small, dark hours early one morning. We were both waiting to clear customs from Mexico. He seems more haggard and gray since I'd last seen him. Bengilla takes my bags, we buy a couple of more beers for the road and are off. The drive to Kinshasa and the "guesthouse," as it is called, takes about an hour.

The first part of the city we come to is Masina, thick with people. It is the most volatile place in the city, because of the overcrowding and the miserable living conditions. Tonight there is bumper-to-bumper traffic and crowds of people, all hot and sweaty even at eleven o'clock in the evening, four and five deep on each side of the road. Trash blows about in the light movement of dusty air that cars stir up as they go by at less than twenty-five miles an hour. Water is sold on the street here in small plastic bags, like water balloons. My colleagues tell me not to try any unless I want to get sick. It is for locals only. There are no awful organic odors, which I was anticipating from what I'd read about the deplorable infrastructure that exists in this part of the city. However, the stench and worse would come I was certain, just like in Da Nang, Vietnam, or Kingston, Jamaica.

A half-dozen roadblocks, with well-armed guards, along the route all require stopping. They ask for cigarettes, food or beer and look in the trunks of some cars, backing up traffic when they do. Frank gives them a less-than-kind "no" when they solicit us and we are on our way again through the city and up a hill that overlooks it and the Congo River.

Finally, we arrive at 66 Allée Verte with its tall metal doors and armed security guards. The moldy, white-washed masonry walls surrounding the property are capped by embedded broken glass bottles and the entry door is protected by barbed wire across its top, as are all the residential properties that I notice thus far. I expect to encounter some of this, based on the research I did on the CIA's website before coming, but the effect is still impressive.

The driveway is on an incline and the swimming pool is visible at the bottom of the drive. The house overlooks a steep valley with houses on both sides.

A servant meets us promptly and takes my bags into the residence where I am to live for the next month. There I meet Tom and Tennessee Tim, brother Marines, who had been aircraft mechanics in the Air Wing of the Corps. They are at least fifteen years younger than I am and thus missed the Vietnam War.

Tom, from Lake Havasu, Arizona, is sporting a cast from mid-thigh all the way down his left leg and foot, with a stainless steel rod connected by some titanium pins coming out of the cast at a number of places. I have to say he is pretty nimble getting around on his hand crutches. At close to six feet tall and about a hundred eighty pounds, Tom is good-looking with a pleasant demeanor and ready smile. In our initial "get to know something about each other conversation," he mentions that he was shot in the house a few weeks earlier and that is what brought about the armed Presidential guards at the entrance doors. There are mixed stories about who did it, a thief or an unpaid, angry pimp. Nobody pushes the subject, certainly not I.

Tim is a smoker and his voice sounds like years of two packs of Camels a day. He is from the hills of Tennessee, where people say "lookie here" if they really want your attention. He is a bit leaner than Tom, a wiry sort with dirty blonde hair and ruddy complexion. Frank, the tallest of the lot, lives here as well but doesn't seem very popular with anyone that I've met so far. He will be going back to McAllen, Texas, tomorrow night.

There is a dedicated refrigerator just for beer at the Allée Verte house. These guys are serious about their beer and other pleasures. The pool outside has a thatched roof hut at one end and some huge speakers connected to a sound system. Well cared for potted plants of all sorts are placed around the property. On the porch leading into the house there is a large cage with an African Gray parrot in it.

All in all, it appears to be a nice place to live and spend my free time when I am not busy flying. The more I fly, the better for Tim and Tom, because when I'm flying they can kick back as soon as they see the airplane off. When I return, they will be there to do the necessary maintenance to keep the plane ready 24/7.

I finally go to bed with the understanding that I will meet Deo, my First Officer, in the morning, and fly the airplane with Frank to get familiarized with the airport. After a light but adequate sleep, I get up, do my toilet and come out to the living area. The mechanics are going to the airport to see Tim off in the Gulfstream. He is taking the President to South Africa this morning. Before they go, Tom introduces me to Pappa Joe and tells me to have him make me an omelet with Piri Piri (very hot habanero pepper sauce, used all over the continent). Pappa Joe was one of many chefs for Mubuto when he reigned. Joe asks if I would like breakfast and I say yes. Shortly, he serves me a full breakfast at an attractive place setting in the dinning room. It is a new experience being catered to like this, one I can easily get used to.

Deo shows up after breakfast and is a gentleman. His English is good and he can also speak another four or five languages. The drive out to the airport in the daylight gives me a clearer view of what life is like here in this sprawling city. We go by markets offering anything and everything. People sell whatever they can or beg at traffic intersections. Women walk by with water jugs and packages balanced naturally on their heads, as if they were unaware of carrying a thing. The sides of the streets are thick with people and there are overloaded trucks and taxis bulging with occupants everywhere. People talking and trucks rumbling, all punctuated with the sounds of blowing horns—life abounds here!

At the airport Deo takes charge of whatever needs to be done on the ground. He sees to the fueling of the airplane and filing the flight plan. In the meantime, someone introduces me to the rest of the ground crew. Zekos and Bart are Congolese and handle the simple tasks of airplane maintenance, so Tim and Tom don't have to do things like cleaning and removing the screws that hold inspection panels in place. When I get into the cockpit of the airplane, I feel, for the first time in two days, that I am in familiar surroundings. It's like putting on an old pair of shoes. I know the Sabreliner, but nothing of the Congo yet. When all is ready, we take a local orientation flight. Again, there is plenty to learn, from the countryside to the air traffic control procedures, which are not as structured as stateside. This is all exciting and beyond what I imagined. I feel like I made a good move coming here and want Chris to share in the experience of it, too.

We return to the airport after twenty minutes of flying west towards the Atlantic Ocean, though we don't go far enough to see it. Tim Roman is at the airport now and on his way to the Gulfstream, which is parked on the ramp in front of the VIP lounge just ahead of where we park the Sabreliner. This is the first I have encountered him face-to-face since we met in the States several weeks ago. He sees me and takes a couple of steps out of his way to shake hands. He says without a smile, "The mechanics will show you the ropes. It's all VIP work. You're on your own." That's it? No attempts at a warm or even friendly welcoming greeting, just: "You're on your own." I am not quite sure, but I think I like that cold approach and suggestion of freedom, although it is a bit sobering.

Chapter 2
From Martinsville to the Corps

Martinsville is a small town in New Jersey, twenty-five miles west of New York City. It lies next to the first ridge of the Watchung Mountains, a foothill to the Appalachians. I spent ages two through eighteen (1950-1966) there. It was country living where I could hunt for rabbits or even deer within a two-minute walk from the back door of our house. This part of central New Jersey during the 1950s was still a place where the Postal Service had Rural Free Delivery by letter carriers using their own vehicles.

The closest town, Bound Brook, is to the southeast. There is a train station there used mostly by commuters working in New York City. The drive to Bound Brook from Martinsville takes fifteen minutes across the valley, past the dam end of the Bound Brook Water Company's reservoir, and down a winding mountain road out of the valley. This is Chimney Rock Road. It follows the brook that fed the water company's reservoir and then by a stone quarry to the flat land south of US Route 22. If you wanted to drive to New York City, a left turn onto Route 22 was the way to go. Without traffic it was forty-five minutes to the entrance of the Lincoln Tunnel, with Times Square at the other end.

The main road across Martinsville is Washington Valley Road, so named because George Washington and much of his Continental Army were all over these Watchung Mountains from May of 1777 to June of 1779, wintering in the southern part of the valley. Driving through Martinsville took about two minutes. It was a complete town, more than just a wide spot in the road. North of the Valley Road was the First Watchung Mountain with the valley and reservoir off to the south.

When traveling from the east on the north side of Valley Road, the first indication of the coming town was a small sign for Doctor Allagrante's office. Next on that side of the road, with a few houses in between, was a general store followed by Martinsville's elementary school, a two-story brick structure with a playground behind it. My younger brother (by two years) and I walked to that school every day from kindergarten through fourth grade carrying our metal lunch boxes. When it rained we wore the yellow rain coats and galoshes that other kids did. It was all Norman Rockwell.

Across from the school, when traveling westbound, is the first of three intersections through town. Chimney Rock Road ends there at Valley Road, where it winds north from Bound Brook. To the west side of the school, on the edge of the parking lot, stood the small public library. Further up the mountainside, behind and next to the school playground was a community center known as the clubhouse. Built in 1920, this two-story structure had a stage upstairs for the local players group. It also substituted as a missionary Catholic Church while its permanent brick structure was being built at the other end of town. Home of the Martinsville Boy Scout Troop, the clubhouse also served as a recreation center in the summer for the local grammar school-aged children.

In addition to the school on the north side, the Chimney Rock Road intersection included Penny's Texaco on the west side and Waldron's newspaper and tobacco store on the east side. The Martinsville post office was located in Waldron's as well. Houses were interspersed between the Methodist Church, the Martinsville bakery, a hardware store, and Tony's barbershop on the south side. The next intersection, a quarter of a mile to the west, where Quarry Lane met Valley Road, held Bueno's butcher shop on the east corner. Opposite the butcher shop was an Esso gas station. The north side of Valley Road contained houses from the school to the Esso station.

The third intersection consisted of Mt. Horeb Road branching off Washington Valley Road and up the mountain a stone's throw from where Quarry Lane ended. The Hoffman House held down the northeastern side of the fork in the road. It was the town bar—originally a stagecoach stop and hotel—complete with daily patrons. A blacksmith's shop and a cobbler were across from the Hoffman House. Westbound on the south side there were two more houses, the firehouse and finally the Catholic Church.

Quarry Lane came north from further down in the valley and ended at the Bound Brook Reservoir, a favorite place to swim—though forbidden by my parents. Until I joined the Marines in 1966, I lived on that road in a one bathroom Cape Cod style house that my father built with the help of friends.

My brother and I would meet my father at Bueno's butcher shop at noontime on Saturdays. He stopped there, on his way home from working a half-day, to pick up the weekly meat order. Mr. Bueno made him lunch while putting together our order and they gave each other a hard time. My father called him Zeke and would complain that last week's roast was tough and the butcher would say my mother didn't know how to cook. They were friends from the west end of Bound Brook where their respective families settled when they got off the boat from Italy.

Seeing my father there felt good, somehow right. He was happy, as he should have been, since he had everything that counts. He had a religion, a healthy family, a job, a house, and friends. Because he and my mother were disciplined, he paid his bills on time, too. He went bowling once a week and took my brother and me to eight o'clock mass every Sunday.

Quarry Lane was paved from Washington Valley Road for a half a mile and then became a dirt road further on to the reservoir, with the quarry swimming hole just before and to the west. The road was an incline that provided sleigh riding in the winter and an ever-present challenge, because I was overweight, for me to reach the Valley Road on my bike. Just walking all the way up Quarry Lane was a chore.

Eating disorders weren't in vogue then. Obesity wasn't a word anyone used. Ridicule was popular though, especially from the other kids. I was taunted by "fatso" or worse names. One incident had me running home to my mother humiliated and in tears after being calling a "tub of lard" by a mean-spirited older boy. Children's capacity for cruelty is difficult to fathom let alone rationalize.

Why I was in this condition is debatable. The Italian influence played a part. The reaction to impoverished times and hunger was to fill up with large amounts of pasta. My mother miscarried more than once before I finally arrived, which made my parents particularly protective. Almost losing me to whooping cough probably added to a "good-he's-eating" approach.

Whatever the reasons, I ended up with a spare tire around my gut for life. I hated myself, hated my body so much that I wouldn't do anything to call attention to it, even refusing to dance when it was time for that. The thought of rejection by girls petrified me. Self-esteem was out of the question. I was always one of the last to be picked when kids chose sides for teams because I was the slowest. Taking my t-shirt off in gym class when my side was "skins" was dreadful. The result was a desperate need for acceptance in adolescence that eventually pushed me towards Parris Island.

Sometimes people would ride their horses into town and have Fred the blacksmith, known as Uncle Fred to some of the kids, shoe them. He wasn't a big burly fellow like Longfellow's village smithy ("The smith, a mighty man is he/ With large and sinewy hands;/And the muscles of his brawny arms…"). He was old and stooped over. His hair was thin and most of it gone, but he was cheerful and loved kids. He had a chicken coop behind his house and I was there one time along with some other kids when he was going to have one of those chickens for dinner. He used a hatchet to chop the head off and then stuck it, neck first, in an old can to drain while he held the wiggling chicken by the feet. He said if he let it go it would have run around a bit. All this and he played banjo and sang songs.

When Fred had a horse for shoeing everything got dramatic, though it didn't happen that often anymore. Fred started the forge by putting a match to just a small piece of newspaper, tucking it into the coals, and then cranking the blower. Soon the coals were hot enough to turn a steel shoe white hot. Fred picked a new horseshoe out of a cardboard box and nestled it into the middle of the fire. When the shoe was ready he would pluck it out with long-handled tongs and start to shape it on the different parts of the anvil with his hammer. All the sparks flying made the scene come alive. Holding the hammer close to the head of the shoe, Fred tapped it once or twice in a less forceful but rhythmic way. He adjusted the position of the shoe every four or five times that he bounced the hammer off of the anvil. It wasn't violent, more workmanlike, and looked like he had done it a thousand times—and of course he had.

The finishing stage was when he put the red hot shoe into the water bucket to cool, complete with the steam and hissing that it made. When he could handle it, he would carry the shoe to the horse. He raised the hoof by lifting the front of its lower leg. The horse cooperated and Fred placed the hoof on his thick black leather apron to check the fit before he nailed it in place. If the shoe didn't fit properly, he took it back to the forge and started the process again. I felt lucky to be there when he was shoeing a horse, because the shop was usually closed. It had had its day.

When Fred died, an Irishman named Shamus Brady took over the business. Shamus had a small forge set up in the back of his pickup truck with everything he needed. A farrier who made house calls, Brady was the very image that Longfellow's poem described—with his big arms and full head of wavy black hair. The old blacksmith shop eventually became home to the first bank in Martinsville.

Today the town is unrecognizable to an older eye who wasn't there during the period when the town evolved into an expensive New York bedroom community.

There was hunting, trapping, and fishing in the hills and streams in that part of New Jersey during the 1950's. My father took my brother and me fishing on the first day of trout season when we were between five and ten years old. The season started at eight o'clock on a Saturday morning in April and we would go to a stream that the State had stocked earlier in the week. Our whole family went to the New Jersey State fish hatchery in Hackettstown, NJ, to observe the process of growing trout for release. Even then New Jersey was a crowded state. Fishermen were lined up shoulder to shoulder on the banks of those streams.

I also trapped muskrat and raccoons with my friend Andrew. He was two years older, a big difference at those ages. He had a shotgun before I did, but I got one for my birthday when I turned twelve—the minimum age for hunting without an adult.

I was fortunate, by today's standards, to grow up in a home with two parents—a father who worked and a mother who kept house and canned wild strawberries that she picked in the field behind our house. In early spring she gathered dandelions and other greens in that field for the meatless Italian soup she made on Fridays.

We lived on what my father made as an automobile mechanic. Sometimes he would do repairs on cars at the house on weekends for extra money. My folks paid cash or didn't buy. I heard "money doesn't grow on trees" plenty of times. There was no foul language in the house, but there were occasional bigoted remarks from either parent. Prejudice about and by the immigrants who came to this land of opportunity was commonplace. People gave—and still give—derogatory names to every incoming nationality. I imagine that if you are near the bottom of the social strata, thinking of others as being even further beneath you might boost your self-esteem.

My father was one hundred percent Italian and my mother was fifty percent Scottish and fifty percent Irish. I always felt the Italian part of me was the more compassionate and sensitive side, while the Scottish/Irish was the tougher side. In some ways my mother had a harder life than my father did when she grew up. Her mother died early and I don't think their stepmother was very kind to my mother and her two sisters.

My father quit high school in his freshman year to help out at home when his father died. Vito Iannone had a miserable job in a chemical factory shoveling coal in the boiler room. Like so many others at the time, his wife and two children stayed in Italy until he earned enough to bring them to America.

There was a story that my paternal grandfather put newspaper inside his shoe when there was a hole worn in the sole. This temporary fix allowed him to walk to work and save the pennies that the trolley would have cost. True or not, it was a great story that I did not forget.

In the Depression, just having a job was an accomplishment. My father worked at the same place for thirty-seven years. He was proud of his work but embarrassed by the persistent dirty hands that went with it. His flat feet kept him out of the service during the Second World War.

Jimmy, as he was known, was well thought of in his trade. His work ethic and motivation for supporting his growing family resulted in his becoming the lead mechanic in an eight-bay garage in North Plainfield, NJ. The owners decided to specialize, and the garage became known for its brakes and front-end work. Jimmy was the go-to guy in central New Jersey if you had problems in those areas. He told me time and again that if I ever became a mechanic he would break my back. Unfortunately, being the hardheaded fellow that I was, his admonishments only fueled my interest in cars and—of course—hot rods. He was a good man and good at what he did. I couldn't have asked for a better model of how to live.

Every summer my father had a week's vacation from his job and the family would travel somewhere by car. When we were young we stayed in a bungalow at Monmouth Beach that his boss owned and spent our vacation time there. We went to the beach and at least once to Asbury Park's boardwalk. The treat for my parents was a visit to the Monmouth Park horse racing track. As we got older there were trips to Washington, DC, Williamsburg and Niagara Falls. In Virginia I saw drinking fountains "for colored only" and knew I was in a different world. My mother and father were well-intentioned parents trying to give their boys a square start in a world somewhat less fouled than the one we are surrounded by now.

The blue-collar life was not what they dreamed of for their sons. The day that my first grade teacher told my mother I was college material thrilled her and, later, my father when she told him. They wanted a better life for their boys than they had. Don't all parents? What they gave my brother and me was as good as anyone could have been given and surely better than most get now. It was a stable, constant household with supper at six, and eight o'clock Sunday Mass with shirt and tie. My father went to work five and a half days a week and bowled on Wednesday nights. My mother cleaned, canned, cooked, washed the clothes, darned our socks, and everything else that mothers did at the time.

There was an annual family fishing trip to Barnegat Bay. We would usually catch flounder and plenty of them. Sometimes we'd catch blowfish, too. My father showed us how to rub their bellies to make them blow themselves up like a ball and he would bounce them on the deck. Everyone was happy, even carefree. My mother was involved just like us. She was strong and hard with a stiff upper lip. My father was really the softer of the two. He wept the morning that I left the house to go to Parris Island and when I boarded the airplane to go to Vietnam six months later. So preoccupied with my own adolescence at that time, I had no appreciation of what a decent and good man he was.

Once a year we would all go to a Yankee game. I got to see Mickey Mantle play and the rest the Yankees of that era. I had no idea at the time how significant those players would become to the game. Yankee Stadium was magnificent. The grass was so green and the new white baseballs were a stunning contrast to the balls my brother and I played with, which were old and sometimes held together with black tape. The public address system at Yankee Stadium was only used for the National Anthem, one time through the batting order, and then to announce a pinch hitter or relief pitcher. No other music or bullshit, just the sounds of the crack of the bat, the roar of the crowd, or Mantle kicking the water fountain after striking out, again. It was another example of the illusion of simpler times. Few people knew of the Mick's sordid problems. As the idol of men and boys alike, Mantle had little chance of surviving so much adulation without hiding somewhere or in something.

My father's family all lived in Bound Brook. Leaving Bound Brook even just fifteen minutes away to marry a non-Italian and a non-Catholic woman was a bold move on his part. My mother and father moved in with his family when they were first married. It was the beginning of her indoctrination to the Italian way of life. At first, my father's sisters would not allow my mother to even clean the house because, after all, she wasn't Italian so how could she know how to clean properly? She got through it and even became a good cook by their standards. She could make her own raviolis from scratch with the best of them.

Bound Brook was where my father's father came from Ellis Island. Vito Iannone is the name on his gravestone. His wife, Philomena, came later when he had made enough money to pay her passage. The family grew to include three sisters and three brothers in one house. When my father was able to buy a small, half acre piece of land in Martinsville for six hundred dollars, they all worked it as one big garden, growing mostly peppers and tomatoes. After he built the house, they kept a garden there for many years eventually planting four apple and two pear trees as well.

My brother and I visited our Italian relatives often and those visits were always good. Our cousins were happy to see us and we usually got to drink soda and eat cake for one reason or another. The Iannones were more expressive than my mother's family—Mediterranean temperament versus British reserve. It was just a little more formal to visit my mother's relations, whom we saw less often because they lived twice as far away.

My mother had a twin sister, Ruth. Aunt Ruth and Uncle Joe lived in Princeton and had two daughters. We got a briefing from my parents not to act like "wild Indians" when we got there. Aunt Ruth was strict like my mother but she was nice to us as were all of my aunts and uncles on both sides of the family. My mother's other sister, Aunt Evelyn, and her husband George had three boys and lived on top of a hill in a house with lightning rods on the roof—a novelty to us. They had a small boat in the Millstone River with an outboard motor on it and a tractor to cut the lawn that surrounded their house. There was a huge, regulation slate-top pool table in their cellar as well.

Adolescence came on me like a hard rain. Of course, girls frightened and attracted me. I wasn't alone in that forest of raging hormones and questions about life, just a little more awkward than most because of my weight. I think it made me more desperate than most for peer acceptance and may have been the underlying force behind the reckless behavior that didn't stop as an adult.

At twelve years old I hooked up with a group of boys who were as anxious as I was to grow up. We played poker, drank beer and, naturally, smoked cigarettes. We even tried sniffing glue. Some of us developed a twisted obsession to be bad. Being known as a "badass" was a very desirable reputation. I found that world of intimidation, so prevalent in male behavior, both scary and exciting. I drew a lot of attention because I was big for my age—almost six feet tall and over two hundred pounds—which made playing football in high school a foregone conclusion.

One of the boys in the group, Lance, had a father—Charlie—with a drywall business. Lance became quite the businessman himself. Once he found a neighbor who was old enough to have a Social Security number and drive, the door to the American form of rapacious capitalism opened. Lance put together a crew and he was the boss. We were twelve and thirteen-years-old, carrying sheetrock into houses or sanding the edges smooth, eating all of that dust but making good money.

The way the business worked was that Charlie's men nailed the sheetrock to the studs. The edges of the boards met at the corners or the middle of the walls or ceilings. These joints were covered with Spackle, a mud-like substance, and paper tape placed over that. A flat-bladed knife was drawn across to smooth out the lumps. When the Spackle was dry, more applications of mud were applied before being sanded smooth. Nailing the boards up and spackling them were the skilled parts of the drywall business. The carrying and sanding that we performed were the unskilled parts.

This job led to my getting drunk for the first time at twelve years old with my sidekick, Allie. Charlie introduced us to that portal into the land of altered states. We drank screwdrivers with him in the kitchen and all pissed off the back porch. Charlie gave me the nickname of "Skinny" that first night. It wasn't a mean dig at my physique or taken as that. Another friend, Craig, picked up on it and it stuck.

Charlie was about five foot eight inches with a full head of wavy black hair. He was a smiling ladies' man, the master of ceremonies at the local 4-H horse show and good at getting laughs from the crowd. He learned to ride in Missouri where he grew up, and, given an occasion, would put on his cowboy attire, saddle one of his cutting horses from the stables behind the house and ride into Martinsville tipping his hat to the ladies. Mounted on a silver-trimmed saddle atop a beautiful horse, Charlie made their hearts beat just a little faster. My friends and I loved him.

Lance kept the book with the figures showing the pay due everyone. As young boys, without business sense for the most part, we felt we were all on an equal footing and would share jointly in the money paid for each job. It was a surprise when our friend and leader made money the week we worked and he didn't. It seemed to us that he was stealing our hard-earned pay. Lance made it clear that if you weren't happy you didn't have to participate. He handled the money and that was it.

The oldest of us, Billy, the one with the Social Security number, had a new Ford convertible with a big V-8 motor in it—stylish crew transportation. Financing for the car was arranged by Lance, always the businessman. After each job we would stop at the closest Dairy Queen and have ice cream—not ten-cent cones but hot fudge sundaes! Lance would keep the tab in the book and pay the bill. One week I ate so much that I owed him money. Sitting in a convertible eating all that ice cream was the best part of the day, never mind how our work clothes stank of drying sweat covered with Spackle dust.

We were all over central New Jersey going from one new development to another, making piecework wages. We got paid by the number of sheetrock boards that we carried into the houses or for which part of the Spackle we sanded. Sometimes we made ten dollars an hour—big money in 1963. A house would have a dollar figure for the whole job. Charlie and Lance would often haggle over the price and the amount to be divided up amongst us. That amount was, of course, determined by the Lance.

One day we saw an old, three-wheeled Harley Davidson police motorcycle with weeds growing through it parked in a farmer's field. The farmer said it ran but needed a battery. He sold it to me for twenty-five dollars. I drove it all over Martinsville at night with my friends hanging on the back using a flashlight to see ahead. It had a working first, third and reverse gear. This was one rusty piece of junk, but we loved it. We did have fun on that thing with three and four of us hanging on to it while it shimmied and shook with its bent frame. One handle had the timing advance and retard control, which could make it backfire. Noises at that age were so exhilarating.

Soon I ran out of places to hide it. I couldn't just take that home at twelve years old, and my friends' parents weren't big on letting me leave it on their property either. The pressure was building as I approached the time I had to go away for a week to Boy Scout camp. I did the only logical thing I could think of. The day before I had to go to camp I drove it deep into the blackberry bushes behind our house. I told myself that my parents might not notice it.

After about three days at camp I got a letter from my father. He asked how I was doing, hoped all was well, and "Oh, by the way, James, I found your motorcycle but don't worry I took care of it." He gave it to one of the men he worked with. I thought it was a fair enough punishment. At least he didn't go on and on about it.

We started going to work very early in the morning, before six o'clock. To our delight one morning, as we passed Johnson's fruit farm stand at the eastern edge of Washington Valley Road, one of us noticed that they didn't put the fruit away at night, just covered it. We stopped and took a couple of baskets of peaches or tomatoes and the fun began. Mischief was our friend after all. From the moving car we pelted any targets that enticed our bent little minds. The lads went to the well once too often though. Farmer Johnson and his sons were there to greet my friends one Monday morning. I escaped that confrontation because I had gone to Boy Scout camp the day before. Timing is everything—sometimes.

We all had shotguns. Lance had a lever action Winchester saddle rifle, too, just like a cowboy in a Western movie. Shooting tin cans off fence posts was good stuff. Somehow we managed not to shoot one another. Idleness being the devil's workshop, one day we found a twelve-gauge double-barreled shotgun just lying around my friend's stable. It had orange paint on it and some rust. One of us thought it was a good idea to cut the barrel down with a hacksaw and we were off. We did it in steps. First we cut six inches from the muzzle and then another six until we got to the forestock. The barrel was about twelve inches long by then. Next thing to go was the stock. When we finished, it was a double-barreled, twelve-gauge pistol. Amazing that one of us didn't get shot or at least peppered with a few pellets that afternoon.

Like most boys my age, I grew up watching movies with John Wayne and John Garfield from the World War II era, and the war was usually the subject matter. Surely I wasn't alone when I got caught up in that terrible part of male adolescence, questioning whether I would be a disappointment to my father.

I remember being at the football awards assembly and along with Allie, my friend, drinking buddy and general class clown, getting a lowly Junior Varsity letter. I thought it embarrassed my father as much as me. I knew it was what I had earned, though. I didn't like football but I had no real choice since I was so big. Everyone just presumed that I would go out for it. Being overweight prevented me from developing any real athleticism. I didn't play much in the games because I wasn't very good. Practice was the worst part of it and I dreaded it daily. I sometimes ended up vomiting from the excessive exertion. The Corps was going to provide me a way of settling all of that self-doubt and loathing. I just didn't know it yet.

In 1963, I resisted the college preparatory program in high school. I didn't like studying or working so hard on the research papers in English and US History. I'd much rather take auto and machine shop classes. The immediate gratification of hands-on results did it for me.

Also, the talk I had with the head guidance counselor, Mr. Black, helped sour me on academia and turned out to be so ironic. When he asked me, "What do you want to be?" I said, "I want to be an airline pilot." This choice grew out of a seed planted by a hobby of building and flying model U-Control airplanes. "Well, you have to take calculus, physics…"—and on he went. He lost me in less than thirty seconds. Truth is, you don't need all that to fly. A little trigonometry helps, as does a sense of the sciences, but they aren't even a prerequisite to flying a jet.

An even temperament is the most important qualification in flying: the detachment needed to separate yourself from all of the distractions to your senses that are assaulted in a noisy cockpit. Focusing on what really matters at the time, particularly in times of emergency, is absolute. A cardinal rule in the cockpit is, "fly the airplane first then talk on the radio." When I look back at myself at that age, I see someone with the intelligence to be an engineer, but who lacked motivation, which is, after all, the key to all learning. Proper guidance could have made the difference. I don't have many regrets, though. I did get to fly the jet and in the African bush at that. Talk to any professional pilot about where I flew, and if he knows, you'll be able to read it in his face. Chances are he will be clueless, but I am getting a little ahead of myself here.

The answer to all of my confusion and indifference ended up being the Marines. If I had what it takes to be a Marine, they would make me tough. Just turn myself over to them and the rest will take care of itself. I had no idea the intensity involved in giving the government a blank check on my life. They didn't cash in the whole check though, as they did with so many others in that era who never got to be twenty years old. They did, however, take most of my remaining innocence and gave me the change in cynicism. As life went on, it became apparent that I got much more than I gave in the exchange.

I preferred working on my '57 Chevy to playing football or anything else. The rule in our house was that I had to pay for the car and my insurance or there would be no car. I could borrow my parents' car, but that wasn't good enough for me. My father went with me to buy the car—auto mechanics was his livelihood after all. We brought the Chevy home and he helped me rebuild the engine to make it a well running, dependable six-cylinder car. That wasn't good enough for me, though. I had to have the popular hot rod engine of the time and it wasn't long before I pulled the perfectly good straight 6 out and put in a 283 cubic inch V-8, bored out another eighth of an inch to enlarge it to 301 cubic inches. I also thought that three carburetors would be a good idea, and on they went. This move tried my father's patience, but he left me alone after some initial challenges about the lack of wisdom on my part. He just shook his head a lot.

My friends and I graduated high school in 1965. I stayed behind while most of them went off to college. My family did not have the kind of money it would cost, even if I wanted to go, although I am sure a way could have been found. I knocked around at different jobs and it wasn't long before I started to wonder if I was doing the right thing.

Finally, my father took me to work at the garage that he ran. If I insisted on a mechanically-oriented career path, then he would teach me properly— his way. For months all I was allowed to do was take the brake assemblies apart, after I had learned how to jack the car up properly and set the jack stands in the right places. I washed all of the parts and laid them out, in the order that I had removed them, next to their respective wheels for his inspection. Attention to detail was the rule. Soon I was cutting brake drums on a lathe, arc grinding new brake shoes to fit the cut drums and rebuilding power brake units.

I took a two week-long carburetor course given by General Motors at a local facility of theirs. That generated some talk of the General Motors Institute in Detroit that John DeLorean started when he was designing the GTO. However, the good feeling of working with tools did not last very long. The shine was wearing off it all.

I started thinking of college when I heard that my old high school line coach, Mr. Kane, had gone on to coach at Millersville State Teachers College, a small college in Pennsylvania. I called him to inquire about going there to play for him. He asked about my SAT scores. I had a 396 on the verbal portion, which was short four points of the 400 score required. It did not mater that I had cracked a thousand points when combined with the math portion.

Coach Kane said I could come out and take another test there and maybe score high enough. I went and took the test but again I came up four points short. "Who does this?" I thought. When I saw him that afternoon to discuss the results, he was visibly upset, with tears in his eyes. Carl Kane was a hard man and to see him like that was awful and chilling. A student there told me that he had gotten word earlier in the day that his brother had been killed in Vietnam. There was nothing more for me there so I drove back home.

Chapter 3
Parris Island

While listening to the radio on the drive home from Millersville, a Marine recruiting advertisement came on the air. It was as if the fidelity of the radio dramatically improved. The timing was spot on and hit me like an epiphany. The Marine Corps was offering a two-year enlistment, deviating from their usual requirement of a three-year minimum commitment. A "twelve month and twenty day tour" was the current Western Pacific orders that Marines going to Vietnam received.

At the time, unbeknownst to me, all physically fit males over eighteen were subject to a six-year military obligation: two years active duty followed by four years inactive reserve duty or six-months active duty with five-and-a-half-years active reserve duty. This conscription was administered by the Selective Service through the random assignment of numbers from low to high. If your number came up, you would get a letter with a salutation stating that "Your friends and neighbors have chosen you …" The marines hadn't drafted since the Korean War, but needed to in 1966. Some who thought they were going into the army at the induction center in Newark ended up randomly selected to go to Parris Island.

Avoiding the draft in the 1960's became an art form for the "non-adventuresome" male citizens who were on the receiving end of that warm letter. Those who could afford and attend college got an automatic deferment from their local draft board for their time in school. It was a bit more challenging for the rest of population to avoid getting drafted.

The sudden build-up for the Vietnam War required more troops and right away. I didn't know from Vietnam except for a few glimpses of photos in The Daily News, the only newspaper that came into our house. As it heated up, the Vietnam War was going to make the draft a political issue. Suddenly, there were songs with lyrics like, "Hey all you mothers out there, be the first one on your block to have your boy come home in a box." The country was en route to bitter polarization.

The seed for enlistment had been planted in me years before by men I met growing up: a couple of schoolteachers and a man who worked for my father. They had taken part in the wars of their generations in the Pacific or Korea or both. There was something about them. The one who had been in both wars said they took him to Korea in chains because he wasn't going otherwise. I believed him. Before I went to Vietnam I tried to get him to talk about combat or at least give me some idea of what it was like. All he would say is that you just don't know how you will react to it no matter how many times you deal with it. The more I thought about what he said the more it sounded like he had been in the middle of some lengthy, awful situations. Fortunately, I was to get only a taste of it, not a full dose of what intense combat was like.

I had a friend who, like me, did not go off to college in 1965 like so many others in our affluent, mostly college preparatory, high school class. Kenny Kreader liked the idea of a two-year commitment, too. His brother Larry had done three years in the Marines and was also a driving influence on us. Kenny and I went to see the recruiter in Plainfield, NJ. Staff Sergeant Wheatly had a recruiting office downstairs at the post office. He presented a typical poster image of a Marine, ramrod straight without a hint of humor in his demeanor. The creases on his clean, crisp uniform could have cut you. The sergeant asked if we thought we could stand someone calling us a girl. I hadn't really thought of that as the supreme insult before. He told us, "You will come out of Parris Island in the best shape of your lives." That turned out to be true enough. He made no other promises—didn't have to. We were sold before we got into his office. Again, I was fatso and had to lose thirty pounds to get in, but I did. I was sure that this was the right path for me.

My father had flat feet, which kept him out of World War II. That had to add to all the fear and pride he felt when I enlisted. The night that I announced it at dinner there was a deafening silence for a few moments. It took my father's breath away but my mother seemed very matter of fact about it. Again, that stiff, Anglo-Saxon upper lip of hers prevailed. I knew she was proud of her son going "in service," as she called it. At some point, my father managed to say that I should think about all the guys who went before me when the training got tough.

Kenny Kreader and I joined the Corps on the buddy system in which they promised to keep us together in boot camp. Even though we were in the same platoon, we didn't get to say a word to each other for three weeks. Matter of fact, you didn't want to get caught talking to anyone unless you wanted to get slapped upside the head for running your mouth. We flew from Newark Airport on March 2, 1966, bound for Beaufort, South Carolina.

The welcome upon arrival at the Marine Corps Recruit Depot Parris Island (MCRD PI) was dramatic by design. It was the beginning of a ten-day shock treatment where about ten percent are weeded out—probably due to having lost their minds. All new recruits are assaulted and insulted in an overwhelming deluge of tirades, slaps and pulled punches to the gut. They are forced to double time [a fast marching pace of one hundred and eighty steps per minute, thirty-six inches in length for the Marine Corps and Navy] everywhere and in everything they do.

The drama started before we even got off of the bus. A drill instructor got in the front door of the bus and exchanged civil greetings with the driver who had a little chuckle, too. That was the last calm, reasonable conversation I heard for some time. He turned toward us in his crisp uniform, campaign hat and buzzed haircut. He spoke with a surge of energy and viciousness that I never thought possible. This was man as I had never seen him before.

His voice was more than loud: it was a penetrating, frightening, savage bellowing, which demanded to be obeyed. He screamed that when given the command to get out of the bus we would all do so by the count of six. Next to the bus on the parade deck were outlines of yellow footprints painted in a platoon formation. "You will fill those footprints with your feet. I don't want to see any fucking yellow!" The very first order was to do the impossible—even with my size twelve shoes I couldn't cover the painted lines. With the help of a couple of other drill instructors at both sides of the bus door, the verbal abuse began with a rabid intensity. I was so scared that I left the carton of cigarettes I had brought with me on the bus.

From that point on there was no letup from them. They had our hair cut off—all of it—within the hour. Inside of two hours, we were issued our entire kit. All personal effects that we brought were ridiculed in any way possible. The berating of family pictures was accentuated by explicit questions and statements of the most personal kind. The worst was saved for any pictures of girlfriends— with hideous suggestions mostly of a sexual nature that were sick and mean-spirited. Even mothers were fair game.

Everything that came with us was sent home. The Corps would provide us with everything we would need while they got all of that civilian scum out of us. We belonged to them entirely. They marched us to our barracks at night like a herd of cattle. It had been raining hard so they dragged us through the deepest water accumulations that they could find—it was over the tops of our boots— between the buildings of the supply area to the 3rd Battalion's barracks a mile away. This was to be our home for the next eight weeks, where our most basic instruction was to begin and where we were shaped into whatever they wanted us to look and act like.

I was too busy to be scared even though I was convinced these drill instructors were the meanest and toughest men alive. I sensed underneath all the activity that there was still a camouflaged and intense fear, but also a surprising and strangely comforting feeling of security. These brutal warriors were somehow going to take care of us. I realized that if I followed instructions, I just might get through this as so many had before me.

In the barracks we were shown the Marine Corps mess trays that we would eat from. The knife, fork, and spoons were collectively called fighting gear. Nothing that we needed to know was omitted. They showed us how to move through the chow line. They schooled us on personal hygiene and our hands became "dick skinners" to pull that foreskin back and wash that cheese out of there. A sick Marine is a non-combat-effective Marine. Making up our bunks with hospital corners on the sheets and blankets was also covered. When they were finally made, we counted off while standing at attention in front of the bunks. Of course, we had to do it a few times because we weren't loud enough, but finally they put us to sleep. Exhausted. No prayers. They would teach us that in the days to follow.

About an hour later, still dark outside, we were awakened by a swarm of drill instructors running and yelling through the barracks while beating garbage cans with billy clubs. They pushed bunks over, sending slow-to-rise recruits through the air with never-ending, bellowed insults. What theatre! These guys were good at this. I was duly impressed.

By the time we were finally allowed to sleep for a couple of hours that first evening we had already been taught a hell of a lot. This was the beginning of the shock treatment. It only lasted a few days and then tapered off a bit. It consisted mostly of some sleep deprivation combined with relentless screaming and hollering that kept you on edge. The next morning, after we made up our bunks and were all lined up in front at attention, there was a few minutes pause. All was quiet and then a door slammed shut at the rear of the barracks. A drill instructor, in an immaculate uniform of the day, marched the length of the barracks right in front of all of us. He was "lean and mean" as were the rest of the drill instructors. We saw in him what a Marine should look like. When he got to the front of the platoon he inspected every one of us.

He poked those he called a "fat body" in the stomach with his finger. We were told that we could only eat vegetables and meat with no gravy and drink only skim milk. We were to fallout to the rear of the chow line when we got to the mess hall and present our tray to the drill instructor for inspection before we ate anything. Once, I wasn't quick enough getting my tray out of the reach of the mess man spooning out gravy and he got it on my meat. When the drill instructor saw that he told me not to eat any of the meat that had gravy on it and to bring my tray to him when I was done to prove it. I was a "fat body" until the day before we left the island.

The fear of being set back in training to motivation platoon for another two weeks was always part of the incentive used on weak or slow to learn troops. Motivation platoon, if that was called for, was much worse than just going back to where you were in training two weeks earlier. It was jail-like and did not count as time served in this prison called Parris Island. All day long you were punished. Those in motivation would move large sand piles with their buckets from one place to another and back again. One day a week they would have a forced march around the whole island. A forced march is more of a run than a march.

Our platoon "picked up" a couple of motivation recruits during our training cycle who were "motivated" beyond belief. They never lost the level of intensity that came with them. [The Marine Corps officially terminated the motivation platoons in April 1976 after a mentally retarded recruit died from head wounds he received in a disciplinary "pugil stick" fight while in a motivation platoon in Marine Corps Recruit Depot San Diego.]

The other option in the case of not keeping up with the program physically was the "fat farm." You would lose weight there, no question.

During our first week at the island we got physicals and inoculations. I was in line one day and a sergeant pulled me out and asked a captain if I should be sent right to the fat farm being the hog that I was. The captain told me to do ten push-ups, which I grunted out. He then told the sergeant to let me stay with the platoon for now and "see how he does." That was motivating by fear of the unknown.

On one of the early days at the Island there was a great scene in the mess hall. Some foolish recruits started talking while they were having breakfast. Of course, the drill instructors saw and heard them. One of the DIs took corrective action immediately by getting a few steps running start and diving onto the top of the offenders' table. Sliding with his arms extended, mess trays, eggs, grits, and glasses of milk flew in his wake until he arrived at the undisciplined recruit's throat to begin choking him and, of course, scream expletives in his ear. I don't think it was the first time that scene occurred in the history of the island. It was a beauty and got everyone's attention.

They also taught us the very basics of how to wash, brush our teeth, and shave. Explicit personal hygiene was covered with all manner of sexual overtones. For some, shaving was a new experience and they became a bloody mess. Nothing was left to chance. They told us exactly what to do. The sooner you adhered to that, the better things would go for you. Putting on a piece of clothing without the order being given would get you in the shit sooner or later. When they wanted to see that third pair of new trousers, and you couldn't produce anything but a pair that had already been worn, you were in trouble. A key to getting through this with as little pain as possible was to do what you were told, only what you were told, and not get in the front or rear of any lines. Just try to be as invisible as possible. Not easy to do if you are six feet two inches and a "fat body."

We got one half hour per night of free time with which to write a letter home saying how happy we were and how well we were being treated. Anyone who admitted to having any political connections was given a special talking to by the drill instructors regarding what they had to say about the nurturing treatment the Corps was giving them. We also used this time to square away our gear, polish our boots, etc. This was all done while kneeling behind our footlockers—no sitting on the bunks, ever. Our time was spent standing at attention, reading our little red notebook with the information we needed to know or kneeling on the concrete deck busy at our footlocker. This was also time for some of the recruits, also referred to as turds, to work on special problems. There might be a turd off in a corner repeating his manual of arms or another working on upper body strength on the pull-up bar.

Fire watch was our first form of duty in which we were responsible for a post. There were the General Orders for Sentries that applied to the duty. The first one stated, "I will stand this post and protect all government property within view." We would take turns of one hour at a time from taps to reveille and walk around the barracks while the others slept. The "Duty," the person standing the post, wore a silver painted helmet liner, which was usually beneath the metal of a battle helmet. He also wore a webbed cartridge belt and carried a billy club. It was during that hour when you would hear some guys crying or thrashing about while having nightmares–little wonder given the stress level we were under. Since sleep was your only respite from the constant pressure of the day, catching the dreaded 0300-0400 fire watch was crushing. The hour available to you for sleep when your turn finished made it more like losing two hours.

I was sure that I was the most homesick recruit there ever was. I even got weepy in the rack one night. In boot camp I lost fifty-six pounds in eight weeks. The program there was more of a physical challenge than a mental one for me and quite the opposite for others.

I lived for mail call and the kind words. After the first week it was announced that the smoking lamp would be lit. Smokers were advised that this would be an opportune time to quit a foolish habit but those who wanted to take part should fall out on the parade deck at that time. The drill instructor formed us up in a circle and we were allowed one cigarette, which we passed around. We all got a puff. It would be a few days before the smoking lamp was lit again.

We were tested for aptitude and intelligence, a process called G-2. When the G-2 scores came down from headquarters those of us with a minimum score of a hundred and twenty were offered the MARCAD program. The drill instructor told us we would be trained as pilots. I qualified but was afraid of ending up with a longer enlistment if I washed out of the program. All I knew was that two years of this would be quite enough. I didn't want to ask the drill instructor that question and get roughed up for not wanting to stay in his beloved Corps, so I passed on that opportunity.

It was during the period of "shock treatment" that they persuaded the platoon to agree to being trained in the old school fashion, as opposed to by the book. Old school was hands on. And they were the hands. If a drill instructor curled up the front of his Smokey Bear hat—campaign cover—just a little, it meant that he beat his troops. By the book was of course for pussies not real

Marines, and we had already started wanting to project ourselves into the image that these poster-perfect figures presented to us. There was a lot of pressure at the time on the drill instructors not to get caught exercising this manual discipline. If caught, at best their career was over and at worst it meant jail time. Nobody in our platoon got roughed up to the point of hospitalization, but it had occurred in years past.

On the evening of April 8, 1956, a drill instructor named Staff Sergeant Matthew McKeon came into his platoon's barracks after he had been drinking. He took the recruits on what at the time was the standard training march through Ribbon Creek in the marshes that surround Parris Island. The tides were wrong that night and six of his men drowned, including the son of the famous journalist, Walter Winchell. That brought the heat down on the training practices at the Island.

We were given the drill instructor version, which blamed the recruits for not following orders, but the Court Marshall said different. McKeon got a Bad Conduct Discharge after a very colorful trial with the most impressive character witnesses possible speaking on his behalf. They included the Commandant and Chesty Puller, who was and is the most celebrated Marine ever. Lewis B. "Chesty" Puller enlisted in the Corps and rose through the ranks to become a Lieutenant General. He was awarded the Navy Cross five times. At taps our drill instructor would say, "Good night Chesty wherever you are," and then give the command, "Sleep!"

The Corps' basic training had been intensified to churn out Marines at a rate not seen in decades. The training cycle had been concentrated to eight weeks from the usual twelve. When our drill instructors would punish us with excessive physical training it would usually follow a slow learning demonstration by some of the platoon. "You ladies don't want to learn together? Maybe we can do something else together. We'll be the dumbest platoon but the strongest. Push-up position. Ready. Exercise." Push-ups or bends and thrusts were common. The duck walk was another. "You ladies squat down and grab your ankles and quack like ducks." Around and around the barracks we would go, painfully.

When the drill instructor was in a bad mood, things got interesting. Like, "Every swingin' dick in the dumpster," was imaginative I thought. Its amazing how many will fit with enough motivation. There was an SS at the end of any recruit's service number if he was a draftee and that made for all the more misery on Parris Island. "You didn't want to join my Corps? What are you a faggot, a communist or a pussy? Well, what the fuck is it shit-for-brains?" Of course any answer would be wrong.

Another creative form of punishment came about while learning the manual of arms. The manual of arms demonstrates one's ability to handle a rifle—the sacred rifle—in a military manner, smartly placing it on either shoulder by moving the rifle not your head. Also, presenting it to an inspecting officer in the proper way, culminating with doing all this and more while marching and turning to the left, right, or oblique.

The prerequisite to executing all of that is knowing one's left from one's right. Hearing, "Your other right, asshole!" was always, and still is, a source of humor to me. It was difficult to suppress a laugh. After enough recruits would screw up left face and right face drills with a rifle on their shoulders, we would be told to put away our rifles in a calm and almost sweet voice. "Alright ladies put your weapons away." Then suddenly we would be given the command, "Right shoulder footlocker." We were in for it now. If you and the "nut"—as we were often addressed—to your front and rear, knew their left from their right, the commands to follow would only have the discomfort of the weight of the footlocker on your shoulder. For those who didn't possess that most basic knowledge, a footlocker in the face or back of the head was an inducement to pay attention. On balance, these were mild forms of motivation. However, in addition to their superb acting abilities, these drill instructors had some brutal imaginations.

While we were being inspected at the Port Arms position, I was caught looking at the drill instructor. Port Arms is holding your weapon four to six inches from your chest at a forty-five degree angle, with the muzzle up and to the left side of your head. That is the weapon part of it. The rest, except for the positions of the hands in holding the rifle, is a posture of attention, which insists on eyeballs locked straight ahead, feet joined at the heel in a forty-five degree angle, and a few other things.

All of this is done without the slightest movement. Any drill instructor knows that the greatest temptation for any recruit is to take a peek at the drill instructor after being inspected. Junior drill instructor Costello got me. He was the "homey" that I was told to be careful of because he was from Jersey City and Italian. I was fine for the inspected position, but I looked at him and his eyes were waiting for mine two recruits down the line. He swaggered back over to me chuckling as he snatched my rifle from my hands. He calmly asked if I liked him and did I want to fuck him because, after all, I was looking at him. He inspected my weapon and then started hitting me about the head and shoulders with the muzzle end of it. I had it coming.

The squad bay where our bunks were lined up was about a hundred feet long. There was a shower room with toilets and sinks, called the head, at one end. The drill instructor's room, called the "DI House," was directly across from it. A table, about three by six feet, was placed just outside of his room. On that table there were pictures of our drill instructor's recently graduated platoons. There were many gold stars and silver stars on the chests of the pictured recruits. Gold was for KIA (killed in action) and silver was for wounded. We were all going and knew it. Somehow that was not as foreboding as the present issue of graduating from this island.

I don't remember anyone getting roughed up by a drill instructor unless that recruit had made a mistake. It didn't have to be a big mistake, like trying to sneak a scratch at a biting sand flea, just any mistake. Drill instructors would watch each other's platoons for some nut trying to sneak a scratch while in the chow line. After a few minutes you would think you got away with it but then from behind you there would come a whisper, "See me after chow," followed by a bellowing, "ASSHOLE!" That was trouble.

After evening chow there was always a line of that day's offenders at the door of the drill instructor's room inside the barracks. The quiet would be punctuated by the loud slapping on the wall by the next recruit. This was a requirement in order to be given permission to enter. Once inside you would take your licks for whatever infraction you were guilty of during that day. After the ass chewing and a few punches, the private involved would be thrown out of the little room and slammed into the wall opposite the door. "Next!" the drill instructor would bellow, until all had been dealt with sufficiently. I took some lumps once because the drill instructor caught me laughing while he was thumping another recruit. He just knocked me around on the spot right away and I didn't have to wait all day for it.

During these times of "redress," two privates were assigned to take positions at either end of the barracks and appear to be sweeping the deck. They were looking out for the officer of the day or anyone not in our platoon. Basically, they were watchdogs to protect the drill instructor from being caught making Marines out of us. If anyone approached, one of the guards would call out, "Attention on deck." This would bring the hazing—the drill instructor's career-ending part of the activity—to a stop. It was in the privacy of our barracks where the "hands-on" part of our training took place.

Training platoons were in groups of three, called a series. This set the stage for various competitions. Series "drill comp," as it was called, became the most sought after goal of all for our drill instructors. Teaching and learning how to march properly challenged everyone. Hours and hours spent on the parade deck required patience and concentration by all involved. First without, and then with, rifles finally produced respectable enough results to move large numbers of troops from place to place in an orderly, efficient manner.

Guaranteed to get you a slap in the face, the kind that sting, was to say you "can't" do something. It goes to the basic premise that there is nothing a Marine can't do and, "How do you know when you haven't tried yet, you gutless puke?" If you were in the shit with a drill instructor and wanted to make things worse, just tell him you can't when he wants another twenty-five push-ups. Bang, you'll get a fresh one. A black sense of humor helps more the worse things get.

Parris Island has sand fleas, whose intensity was not to be believed. The drill instructors would occasionally give the command, "Git'em!" or "Attack!" Everyone was permitted to scratch for a moment. Sometimes, however, they would give the command, "Let 'em eat." That was hateful. The fleas would go way down into your ears and have their way.

I thought the most severe forms of teaching aids were done at the rifle range. Marines take marksmanship seriously and qualifying with your rifle is very much encouraged. The drill instructor would say, "If your best isn't up to the Marine Corps' worst you're wasting air," or some other derogatory suggestion. Before we even got to the range a recruit in another platoon tried to commit suicide by cutting his wrists but failed. Our drill instructor called for a school circle. That is a teaching formation with all recruits gathered around the drill instructor. He told us of the recruit's failure and how to do it properly. "Any asshole that wants out do it lengthwise not across."

As far as the Corps is concerned everyone is right handed until proven otherwise. Proving otherwise to your drill instructor is a painful process but possible. They are the same way about swimming. Everyone can swim, "Get in the fucking pool." Then with long bamboo poles they would push anyone who tried to hold on to the edge of the pool down and away from it. This went on until that recruit proved their inability to swim by nearly drowning, another painful process. The Corps is big on pain. They like to say it is weakness leaving the body.

A target tells a story about what the shooter is doing. Each shot that hits the target will tell a different part of the story. If someone exhibits the common fear of actually firing, they may jerk the trigger, which contributes to an erratic pattern on the target. You can't jerk the trigger if your finger has a blue fingernail. We spent the greater part of each day for a week dry firing our weapons at black dots on barrels. A squad of ten to twelve recruits lies down in the prone position and makes a circle around a barrel that had black dots every six inches or so all around it. We would squeeze off simulated shots at those dots practicing the technique we had been taught.

The most important of all firing positions is the prone position. It offers the shooter the opportunity to score more points than the other positions in the qualification course. Of the fifty rounds allotted, ten were offhand (standing), ten were sitting, ten were kneeling, and twenty were prone. The twenty rounds from prone make a hundred points possible. To qualify, a hundred ninety points out of a possible two hundred fifty were necessary. Firing a two hundred twenty or better was expert and nearly got you a bye for the last two weeks of training.

The prone position is started from standing at a forty-five degree angle to the target. The left arm is placed through the sling and the hand is on the forestock. The right hand holds the handgrip above and behind the trigger.

Taking the prone position is started by going down to one's knees and leading with the rifle butt while continuing forward to the ground. The shooter ends up with the left elbow under the rifle, the right elbow under the right shoulder, and his torso flat on the deck making a tripod. It is a very stable structure with the pelvis flat and ankles down. Some Primary Marksmanship Instructors (PMI) could start from the standing position, go down to the prone and hit a bull's eye from two hundred meters, blindfolded. That's what extensive practice can do.

The teaching of this most revered subject was the task earned by our PMI. Our regular drill instructors were there keeping an eye on us though. About twenty yards from the target barrels was a shed with bleachers in it where we would assemble for instruction from time to time. There were a couple of simple rules regarding leaving our weapons on the grass around the barrels. The bolt will be locked in the open position, not closed as if it had just chambered a round. The safety will be on. That is a piece of flat metal that protrudes from the front of the trigger guard. It requires about one pound of force to push it to the on position. Finally, the operating rod handle used to pull the bolt back for chambering a round will be pointed toward the sky. Simple rules, right? Like all of the rules at this place they were designed for the least common denominator to follow and understand. Whenever we assembled in the PMI hut one of our drill instructors would go around gathering the weapons that were not left behind correctly. There were always some.

Safety not on and you will put it on with your nose. Kenny told me that was painful, which dovetailed with the usual method of learning motivation: pain. The other infractions were usually paid for with an exercise called bends and thrusts. The offender's rifle numbers were announced to the class and woe to those who didn't remember that bit of vital information. The recruits who belonged to them would claim them from the drill instructor while the remainder of the class stayed with the lecture. All of this took place on thick turf, which required about a hundred bends and thrusts to wear through it to the dirt. Eventually you would dig six divots beneath the grass—first, where your hands went when you bent over to support your weight and second, where the toes of your feet went when you thrust them back to full extension. When you came back to the crouched position your feet would make another pair of holes. By the time you were finished digging holes, you had cracked a good sweat.

The second week at the range was spent firing our M-14s. Everybody knew the rifleman's prayer that starts with "This is my rifle. There are many like it, but this one is mine. Without it I am nothing. Without me it is nothing." Marines have been reciting this prayer for decades. We echoed whatever our drill instructors demanded in training and it all went to a mindset that stays forever. A recent Commandant finally put to rest that whole business of, "There are no ex-Marines only former Marines." He issued a written order that said, "There are no former Marines just Marines." It is a large part of what makes us the worst enemy one can have. Our history more than supports the claims of the Corps being a superior fighting force.

The coming week would be the most important of our training. At Parris Island, the rifle and discipline are the focal points of training, with physical readiness very close behind. Our rifle, the M-14, weighed eleven and one-quarter pounds and we became very close, even intimate. The nomenclature, muzzle velocity, and all other pertinent information were the substance of an inspecting officer's questions. It was a tool that provided a path to superior marksmanship in a place where that would set you apart from the rest. If you scored Expert on the range as a recruit, you at least got a promotion in rank if not a chance at the rifle team. The rifle team is royalty in this society.

A rifle is a "piece" or a "weapon" but never a gun. Sometimes back at the barracks in the evening there would be one nut that had not referred to his rifle properly, marching around the squad bay in his skivvies with his penis hanging out. He would first point to his rifle saying, "This is my rifle," then pointing to his penis saying, "This is my gun. This is for shooting and this is for fun." He would alternate the pointing to coincide with the appropriate lyric. Then there would be the one recruit who dropped his weapon. The drill instructor would tell him that his rifle would sleep in his bunk that night and he would sleep on the deck. The other punishment option to that infraction was an order to field strip the rifle—i.e., take it apart into at least ten pieces—and sleep on it that night.

There are a number of factors that culminate in good marksmanship. One is that done properly the shooter is surprised when the rifle fires. This is true. You sight down the barrel and through the peep sights to get the proper alignment of the front sight blade in the middle of the circular peep hole on the receiver near your right eye. Then after a breathing sequence you take up the slack in the trigger and focus on the front sight blade of the rifle. The target's bullseye down range will be fuzzy because you are focusing on the sight blade not the target. When the sight blade is under the bullseye properly it will resemble a lollipop—really. While you are holding that elusive picture you squeeze the trigger, but when it drifts away you stop the squeeze until you can get that picture back again, at which time you continue the squeeze. This goes on until enough pressure is applied to the trigger for the sear ["The part of the trigger mechanism that holds the hammer, striker, or bolt back until the correct amount of pressure has been applied to the trigger."] to release the hammer and fire. At that moment the shooter tries to recall the sight picture he had when it went off and writes it down. When the target is spotted—marked with a white spot where it was pierced by the bullet—you have the information on which way to adjust your sights. If the bullet strike and your last target picture were the same your rifle is sighted in. Those established windage and elevation settings are the basic "dope" for that rifle. The only other adjustments needed would be in case of wind corrections.

RASBAS. That is the acronym for the shooting mantra. Relax: you should be relaxed as well as comfortable in your shooting position. AIM: for sight alignment, place the front sight blade visually into the center of the rear peep sight. SLACK: take up the slack in the trigger mechanism. BREATHE: take in a breath and release some of it. AIM: get the sight picture of the fuzzy bullseye under the front sight blade. SQUEEZE: the trigger while you have that proper sight picture and only then. The firing should be a surprise.

This squeezing of the trigger is so paramount in marksmanship that there were a couple of draconian measures taken to ensure that even the slowest learners would correct their mistake. One was to hold the recruit's trigger finger in the end of the chamber where the bullet would go and let the bolt "go home." The bolt would forcefully slam down on that finger as if it was chambering a round. I never saw that administered so it may have just been a threat, but I doubt it. The method that I saw used was a pair of pliers squeezed on the fingertip vigorously, which results in a blue fingernail. Same effect really.

The most comical thing I saw at the rifle range was at a morning formation where the platoon lined up to be marched to morning chow. It was a chilly morning and one recruit thought it chilly enough to wear the gloves that we all had been issued. He was immediately noticed by the drill instructor taking us to the mess hall and was asked, very nicely, why he had his gloves on. The recruit replied, "Sir, I thought my hands would be cold, sir." The drill instructor laughed and said, "Look at all these dumb maggots who don't know enough to put their gloves on. Platoon push-up position, ready, exercise. Oh, not you," he said as the offender started to get in the push-up position, "just the rest of these assholes. Private you leave those gloves on until I tell you to take them off." That was three days later. The poor nut did everything with his gloves on for those three days—eat, shower, and brush his teeth—everything.

I qualified on "pre-qual day"—the day before we fired for scores. Those who "went unq'," meaning unqualified, paid dearly that night in the barracks. We had heard rumors of the horrid punishments for belonging to that group. The worst was the ammonia showers. All "unq's" were herded into the shower room, the hot water was turned on, and they would begin to exercise while a drill instructor poured ammonia on the floor. Our drill instructor did everything but the ammonia, although we could smell some, perhaps from another barracks. The abuse went on for hours. Threats of being set back two weeks in training if you didn't qualify the next day were the primary motivation.

I got to basic training during wartime. I heard, "Don't complain about this war. It's the only one we have," many times over. That and meeting the absolute toughest, meanest bastards imaginable—that is, the drill instructors who would be your mother, father, brother and sister—were very impressive to this eighteen year-old, scared youth. Many years later I met another Marine who was in the infantry in Vietnam and he said the "gooks" didn't scare him as much as his drill instructor at Parris Island.

We had a recruit who didn't get the point across to the folks at home that they were to send nothing but a letter in a plain envelope. That order, just like every other order, was meant to be taken literally: nothing, no additions and no subtractions. Girl friends who wrote S.W.A.K., as did those with perfume, got you slapped with the letter in the drill instructor's hand. I got seven letters one night and that was just too many, so he slapped me with each one. These weren't slaps that knocked you down, but they stung. So when a package full of candy bars arrived for a member of the platoon, he was summoned to the front of the squad bay. He was told to open his package. Sgt. Vance, the drill instructor, was all polite and nice to him remarking how nice the person was who sent the candy. After all, the private must have asked for it because the Corps wasn't taking good enough care of him at Parris Island. "Isn't that right, private?" said Vance. That private got roughed up and the drill instructor took the candy bars. He asked Kreader if he wanted one and Kenny said yes. "Open up," said Sgt. Vance. Kreader opened his mouth and Vance stuck the unopened candy bar in his mouth.

Vance came back a few minutes later asking Kreader, "Where is it?"

"Sir, I ate it, sir."

"The wrapper. Where is it?"

"Sir, I ate it, sir".

They went back and forth with Kreader sticking with his story that he had eaten it wrapper and all, and Vance not believing him until another private vouched for him. Kreader barely dodged a beating on that one.

Thompson, another Drill Instructor, was just mean. When he worked you over, the routine was to stand at attention and recite your general orders. They are the eleven orders all sentries are obliged to adhere to. Thompson would punch recruits in the gut while they tried to recite those orders. No personality, he was just mean. Vance was our favorite drill instructor. He had already been to the Nam as a Recon Marine twice and would be going back when his tour on the drill field was finished. He was what is called Force Recon, a parachutist. They go into enemy territory without being seen and gather information. Returning with the information without the enemy knowing you were there was the tricky and valuable part.

Vance liked Kreader because of a couple instances that lead to the candy bar business. When we were out at the range, Kreader was cleaning the mirrors in the head and got to one where another recruit was in the way. Kenny told him to move so he could do the mirror and was told, "If you want me to move, move me." Without words or hesitation Kenny decked him, but cut his hand and had to go to sickbay to get stitches. He was back with the platoon before noon chow. That night during free time Vance was wandering around and saw Kreader's hand. He went up behind him and into his ear asking, "What happened to your hand Kreader?"

"Sir, I fell on a G.I. can, sir."

"What was the name of that G.I. can?" said Vance.

"It was a G.I. can sir. It didn't have a name, sir".

After our two-week sabbatical at the rifle range, we came back to our original barracks to finish our last two weeks of training. There was some hand-to-hand combat training, a very brief course because of the limited time available. There was also the confidence course, which was my greatest challenge. Heights were a big part of that course and they put the fear in me. We spent a lot of time on the drill field preparing for series drill competition. It took almost two days to clean our rifles adequately for the dreaded final field inspection. The result of all this was that those two weeks remaining after the range filled right up.

Running was the most physically difficult part for me. If we weren't running it was marching out on the parade deck until we weren't doing that up to snuff in which case we'd do some more running. I feared the morning runs, all runs. As soon as the command "Double time march" was given, the fear came. It was fear of not being able to keep up and just how many times we were going around the half-mile track. This was the mental part for me but I thought it physical at the time.

The obstacle course was at least a daily event. Sometimes twice in one visit, with another go at the end of the day. One's agility and strength were tested vigorously when trying to negotiate the various obstacles. If you couldn't get through it, you weren't leaving the island and that was all there was to it. I knew that I wasn't the only hog having a hard time of it. The "O course" was challenging! I had very little idea of my physical capabilities until being pushed like never before. They were far, far beyond where I had been or even imagined. High school football practice was nothing by comparison.

Force is the ever-present theme of infantry training. All will yield to enough of it, of course. In bayonet training on PI the instructor apologized for having to teach us a parrying movement. He did so because his orders were to follow the book, which stated we would be taught such a defensive tactic. His preference was that at all times one proceeds straight ahead into the enemy always attacking. We got to demonstrate that attitude on each other with training weapons called pugil sticks: rifle shaped devices with padded ends to simulate a bayonet at one end and the butt end of a rifle (also a weapon) at the other end. The drill instructors split the platoons up into groups and we made circles facing the center. As our turns in the center came up, arbitrarily, we donned some protective headgear in the form of a football helmet with a face mask and beat the hell out of each other. The winner of each bout remained in the circle until someone got the better of him. Displaying aggressive behavior was the most important part. The competitive spirit of the drill instructors was not to be denied and they were all challenging each other with taunts of, "My turd can whip yours." After which, they each paired up a few of their prize recruits and let them have at it for their respective platoon's honor. Those who lost were not coddled.

Our aggressiveness was fueled by having been so put upon in the three weeks prior that taking anyone apart was a pleasure. The Corps' approach to hand-to-hand combat at that time was more of that same straight ahead attack philosophy. Casualties are going to occur but the objective will be met. In hand-to-hand combat, the instructors told us, an encounter with an enemy should not take much more than a minute until one party is dead. Using hands is the last resort. Grab anything available and beat the opponent to death with it. Absent something to use, it was hands, fingers, or teeth to the vital areas of the body: eyes, throat, and groin. Included with this technique was a blood-curdling yell.

The confines of the training schedule only had enough time to make our crude technique somewhat dangerous. It was the aggressive mindset that truly made us a cut above. We believe we are the descendants of the "Devil Dogs" from Belleau Woods. The Germans gave that moniker to the Marines who fought there in the Great War. There is such a history behind us to live up to that we have to be the best. We owe them.

There was supposed to be a bivouac at a place called Elliot's Beach on the other side of the island. Before that, however, we had a forced march to the site where we demonstrated all that we learned thus far—things like assembling your rifle blindfolded in thirty seconds and rolling a proper bedroll so that it had half of everything necessary to make a pup tent. Every platoon there performed miserably according to the Commanding Officer, who declared that instead of a bivouac as planned we were going to run all the way back to the mainland. This of course, meant we would be in full gear—packs, rifles, helmets and canteens. He followed it with a baited question. "Does anyone think they can't make it?" No one was foolish enough to say anything.

It was a grueling run and I made it, my shining moment, without falling out as so many others did. Those who fell out were encouraged to continue by the drill instructors who were behind every platoon. Of course to fall out was not simply to stop running and rest or walk, no, there was significant motivation applied to those who straggled. They would be kicked along for some time before being pushed off the sandy dike of a road that we were running on and down into the marsh with the accompanying derogatory expletives and threats.

Kenny saw me at my absolute best and worst. He knows me better than anyone else. He has seen me run and vomit at the same time, but never falling out of a run. It was the running that was such a personal challenge. Everywhere we went we ran. The sneakers and shorts they issued us were never used. We ran in boots and when we were issued rifles we ran with them at port arms. Every time we started a run I was scared that I wouldn't be able to make it, but I did. That was the personal growth of confidence in myself that I only recognized later. Arrogance came as well. I have only met a couple of Marines that weren't arrogant and maybe that was because I didn't know them very well.

Before our final inspection we had the Physical Readiness Test (PRT). In addition to being able to do a certain number of exercises in an allotted time period we had to run three miles with helmet, pack, rifle, and canteens inside of thirty-six minutes. Final Field Inspection was the last day of basic training. We had prepared for days, really the whole time we were there was in preparation for it. We spent a whole day sitting on our buckets cleaning our rifles with hot soapy water and toothbrushes first and then sparingly applying some WD-40 to keep the rust away. A rusty weapon is a court martial offense in the Corps. Sitting on our galvanized buckets for those hours left an imprint around your ass so deep that it remained there for days.

For the inspection we wore the uniform of the day, which was called summer service uniform-A or just "trops." It was short for tropical, which was lightweight wool. On our chests we wore our shooting badge, Expert, Sharp Shooter, or Marksman in descending order of scores. Mine was a Marksman badge. I was disappointed but it was good enough. Above it there was also a ribbon that we wore called the National Defense ribbon. It was approved because we were serving while the country was involved with the Vietnam business. It was referred to as the "Fire Watch Ribbon" mostly because we hadn't done anything to get it and we already knew the Corps wasn't big on uniform gadgets like the Army.

When we graduated, Kenny got the prestigious 0311 Military Occupational Specialty of infantry rifleman while I got the lowly MOS designation 3516 of truck mechanic. Of course there were many who thought me the fortunate one, but John Wayne was never a mechanic or a clerk or a cook in the rear with the gear and the beer. Those infantry bragging rights would forever elude me.

I had no clue as to how life-changing those eight weeks would be, how that personal success would make other of life's challenges small in comparison. Leaving the island had my head so full it could have exploded with pride from accomplishment and fear of the coming unknown at the same time.

Graduating from Parris Island was grand. My parents and brother came, all quite proud, as I was some thirty years later when I saw my son graduate at the very same place. It's a special place. For me it was the right place. I wouldn't know for years how much more the Corps gave me than I gave it. It is always with me. It is my pride.

Chapter 4
Remainder of Active Duty

The morning after graduation day the new Marines from Platoon 361 and the other two platoons in our series left Parris Island for Camp Geiger. This time we were on Greyhound buses that departed the island almost daily. Camp Geiger is the home of the Infantry Training Regiment (ITR) at Camp Lejeune, North Carolina. All Marines are riflemen first, cooks and technicians second. There, those of us who were destined for the infantry would get six weeks of infantry training while the seventy to eighty percent remaining got only four weeks before going to schools in their military occupational specialty. From ITR or schools it was on to the Western Pacific—WesPac - meaning Vietnam for the majority of us. The rest would go to the Fleet Marine Force, FMF, and follow along shortly anyhow.

It was an early morning departure–zero dark thirty. All of our drill instructors were there, some with tears in their eyes if you got close enough to see. They were justifiably proud of their work with us. We came a long way in eight weeks with their help and encouragement. Some of them had gotten close to us in a special way. No hugs or "touchy feely stuff" by any means. More like a "brothers in arms" relationship as we were on our way to being peers. We were all going to the same place eventually. No one returns the same from war even if they came home alive. We had a certain kind of love for those who trained us while weeding out the weakest and making the rest of us stronger. Of the original one hundred and ten recruits that our platoon started with, seventy-six of us graduated together. Some were set back in training and would catch up later while others were discarded with a general discharge.

These men who wore the flat-brimmed Smokey Bears covers, who lead the chants while we ran, who were always impeccably uniformed, had attacked our most vulnerable features relentlessly to tear us down and if we didn't break they built us back up to a formidable fighting machine that would follow any order given. Their cadence calling while we marched has a beauty that is imprinted in any recruit's heart who marched with a rifle on that island. Just by graduating we had proved a great deal to ourselves. Looking out the window of that bus as we rode off the Island seeing those who still had many weeks of training left, of marching and running was a feeling of accomplishment I had never imagined possible.

Infantry Training Regiment was very different from Parris Island, even fun at times. Physical demands were still present, but the harassment and abuse were considerably less. The best part was firing all of those weapons, including machine guns and rocket launchers. Happiness is a belt-fed weapon. Operating one gives you a feeling like none other. Throwing grenades and demolitions were a close second. The weapons we didn't fire, like the flamethrower, were demonstrated to us.

The M-1 rifles we used were left over from WW II, as were the C-rations that we ate in the field. Lots of other classes, from first aid to venereal diseases, were taught while we sat in bleachers after humping our packs and those heavy rifles for miles in between the different ranges. There were also subjects like the Geneva Convention and NBC (nuclear, biological and, chemical) warfare, which made death by a bullet seem quite humane and preferable.

The lengthy marches between the different ranges made for enough fatigue that staying awake in the bleachers for classes was another form of training. A class of nomenclature and operating procedures preceded the actual firing of all weapons competed with sleepiness. The rule was that if you were tired, about to go to sleep, just stand up at the side of the class but do not continue to sit and get caught falling asleep.

The punishment was not like boot camp, but it was effective. After being rudely awakened by the instructor in a survival class you might have to hold a poisonous snake while you stood at the side of the seats anyhow. Or if it was a hand grenade class, you would have to hold one, off by yourself, with the pin pulled. The C-4 was probably removed but that was not what we were told. Just don't go to sleep.

Discipline, discipline, discipline was the heart of the training. Don't get a good Marine killed because you are an asshole. Don't get your platoon wiped out because you can't suppress a sneeze when set in an ambush and a company of Viet Cong comes by.

There was the John Wayne course using live ammunition and pop-up targets. The technique to be learned was how to use the rifle's recoil to improve accuracy. By aiming low at first the weapon climbs with recoil so from the knees or groin area as a starting place you should finish with a few rounds in the abdomen. The course was through the swampy parts of Camp Lejeune with life-size targets popping out of the ground or from behind a bush. The enemy targets had a little red light simulating a muzzle blast. Some were women bearing water or carrying a child. We weren't supposed to shoot them.

Our weapons were so old that they often jammed. When we were first issued the M-1 the proper way to deal with this common malfunction was demonstrated. First order of business was placing the butt on the ground near your feet and pointing the muzzle as far away from yourself as the length of your arm would permit. Then you raised your right foot and brought the instep of your boot forcefully down onto the operating rod handle to drive it to the open position while keeping your arm stiff. This procedure clears the weapon but if the boot slips off and a round goes into the chamber the locked elbow will keep an accidental discharge from going into your head. That was the theory, but I met some who could overcome the best of plans.

More black humor was prominent at the gas chamber. This part of training was always built up into a horror show by those who had been through it already.

(Just like the guys coming out of the buildings where we got all of our inoculations back at Parris Island. They said it's a square needle the corpsmen were using while they held their arms feigning pain, some of them bleeding. In truth they used what looked like inverted spray guns that would shoot the vaccine into your arm as you hurried along walking by the Corpsmen. There would be a number of them on each side of the line and they would get you as you passed by. Bang on one side and then the other often while you were still looking back at the first one.)

For the gas training we used World War II gas masks, leaky antiques. The idea was to get us exposed to gas, so leaky masks fit right in the program and were cost effective as well. For this training we were allowed to put the gas mask on before we went into the little wooden building with the "gas chamber" sign on the outside. When we were first issued the masks it was always a surprise exposure. They showed us how to put them on and then as soon as we had them back in their pouches we heard the sound of two canisters popping open. An instructor yelled "GAS" while two other instructors instantly appeared in front of the small bleachers that we were sitting in for the class and sprayed us with a foggy CS tear gas. Leaky masks or not, you didn't have time to get them on.

The gas chamber exercise was preceded with horrible scuttlebutt, which ended up being partially true. For most of us it was a first and very unique experience—that is to say, awful. Its effect was disorientating as well as uncomfortable. That is the very reason it has been part of the training for some time. The use of mustard gas by the Germans at Belleau Woods in the Great War is deep in the fibers of the Corps history. In June of 1918, in a space of twenty-four hours, 1,087 Marines died a miserable death there, most from mustard gas.

We lined up at the entry door of this wooden shack and went in a squad at a time wearing our gas masks. We got in there and saw an instructor inside a dimly lit room that appeared clear of gas. The effect was eerie, without the fogginess that the canister CS had spewed into the bleachers. He gave us another short lecture about gas and what to do and not to do. While he took his sweet time talking about the subject you felt the CS gas burning in your lungs as the mask leaked away. When he finished he told us he would give the command to remove our masks individually so we received a real dose of the gas.

"Become familiar with it," he said. When at a position of attention in front of the instructor, he ordered us to stow the mask in its pouch and "Breathe it in." Then he had us recite some technical weapon information, sing the Marine Corps Hymn, or carry on whatever whimsical conversation he fancied. After you had been exposed to enough gas to satisfy him of your sufficient familiarity, you were told to leave the building, which began the comedy.

To rid yourself of the gas you needed to run while shaking your arms. This helped remove the gas from your skin and clothing quicker than just standing still. Touching your skin would press the gas into the skin and burn even more. All of this transpired while snot and mucous were coming out of your nose and hanging down to your knees. It was all so distracting and disorienting that many forgot to look where they were going. It was "Show Time" now. All of these green, dressed, bald headed, snot slinging, cursing young men running into trees and ending up all over the ground was beyond funny, especially after you were finished doing it yourself. Somehow I managed to pay attention to where I was going. I must have learned from watching the first guys. The "don't get in the front or back of any line" rule still applied.

After Infantry training we all received what is called boot leave. Go home for a few weeks to feel very much out of place. The recent life-changing experience made relating to former friends strained. Many of us got orders to WesPac, which meant the Western Pacific region, i.e., Vietnam, right from boot leave. I was sent back to Camp Lejeune but stayed only a few weeks and volunteered for WesPac at my first opportunity. The sales job done on me at Parris Island was complete. I wanted to go and be part of it—a bride not a bride's maid. Clearly I had joined the right branch of the service to accommodate this foolish mindset. It didn't matter whose idea it was, I was on my way.

My orders were to report to Camp Pendleton, Staging Battalion. Staging was a training regiment and was my first exposure to some real mountains—West Coast mountains. This extension of infantry training included the addition of survival courses, abandon ship exercises, and many long forced marches for conditioning. Getting caught in the escape and evasion (E&E) course meant being taken as a prisoner of war to the simulated "VC camp" and being interrogated possibly with a water method. The ones that the aggressors selected for that special treatment were tied wrists to ankles on their knees backwards and water was poured down their nose. Besides avoiding the simulated POW treatment, another benefit of completing the E&E course without being captured was that you got water, a cup of rice, and an orange. That was it for the day except for the two canteens of water that you started with. These were the days of water discipline—preserving supply by restricting drinking—when nobody heard of the importance of proper hydration.

We got liberty on Sundays and for many it was off to Tijuana to release some built up tension and drink at places with names like the Blue Fox. Most of us weren't old enough to drink in California and, besides, Disneyland just didn't pack the punch that TJ did. When staging was completed, we boarded a ship, the USS Simon B. Buckner, in San Diego harbor on 9 September 1966. For the send-off there was a small military band on the dock along with some family and friends of those departing. It was all very low key. Nine hundred of us joined the same number of soldiers from an Army military police battalion at Fort Ord.

Off we went on the morning tide steaming to White Beach, Okinawa. Life aboard ship was just one more part of my education on my way to the University of Southeast Asia and the I Corps campus. We were WESTPAC bound and as soon as we lost sight of land ten percent of us got seasick. Many chose the upwind rail to relieve this new sensation, much to everyone else's dismay. Most of the time at sea on a troop ship is consumed with waiting in line for chow. The chow line for every meal wrapped around the entire deck at least twice. Time passed with four-handed double deck Pinochle games that moved with the mess line.

After chow there was physical training or other classes on everything from the M-60 machine gun to gonorrhea and syphilis. We were warned of a special venereal disease that they called the black syph. Get that one and you weren't allowed back in the States, or so they said. Always wear a rubber, piss, and wash after. That was the message. There were two movies for the whole seventeen-day voyage—*Thunder Ball* and a boring documentary called *Why Vietnam* narrated by President LBJ. We had been force fed the Why Vietnam film many times in staging already.

Traveling via troop ship isn't a Carnival Cruise to the Caribbean. The one that we boarded in San Diego, the Buckner, a merchant marine vessel, was not overloaded like the ones in WW II, which had men sharing bunks and sleeping in shifts. Our ship was crowded to the point of using half of the brig to hold regular troops, not prisoners. It took a day to get the ship loaded. The troops boarded by climbing rope nets. Scaling about three stories with all of your gear hanging off your back is a job—and a long way down if your hands fail.

I was billeted in the half of the brig allotted for troops with brig rats in the other half. Our bunks were stacked five high with a two-foot aisle separating the rows. The troops above you helped keep you in the bunk in rough weather. The brig is in the bow of the ship providing the most motion of anywhere else on the ship as the sea got up. The prisoners in the brig part of our compartment roughed up an abusive guard they didn't much care for and were ordered to be put on bread and water, AKA piss and punk, for some days.

Some of the nine hundred of us were to be used as much needed replacements for what was left of Third Battalion, Third Marine Regiment (3/3). They had returned to Okinawa to regroup from a rough go of it in Chu

Lai, which is south of Da Nang. After a week of more training, to keep us occupied during the day, we were given our assignments. I was attached to H&S (Headquarters and Services) Company of 3/3. We boarded ships and steamed for the South China Sea awaiting the beginning of Operation Prairie in the Demilitarized Zone (DMZ). The DMZ was a ten-kilometer strip of land that separated the two Vietnams: North (the Democratic Republic of Vietnam) from South (The Republic of Vietnam). There were a few more weeks of shipboard life, but this time it was a regular Navy ship, the USS Iwo Jima. This meant better chow. At night we passed the time watching fire fight tracers onshore from the fantail. There was more entertainment in the form of "smokers." One Saturday on the hanger deck of the Iwo, Navy vs. Marines paired off in three, two-minute rounds of boxing. There were some very spirited matches due to the intense rivalry between sailors and Marines, who often refer to themselves as the male part of the Navy.

When the landing finally came, it was a large-scale helicopter assault. The infantry line companies of Third Marines went right into the bush next to the DMZ and were immediately in the shit. I was assigned to a motor transport company at Đông Hà, the logistic base closest to the DMZ. I stayed there for my whole tour except for R&R (rest and relaxation). I had five days in Kuala Lumpur, Malaysia and three days at China Beach near Da Nang.

It was the end of the dry season when we got to Đông Hà and soon it became a sea of mud. The roads were boot-deep—step off to the side and it was mud up to your knees. That is what happens when lush vegetation is torn off the surface of the earth in a rainy climate. My unit, called FLSU#1 (Force Logistics Support Unit #1), had a compound approximately two hundred yards square with a slight slope that faced a small Vietnamese village. Multiple strings of plain barbed wire fencing woven through rolls of barbed concertina wire were on that side of the compound, with two sandbagged bunkers at the corners with guards at night. The other sides of our compound bordered other base units and not the village.

Seabees, the Navy's combat construction branch, built a number of plywood shacks called hardbacks. They had corrugated metal roofs and screened-in sides for us to sleep in instead of tents. Similarly constructed work areas were used for maintenance of trucks, radio equipment and weapons. Wooden pallets were put down for walkways between the work and sleep areas. There were outhouses and a unique urinal setup in back of the hardbacks. Empty rocket shipping tubes were sunk into the ground to carry the urine down below the surface. We also had some showers set up nearby. Trenches were hand dug about five feet deep right behind the hardbacks. They formed a zigzag pattern to cut down on the casualty radius should there be a direct hit. A casualty radius is a zone emanating from the point of impact of some piece of ordinance, in which half of the personnel are killed and the other half wounded. Once we finished digging and sandbagging the edges, to cut down on the erosion from rain, it was home sweet home.

The Seabees also built a number of towers about seventy feet tall around Đông Hà and the other bases in the neighborhood of the DMZ to triangulate on the enemy firing positions. Rockets leave telltale red trails when fired. Interlocking sightings from the towers gave artillery batteries a target for a fire mission. Those towers were put to good use during the second half of my tour. There was cooperation between these bases to counter attacks from Charlie, as the enemy was called. The base under attack would hunker down with the other bases returning artillery fire to the enemy sources that had been located via the observation tower coordinates.

My first assignment when I got in country was mess duty for thirty days straight. The field mess hall was a large hardback about a quarter of a mile down the muddy road from our compound. The day started at 0400 and lasted until 1900 when all was cleaned up. These were mostly dreary days with lots of rain, but a USO show came once. It was very low key, not Bob Hope by any means. No stage, just a gathering in the mess hall with Martha Raye. In her uniform and still in the Army Reserves as a nurse, she was great. Genuine, upbeat, good to see—and she made you feel just a little bit better. She didn't have to be up there by the DMZ. This was I Corps and mostly Marines.

Mess duty was followed by a shit detail, literally. It was a month of "burning shitters." That detail was comprised of pulling the half-barrels from under the seats in the outhouses, pouring diesel fuel in and lighting them on fire. After they burned for a little while they need to be stirred around, like a saucier might do, to aid in the reduction. Eventually we would dig a hole and bury what remained. By the end of the day you smelled like the shitty smoke.

From that detail it was the motor pool for me. I'd made Private First Class by then, but it didn't keep me from more shit details, like filling sandbags all day or building bunkers. It was the binding of filled sandbags that grew two blisters on your hands, in the same places every time. I was assigned the position of driving the company commander's jeep for a few weeks, but wasn't quite squared away enough to hold it. From that I moved to the water truck. It was a beat-up two-and-a-half ton 6x6 with no roof. The water run amounted to going around the airstrip and hooking up to trailers, called water buffaloes, at a number of places, taking them to be refilled with potable water and returning them to where I picked them up. One stop was the ration dump, which was usually good for a case of C-rations. This is a trading process called scrounging and is part of military life, especially in the chaos of a war zone. Another destination was graves registration, where they cleaned up dead Marines for shipping to Da Nang—they had fresh sheets, which helped. Everything moved by truck.

I tried to maintain some class when at all possible—going to the shower in a terrycloth bathrobe, cooking Italian in the hardback with Richard Lisante. It is possible to boil spaghetti in a helmet. We would get some canned tomatoes and spaghetti, imagining we were home in Jersey and Brooklyn respectively. My relationship with him would become the most influential of all. He talked me out of the foolish notion I had of extending my tour to get into a line company. This is a bullshit war he would say.

My tour in Vietnam was, for the most part, unremarkable. I never got a scratch. In fact, for the first six months it was quiet where I was in spite of being about six miles south of the DMZ. Then we started getting hit by rockets and artillery, but still nothing like the other Marine bases along the DMZ. Khe Sanh and Con Thien were sometimes shelled around the clock. Compared to being in a line company, I was in the rear with the gear and the beer—although beer was hard to come by.

There was plenty of beer in the ration dump, but it went to the Staff NCO club instead of to the troops, whose ration was supposed to be two cans per man per day. When we were lucky, we bought hot rusty cans of Ballantine from the gooks across the concertina wire. We had no ice so we put them into gasoline cans for cooling. When you took the cans out, the rapid evaporation of gas on the outside of the can took some of the heat out of the beer. The aftertaste of gasoline on the metal cans almost made it not worth the trouble—almost.

The times I got to drive a wrecker were high points. It was a five-ton truck that had a crane with a cable attached to a hook on the back where the bed would normally be. There was a small seat up on the side of the crane with controls to move the boom right, left, up, down, extend, or retract. Driving the wrecker got me out of Dông Hà and north where the action was. I drove up next to the DMZ a few times, but was never under fire. I was sent up there to change out the gun barrels on the M110 8-inch self-propelled howitzers. The terrain is mountainous with rocky gorges and thick, lush-green vegetation. A young, foolish, bulletproof fellow, I didn't wait for other vehicles to form a convoy. It was only the armorer, who knew the gun we were going to service, and me. We drove north up Route 1(National Route 1A, the trans-Vietnam highway, location of numerous battles during the Vietnam War). The whole business took less than a day so on the way back we stopped at a little hooch on the side of the road in Cam Lo for a beer. It was Tiger beer known as tiger piss. Heineken it was not.

The wrecker was not an everyday operation so it was back to the motor pool more often than not for me. One day I was told to pull a radiator out of a truck. The lower hose resisted my attempts at removal so I cut it off. That was the end of my posting as a truck mechanic. "Get him out of my motor pool," said the Gunnery Sergeant in charge.

Then it was out to the perimeter of the base with the other shit-birds.

I got to like it and, since few asked for the duty, I was there for months. We lived in two-man fighting holes spaced along our side of the barbed wire fences. Boredom was usually the order of the evening, though. One night a dog set off a trip flare in the wire and by the time we received and accepted the cease fire order there wasn't much left of that dog. Eighteen-year-old lads with idle machine guns get bored easily. We even cut the parachutes off the flares launched out of the hand illume rocket tubes and fired them at the Marines in the outpost a few hundred meters from the wire.

When the rains came and I couldn't even see the wire, I wondered how secure this perimeter could possibly be. I was out there the first time Đông Hà got hit with rockets. One came down, loud as a freight train, and hit right in front of our hole, throwing dirt all over us. Private Imbragno had prayer beads in his hands and said he did a couple of rosaries in record time.

The attacks started in April of '67 with rockets every few weeks, forty or so rounds spread over the whole base. Đông Hà had grown to about three square miles by then and apparently worthy of being a target. The frequency started to increase but not the quantity.

Some nights when there was activity nearby, Puff the Magic Dragon would show up. An Air Force C-47, this was the military gunship version of a World War II era DC-3, with three General Electric 7.62 mm miniguns mounted in the rear and side. It is described as a flying Gatling gun composed of several machine guns. The miniguns had such suppressing fire power that they could put a bullet every 2.4 yards in an area fifty-two yards in diameter in three-second bursts. Puff also dropped flares that made it bright as day. The racket the gunship made was what a fire-breathing dragon would have to sound like—a roar and a solid column of orange-colored tracers that burned out halfway to the ground. Its nickname was very appropriate.

When there was enough enemy activity in the area, our lines were augmented with grunts. That's when I met Sergeant McCoy. I was in the command post tent operating the radio when his platoon was assigned to our sector. He had just returned from the hospital in Japan where his lower leg was mended from machine gun fire earlier in this, his second, tour. He was the image of a nail-eating, broad-shouldered Marine. It looked like he was lucky they didn't amputate that leg. He slept in the tent when he wasn't out checking on his men, which was often. Sergeant Mac was a good dude from New York City whom I would have followed anywhere.

There was a radio station from Hanoi that we could receive and as hokey as it sounds the broadcaster's name was Hanoi Hanna. She told us when "they" would visit us (Đông Hà), Camp Carrol, Con Thien or others along the DMZ, and was much more accurate than our intelligence. When our G-2 said we were going to get hit we got a good night's sleep; they seemed infallibly wrong. These rocket assaults were mostly what are called H&I (harassment and interdictory) fire—spread out, not concentrated. They gave you something to think about if you let them. When the incoming became almost regular, some of us started to sleep on top of our bunkers so we didn't have far to go to get in them. I remember feeling their claws when rats ran across our backs as we were trying to sleep on those bunkers.

At the end of my tour, when I was what is called a "short timer," we were getting incoming rounds most mornings. Just a few, but sometimes they were accurate, like the time they set off the ammo dump. There were secondary explosions for hours. The base at Đông Hà had really grown by then as had the ammo dump. The gooks maintained some artillery pieces in the mountains of the DMZ on railroad tracks. Along with the dull roar from the ordnance, an inch or two of dark gray could be seen at the horizon after the B-52s would carpet bomb. After the smoke cleared, the North Vietnamese would fire a few rounds from their artillery just letting us know they were still there. There was some pattern to it all and I could feel myself looking towards the bunkers after seeing the gray smoke, especially the shorter my time in country was getting.

The standard tour for Marines was supposed to be twelve months and twenty days from shore back to shore—i.e., time from when you leave for WESTPAC and return back in the States. Grunts like Kreader were supposed to be out of the bush and in the rear in twelve months. I lost a friend who was still in the bush after twelve and twenty. In that last twenty days you were supposed to have a flight date home. I was getting nervous and angry after my twelve and twenty came and went with no flight date, while I was still running to the bunker every few days. These are by no means outrageous examples of the Corps fucking over their troops. They did it with aplomb and my guess is they are still good at it. You hate it when you are in but love it when you are out.

The most singular incident of my tour occurred on September 25th, 1967. One well-placed artillery round hit our compound, with another Marine between me and where it struck. You don't hear artillery incoming like rockets when they are going to hit you. I'm not sure if it's the velocity of artillery rounds or the arc a rocket travels that causes the audible difference. This shell landed about twenty-five yards in front of Francis Mahaney. At the moment it went off all my senses were consumed by the sound and shock waves from the explosion, which was followed in slow motion by a silent pause. Despite the confusion, I knew enough to be heading for the bunker. Before I reached it, I heard Mahaney calling me by my nickname, "Moose, Moose." I turned around and saw him holding his very bloody abdomen together with both hands and one of them was a mess. Then another Marine was coming from the direction of the explosion clasping his neck with one hand, his other hand reaching out. The arterial blood from his neck wound was pumping arm's length. Several of us got them into the bunker and

I called a corpsmen to come from the next compound where there was a Recon Company. The corpsman promptly stuck a tube in the still-pumping artery to channel the flow and bridge the void to the head of the Marine's injured neck. There was a truck near the bunker so the corpsman and a couple of others put the wounded in the back and I drove them to the field hospital. There were still rounds coming in and just after we drove off another round hit where our truck had been standing.

Mahaney saved my life that day without intending to, but saved it none the less. During the last month of my tour the company clerk was looking for anyone who could type at all. I went for it and spent my last month in a tent typing reports. Francis worked in the same tent with me. We had tables for desks with our typewriters on them that faced each other. We were a couple of Remington Raiders. The day of the artillery attack he asked me a question and I was in a cranky mood having just been told—again—no flight date today. I told him to fuck off and as he took a couple of steps away the round went off in front of him. The explosion left a silhouette of him behind where I was sitting at my typewriter. The shrapnel that he caught with his gut would have taken my head.

As expected, I survived Vietnam because I was in motor transport. Kreader got away with it, too, in spite of being a mud Marine. He was in some fierce battles in which, twice, men were awarded the Congressional Medal of Honor. He volunteered to be in a CAP (Combined Action Platoon) unit. This consists of one squad of Marines and three squads of South Vietnamese troops living in villages. It was riskier duty than a regular line company.

I didn't go to Vietnam with any kind of moral purpose or agenda. I just wanted to see if I was tough enough to be a Marine and they turned me out. I spent my nineteenth and twentieth birthday in Vietnam—from October 1966 to October 1967—rotating home just before the major North Vietnamese Tet Offensive.

My father passed away two weeks after I got back and I still had six months left in my enlistment.

When I was released from the Marine Corps on March 1, 1968 I was twenty years old. I had taken part in a war and returned with all of my limbs. Vietnam was no longer an issue for me while most young men my age were scrambling around trying to avoid it. I don't think many of them knew that their dodging the draft showed wisdom beyond their years. No one gets through a war without being carried out or carrying out some form of baggage, as in physical or emotional scars. However, for many draft dodging also showed an absence of conviction and taking responsibility. Pacifism is one thing and running away is another. Some were just scared and the rest petrified. I felt that someone who wouldn't go when their number came up in the draft but suffered the consequences for refusing was okay. Going to jail might be the most honorable way to demonstrate one's principles. If you ran away, perhaps to Canada, stay there.

I didn't think much of the Carter forgiveness plan of letting them back in the country. For that matter, I can't forgive Jane Fonda's shenanigans as youthful indiscretions—not that she could possibly care about my opinion. She was the reason some good men were hurt in dreadful ways at the Hanoi Hilton even more than they already had been.

As I got older I thought teenagers were absolutely the right ones to go to war because they didn't yet know how good life might be. They could also be trained to do whatever they were told to do without question. The latter is an absolute necessity in trying to command soldiers effectively in the face of the madness of combat.

When I got home from Vietnam and out of the Corps all directions were available to me and I didn't know which way to go. This wasn't such a good formula for me given the state of the country culturally and politically. I am sure I was not alone in that place either. It must be a given of war that the returning will need some help screwing their heads back on right. Sending eighteen-year-olds off to war and treating them indifferently at best when they return is just flat wrong.

Chapter 5
Local 779

In 1968, making four dollars and sixty-five cents an hour was good pay. That's what a union laborer made working in what was called the building trades. Laborers would be sent out to work on construction sites with masons, carpenters, plumbers and excavators. Local 779 had a thirty-five hour workweek: eight o'clock in the morning to noon, with a lunch break for thirty minutes, then twelve thirty to three thirty—anything else was overtime at double time. These were some of the conditions negotiated by the union and agreed to by contractors who did work in the 779 territory.

At times it is next to impossible to get membership in construction unions, especially the ones that pay well, like ironworkers, operating engineers and electricians. Nepotism usually prevails, but sometimes you can pay the right guy and you're in. I once had an opportunity to join the operating engineers union for a thousand dollars, but didn't take it. Looking back I'm glad I made that choice. Otherwise, I might never have ventured out of New Jersey or flown a jet in Africa.

I had a friend whose father was a union carpenter. He put a word in with the business agent to get work for his son. The business agent, or BA, is paid from union dues membership and is responsible for finding work in the local's area of operation. It is an elected position that pays foreman wages all year long. Louis Conte was the BA for 779 and nobody worked as a laborer unless he said so—not unlike Johnny Friendly in *On the Waterfront*. The membership was not composed of too many rocket scientists or Eagle Scouts—quite the opposite really—but there were a few students like myself rounding out our educations.

Louis arrived at six AM in his office next to the hall, where he got phone calls from contractors and shop stewards looking for men or advising him of problems like a pending layoff. After a call that was usually full of hollering and profanities, he came out from his office to see who was in the hall waiting area ready to go to work. Then he went back in his office and after some time, and maybe even more calls, he shouted out someone's name. That person would go in the office and Louie would say the name of the contractor, where the job was and who to see.

Louie stayed at his office until about ten. The rest of the day he went to worksites checking in with the shop stewards to see if all was going as it should. The local's territory needed inspecting as well to make sure there was no building construction without union representation. I heard that he could often be found at the horse track, a popular place for many in the local.

A small local in East Orange, NJ had a BA by the name of Carmine. His influence was so strong in the building trades that he would arrive at a job site in his chauffeur driven limousine. The chauffeur would get out, blow an air horn and the whole job would stop until Carmine's shop steward came to the car and they spoke. If everything was okay, his chauffeur would blow the horn again and everyone would return to work. If there were any issues with a contractor, the job would not go on until it was straightened out to Carmine's satisfaction. I am sure he had picket signs in the trunk of that limo for ready use.

This is an example of how strong the construction unions had become. Like a pendulum, labor struggled and fought its way up from the time when excavation was "fifty guineas in a ditch." When one fell over from exhaustion he was fired, and another hungry immigrant hoping to feed his family took his place. My grandfather shoveled coal in a chemical plant. He would walk to work to save the nickel trolley fare. How soft we have become.

Working on construction is still a hard place but with considerably better conditions than the old days. That pendulum has gone to the other extreme for labor. When a contractor bids a union job he cannot plan on getting much more than four hours of work out of a tradesman in an eight-hour workday. It's the reason it costs twice as much to build the same building with union workers than non-union. When you are on the receiving end of the good wages the injustice of it all doesn't bother you so much.

My friend Billy knew I was looking for work and said he would talk to Louie that night. There was work so nobody was at the hall. Anyone who wanted to be working was and contractors were calling for more help. I went the next morning and after listening to the litany about having to buy a "book" and agreeing, Louie sent me on my first job. The book, which was membership in the union, cost $160 at that time and was payable in installments. There were also monthly dues to be paid but all of it seemed well worth the price given the wage rate.

The job was with a brick laying company called John B. Kelly from Philadelphia. I went to find the shop steward, Frank, and he was at the mortar mixer, of course, which is the best laborer's job. Frank took me to Phil Manual the foreman who put me to work "rolling block" on a flat wheelbarrow. All day! It wasn't long before the monotony had me questioning the four dollars and sixty-five cents per hour as such good money. I was soon to find out what the word "conditions" meant when I went out on my first job. I knew only enough to bring work gloves with me. Payday was Friday and a little accountant-type guy came with a ledger. He had someone with a holstered pistol stand behind him while he handed out the cash-filled envelopes.

I had no idea what "killing the job" meant or "who do you work for?" The second was an uncomplimentary remark that refers to someone being a company man and not a local man out of the hall. At first I couldn't believe things like only four twelve-inch blocks to a flat wheelbarrow or six eight-inch blocks. I thought the guy telling me that was setting me up to be fired because so many more could fit. I also thought being hired and paid good wages meant you worked hard for the company that was paying you. I knew nothing.

A compliment when speaking of a laborer who worked out of the hall was to refer to him as an "artiste." The accent goes on the second syllable. The art was being able to give the appearance of working without getting much done. Pick a plank up and carry it around the building. When this kind of behavior is multiplied it will add time to the job. It just seemed wrong somehow. I'm not as clean as the driven snow but there were a number of other things to come that wouldn't sit well either.

When a contractor came into a local's territory they would be required to hire a certain number of men from that area's local based on how many of their own men they wanted to bring in. It was a two-way street because it allowed a contractor to bid a job, away from his base of operations, without having to travel with a full-time work force. The downside was that the contractor had to get along with the business agents no matter what trade or trades were needed. If they got along, the respective BA would send men who worked reasonably well and, if not, he would send one of his "beauties." A "beauty" did next to nothing on the job except affect others by talking to them and keeping them from their work.

I was on a job once when a small contractor came on the site with a crew of hard working company men. He had to hire at least one local man and the only one Louie had at the hall was one of his "beauties." By ten AM of the first day on the job the foreman came up to this local man, paid him off with two weeks pay and told him not to tell the BA. He also told him to get off the job before he ruined his crew. On a much larger scale a contractor was put out of business in Atlantic City due to a poor relationship with trade unions while building a casino.

Working out of the hall meant you could go out on jobs that lasted for one day or until the job was complete. Some jobs lasted years, but not many. There are a lot of concrete pours common in the early stages of a building. The footings are first and then the ground floor, after the rough plumbing and electric went in place underground. The floor is usually four inches of concrete, on a wire mesh with a plastic vapor barrier under it. A crew of six laborers can empty ten cement trucks or more by noon. It depends on how far they have to take it, often by wheelbarrow, from the truck to the placement of the concrete. All subsequent floors are concrete, on corrugated steel, which is pumped up in a four-inch hose.

These were the big jobs. If you go out of the hall when a big job starts, to work for the general contractor, you can be there for the whole job. Otherwise you might get work with one of the many subcontractors—masons or plumbers. All trades need laborers at one time or other and in the late 60s and early 70s there was plenty of work to be had out of the hall.

A standard procedure for some laborers was not to work in the winter and collect unemployment instead. It's a simple matter to be laid off from a job. All you had to do was tell your shop steward that you wanted your money and all that the company owed you would be there at the end of the day. No one disputed whether you were fired, quit or were laid off when it came to collecting unemployment. No job search was required because you paid a business agent to find you work. If the state wanted to call Louie for validation they were welcome to do so. He would of course cover for his men. If you were laid off because the job ended and Louie liked you, he would send you to a job, usually the next day, when there was work.

In those days there were certain routines followed on jobs. The shop steward came around to get the coffee order for the "coffee break," which was another contract condition between the company and the local. Sometimes he would also take your number for what morphed into the state's lottery. The winning three-digit number was the last three numbers of the local racetrack pari-mutuel total dollars that day. It certainly seemed like a random enough number to bet on. When the mob controlled this, the payoff was significantly larger than what the state pays now for the pick three. You could give the steward your numbers and a dime or quarter if you wanted to play. If you picked the correct number your cash would be there the next day.

I ended up in Louie's favor early on. I was of Italian decent, worked hard, and didn't cause trouble. I even wanted work in the winter when few others did. The breaks in the college calendar for Christmas and those in between some flying jobs were times that I fell back on construction to make a buck. He started to send me out as a shop steward occasionally. They weren't the big, good jobs but I liked it. It helped offset the pain that goes with working outside in the winter weather. The shop steward by definition is the union representative on the job. My friend Edmond, an engineer, says, "He's there to make sure nobody works too hard." That's part of it, but I had a lot to learn.

Louie sent me out as a steward on job with a bricklaying crew and, as was usually the case, the labor steward mixed the mortar. There is another rule that says laborers build scaffolds only up to three stories and then a carpenter has to be hired to add his expertise for safety. The scaffolds have to be tied to the building at the third story, which was supposed to be a carpenter's job.

There was a carpenter on the job as per the rules and all of the scaffolds were put up. The carpenter was going to be laid off at that time, which a contractor would often do to save money by having laborers take the scaffolds down. The carpenter came to me complaining about it. He said that a carpenter was supposed to be there and that his business agent, Sam Barret, would picket the job if only laborers were used. I was the young, naïve steward and said, "I'll call Louie tonight." I thought that this was a clear breech of the rules and couldn't be allowed. When I got Louie on the phone and told him of the problem, he said, "Fuck Sam Barret and his carpenters." That was the end of it, but not the end of my education in construction and unions. I had completely missed the obvious conclusion that it meant more work for laborers without the carpenter.

Working on construction for years served me well when it was time to build a house. My experience in the building trades made me sure that I could build a masonry structure. Having grown up in the house that my father, whose trade was not carpentry, built with his friends was an influence. That coupled with my own arrogance in believing I was capable of most anything I put my mind to, was all it took. Of course I did need the setting that allowed me to do it and the Veterans Administration provided it in the form of a mortgage.

Chapter 6
Private Pilot

Dariush Khosrovschahi was a high school friend who introduced me to aviation. He returned from a tour in Vietnam as a crew chief of a Huey and insisted I take a five-dollar introductory flight. "Okay," I said, and we went to Somerset Airport in Bedminster, New Jersey. A half an hour in a Piper Cherokee 140 was all the flying needed to gut-hook me. This was an epiphany—flying was something worth doing. I had been discharged from the Corps for a year, getting high every chance I had and going nowhere in a hurry.

Working out of the laborer's union hall did not do much for my intellectual growth. The characters I met on the job were a crude lot for the most part. My father's death removed a grounding influence, which may have kept me more in line—I don't know. Being as free as I was just then may not have been such a good thing for me. Flying offered a worthy and serious channel for my mental energies. The first flight was life-changing.

I knew Michael Bernat from Martinsville. He was tall and thin, two years younger than I. While I was in Vietnam he was convicted of marijuana possession and sent to the reform school in Jamesburg, New Jersey. In 1969 our girlfriends were friends and we spent time together after his release.

Michael was a marijuana dealer and quite comfortable with it. He became addicted to the money it brought him. His was a world of sex, drugs, and rock 'n' roll. We accidentally ran into each other in the mud at Woodstock in the middle of those four hundred thousand beautiful people. Country Joe and the Fish were playing the Fish Rag and I was wearing my jungle boots from Vietnam for the occasion.

Shortly after Woodstock I went to Europe alone. I was hardly by myself, given the number of similarly appearing Americans littering the continent, as they do every summer. While I was there Michael was in Mexico making connections in the marijuana business. We stayed in touch. Getting the money in place for flying lessons was not so easy and cost me for the rest of my life. The introduction to flight came during the readjustment to the drug world of the late sixties. There was Woodstock, not to mention Timothy Leary. And I turned twenty-one. I was lucky to get through it all as well as I did—never met a psychedelic drug I didn't like. Eventually, I got caught importing a controlled dangerous substance—marijuana—and I found myself locked-up.

When I came back to the States from Europe I went to California. There was another veteran I knew from high school who was living on the San

Francisco Peninsula and taking advantage of the California education system. This was the home of the Grateful Dead after all. College was cheap as were airplane rentals. This was where I put the flying plan together. I just needed money. So, when Michael asked me if I wanted to drive a load of pot from El Paso to New York, I was all over it. It took some time to put this scam together but once the advance work was done the first time, repeating it became easier.

I went to Texas and got a driver's license in Waco, then met Michael in El Paso, where he bought a pickup truck with license plates to indicate the truck was from the Rio Grande Valley. If you get stopped with a load, the fewer things out of place the better. Look like you belong there. I had short hair and an appropriate hat. Now it was the wait, the hard part. Michael had a girl from California flown in to go along and complete the image. She had a boyfriend, Chipmonk, who was a roadie for the Stones. She minded her own business, drank soda and chattered mostly, not demanding conversation, which was fine with me.

Finally, the call came. The Mexicans were ready to load the truck. I went to a bar next to the Rio Grande River, parked the truck, left the key in the ignition and went inside the bar. I had a Lone Star beer and shot some pool until I saw the truck had been moved—indicating it was loaded. Now, it was show time. I drove back to the motel, checked the load, put all of the camping gear and other eye-distracting props in the back of the truck, and we left. The truck was a standard size Dodge pickup with a four by eight sheet of plywood over the bricks of marijuana, which were placed edgewise on the floor. The plywood made a false floor about five inches deep. We had an externally mounted gas can on the tailgate to keep it from completely opening when the can was in its holder. This made the false floor barely noticeable.

I decided on going north through New Mexico from El Paso to get away from the Texas border as soon as possible. It was a longer trip but getting busted in Texas would be brutal and I had been there long enough. We still had to deal with the immigration checkpoint station like many others all along the Mexican border. They were usually within twenty miles of the Rio Grande and known to the locals as wetback checks. I had driven right by the one on the northern route out of El Paso a few days earlier and noticed an exit to an overpass going west a half a mile before the station. There was no one in the checkpoint at the time.

Now, at night, I could see from the bright lights of the station that a trooper was waiting. I made a quick decision to exit the freeway and go around his position towards the west via the overpass. Maybe he wouldn't see me. Fat chance, but I was already committed. He saw my move and pursued.

"Can I see your license and registration, please? Let's go take a look in the back." Calmly, after a pause, he said, "Where you going?" He looked at the contents of the capped truck bed with his flashlight. I told him we were going camping a few miles out. "The last fellow who went around my station was carrying marijuana." He handed me the registration and turned back to his car. I tried not to stumble as I walked back to the driver's door.

Money taken care of, selecting a flight school was next. The airplane and instructor time came to a thousand dollars. I took ground school courses in a junior college to prepare for the written exams required by the private license, instrument rating and commercial license. There were other courses I enlisted for, like SCUBA diving, judo and another go at calculus. After passing the ground school exam, I attacked the business of learning to fly by joining an inexpensive flying club in San Jose.

During ground school you don't have your hands in control of a flying airplane to effect movement so the subject matter can become quite dry. Bernoulli's Law and some Archimedes aren't too difficult but the absolute worst, guaranteed to put you to sleep quicker than Ambien, are the FAA regulations you had to make friends with. There was no getting around any of it, however, with some practical application, the ground school began to fit, and even the regulations made some sense. The FAA language is a fight all the way though.

Before flying, the legs of a landing pattern were just memorization. Names like upwind, crosswind, downwind, base leg and final were boring. In the airplane and flying those legs, the descriptions given on paper about crab angles and ground speeds all became clear. It was a relief to think I wasn't so obtuse anymore. Understanding the relationship that the airplane has to the ground as a result of the wind direction and speed is basic: ground referenced maneuvers. The traffic pattern is one of the most important concepts to grasp, since it applies to the conduct of all airplanes approaching or departing an airport.

The standard landing pattern is flown with left turns to keep the runway in the best position for the pilot to maintain visual contact. There are signals on the ground reinforcing this or indicating a deviation from the normal procedures as in a right traffic pattern for a particular runway. This may occur for noise abatement purposes. Farmer Jones may have a turkey hut right under the left base leg of a runway and airplane noise overhead causes all those turkeys to bunch up in a corner out of fear, smothering some in the process. So to keep peace the pattern is changed to right traffic.

Contrary to what some may think, not all air traffic is directed by a ground controller. Some airplanes have no radios in them. When I first started flying a coast-to-coast flight remaining clear of radio controlled airspace was not difficult. Such a flight might not be possible today, with so much restricted airspace.

Harmony is maintained by pilots anticipating the routine actions required of them. So, radio or not, there are expectations, not surprises, when landing, taking off, staying in or leaving the traffic pattern. Runway numbers are determined by their alignment with the compass rose to the nearest 10 degrees.

Runway 09 will be towards the east (90 degrees) while runway 27 will be west (270 degrees). Verbal directions coming from the tower with "Left" in them means you will make a turn to the left at some point. "Enter a Left base for runway 27," means when you are in a position to land on runway 27 you will make a left turn to become aligned with the runway. When there is no tower control, the pilot with a radio-equipped aircraft announces on the common radio frequency he will be entering a left base for the intended runway followed by announcing his final turn.

There is a term often used in aviation confusing to many people. The word is "stall." In everyday life it means the engine in the car has stopped, usually from an idle or from poor clutch engagement technique. Not so in the world of aviation. This is where Bernoulli's law comes into play. Explaining why an airplane flies can be a lengthy discussion about pressures and angles of attack by an airfoil.

There is a very simple demonstration to help visualize this source of magic. Hold a hand out of a car window flat, parallel to the ground. Through moving air, it will create a lifting feeling if the front of the hand is slightly angled up. The back of it feels lighter and a relaxed arm allows the hand to rise. If angled beyond a certain point (the critical angle of attack) the back of the hand no longer feels light and stalls. The air flowing across the back of the hand ceased to stay close to the skin and eddied, as visually depicted in a stream with water rushing by a rock. So "stall" in the aviation sense means an airfoil is no longer creating lift and in the case of a wing it will fall down—straight down if sufficient air moving across the wing is not promptly restored to a smooth flow.

Familiarization with and mastery of any aircraft includes "slow flight," flying at minimum controllable airspeed (MCA). There is a horn to warn the inattentive pilot of an imminent stall. It saves lives. Flying at the slowest possible speed so as to remain in the air without stalling demonstrates a pilot's airmanship (touch). The power is reduced but the airplane altitude and heading are maintained with the use of adjustable trim tabs and diligence. As the decreasing airspeed approaches stall speed the power is increased. From this configuration you can explore the wing's behavior as it nears the stall.

The air beginning to eddy over the surface of the wing feels like a fish is nibbling at it. The further you go into the stall the more the airframe vibrates and then shakes. Making turns in both directions in slow flight establishes and builds the confidence necessary to develop a real feel for an airplane and what it is about to do. One side of the wing may break from the air before the other side and lead to a spin. Recovery from there is practiced in training but a demonstration is not required in the private exam.

After three or four lessons all I wanted to do was solo. I had my flight physical medical certificate, which a student pilot was required to possess when flying solo, in my wallet. I wanted the instructor out of the airplane and to do the flying myself. He was a decent sort, but getting the first solo out of the way was significant to me. The curious thing about the first solo is it happens when least expected. Mine was at about ten hours' worth of instruction and I was in the middle of a terrible hour of bouncing the airplane on the runway and not keeping it straight or on the centerline. I was just awful. The instructor said, "Pull it up over there," pointing to a parking area near the end of the runway. Maybe he was going to make me walk back to the hangar.

He told me to leave it running and opened his door. He looked at me, asked to see if my medical was with me and then said, "Just take it around the pattern and come back and get me." I was more than surprised, happy and a little nervous now. The rest of it was academic. I did my solo, making the best landing of the hour and after I parked the airplane at the school ramp, we went inside where he cut the tail off of my tee shirt and wrote my name, number, his name and date. Then he hung it on the wall with all the rest of them.

The shock at being turned loose to solo came after a bad hour of landing practice. The student is astonished because in his mind the landings should be good, his best so far. No. The instructor is looking at the student's ability to recover from those demonstrations of miserable airmanship.

After signing off my medical, "Student cleared for solo flight VFR conditions only," my instructor gave me his two rules: (1) I was always supposed to check with him first about going anywhere except the home field, and (2) the weather had to be good, with light winds at most. I was pretty compliant about following his rules—at first. I wasn't and am not without fear when it comes to flying airplanes. Being in control makes it all okay, except when the weather has your hair standing on end.

I practiced those landings for an hour at a time every chance I had. Even at the early stages of flying I knew I would be judged by my landings. Another requirement of the private license was the dual cross-country flight to an airport at least fifty miles away from point of departure. It's an exercise in planning as much as anything else. Dual always means with an instructor's supervision, so— as is part of my nature—I wanted the solo cross-country without a baby sitter. We did the dual version uneventfully and after he approved my plans for the solo flight I was ready. He gave me a short lecture of dos and don'ts, but apparently not emphatic enough. Adherence to the flight planned is paramount in the instructor's mind. His license is at risk in these operations, especially when the student deviates.

I took off on this exciting solo flight north to the Napa Valley, made the first approved landing to a full stop and took off again. On the way to the next airport I noticed a sod airstrip and liked it, narrow as it was. I landed there and realized how much softer it was than the macadam surfaces I had been using. I imagined ag planes with tailwheels and felt warm inside. The Cessna 150 is a tricycle gear-training airplane, and not the stuff of my dreams although it was a means to an end. After finishing the requirements of this flight I headed back to the home base.

It was debriefing time and to my surprise it became ass-chewing time. Instructor Jim became unglued when I told him about my ad hoc inclusion of the narrow grass strip in my curriculum. Up one side and down the other he went. What if something happened? Of course he was right and I had acted irresponsibly, but I liked the grass strip.

The rest of the private pilot's course went without incident and I finished in the minimum time permitted. After taking the practical exam with the local FAA designee, I knew this was only the beginning. There was the instrument rating, the commercial pilot's license and multi-engine rating to earn, plus, if I wanted it, the instructor's license. Where to continue my training was the only question. Now, though, I needed to get back to earning money.

My friend Edmund, the engineer, offered me a job in New Jersey. I needed the work and decided to risk a friendship by working for one. Edmond was a member of 779 while he was going to college. He knew the difference between building trades and heavy construction—poles apart regarding working conditions and pace. He had been in a ditch with a shovel before wearing the white hard hat of a boss.

On building trade jobs, you rarely saw a short-handled shovel. They were all you saw in heavy construction. It speaks of the work intensity. A short-handled shovel requires you to bend over and put your back in play whereas the long handle gives way to a lazy pace of working. I saw guys on heavy construction who used a shovel as if they were playing a fine instrument. It is an acquired skill coming from considerable practice. Once you can do it well watching someone who can't makes you sick.

On Edmond's job we worked. The only reason I was on the job was because of him. This paving company didn't hire white Americans because they couldn't keep up with the "pork chops," Portuguese laborers. They arrived in this country weighing little more than a hundred pounds but after three or four years were about one-eighty with a physique like the proverbial fire hydrant. I had never seen people who could work as hard in the humidity of August. Many of them went home in a few years to a rich retirement with their saved money.

Chris and I met in a restaurant where she was waiting tables. Mister Smith's was a bar and grill run by a friend of mine, Jimmie Codd. He was introducing me to bartending on a part time basis while I worked construction during the day for Edmond. Chris came into my life and eventually became the grounding I so desperately needed. Not quite soon enough though. My relationship with Michael was already in place.

There were times in the beginning when I wanted to run away from her, knowing where the attraction was taking me. Shades of the M word were creeping into my head. I had a couple of other girlfriends since coming home from overseas but she was different. By the time I realized the seriousness of the relationship I was helpless.

This was the summer she graduated college in a soft job market. The only places where an English major with a teaching degree could get work were Appalachia and Alaska. My plans were always to go back to California and I asked her to go with me. I had a friend working at a ski resort on the north shore of Lake Tahoe. He rented a house and had a room available, if I wanted it, and off we went to Truckee, California. Life was good.

We spent the winter in the Sierra Nevada's at 5800' above sea level, snow and all. After working in Reno for a few weeks driving a taxi I got a job at the ski resort, North Star, where Norm worked. It wasn't far from Squaw Valley where the 1960 Winter Olympics were held. There were two other couples with us in a large A-frame house. The view of Lake Tahoe from the mountains in a winter wonderland was second to none. My job as the night maintenance man provided me with an ID card as my lift ticket. I was also entitled to a free guest pass daily so Chris was solid, too. Learning to ski in California was the highlight of the winter.

Then Michael called one night. "Do you know what a Lockheed Lodestar is?"

"Yeah."

"Want to fly one?"

"Yes," I said, and soon was off to New York, where the scam took shape.

I had seen pictures of the Lockheed Lodestar in aviation magazines. It's a large twin engine (1200 horsepower each) piston-driven airplane Howard Hughes sported around in with starlets. It could fit ten to fourteen passengers or close to two tons of well packaged pot.

My flying experience at the time was minimal. I was a private pilot who didn't even have a hundred hours total flying time. My personal arrogance prevailed where caution was needed. The money would pay for the flight training while I waited for the VA to reimburse me the ninety percent my military service qualified me for. (The flight training part of the G.I. bill required the veteran to have a private license first and then they would pay ninety percent of approved programs.)

Federal agents were involved before I even arrived in New York. The original plan was for me to fly as co-pilot with a pilot from Chicago who had the Lodestar, but all that changed when I got to the city. It changed because he got caught bringing in a load and took the government's offer of a reduced sentence to set up a group of smugglers. I was too green to see this coming, but the others involved should have recognized trouble brewing. There was a replacement pilot who was a "friend" of the original pilot. Raymond Justinic (an undercover

DEA agent) had a Piper Navajo to use. A Navajo was not nearly as exciting as a Lodestar, but it would do. By then, I was hooked for the flying adventure and quick money.

We all met at a restaurant near LaGuardia Airport and once we discussed the plan—except the destination—the government had the elements they needed in place. If we brought a load into the country everyone at the table could be indicted for a smuggling conspiracy. The destination was yet to be determined and I would reveal it to the pilot at our first fuel stop in the States.

The logistics of the operation had to be worked out. Where to unload near New York was important. Refueling needed to be considered. Michael had the connection in Jamaica and there were other partners taking care of the retail end at the destination. I had a pilot's license making me capable of renting an airplane. We needed to go to the airport where we would land the loaded Navajo to make sure it was adequate.

I rented a plane at Caldwell Airport in New Jersey and four of us flew to Pennsylvania. I was such an inexperienced pilot I nearly got lost looking for Bendinsky Airport. The airstrip was on a ridge of a coal mining mountain south of Scranton. After making a low pass over the old unmaintained runway, I landed on the fairly smooth gravel surface. There were a few rundown shacks and remnants of old hangers with vegetation growing all over them. Trees were closing in on the once forty-foot-wide runway but we considered it acceptable. The area looked abandoned. On the aeronautical chart there was a red X depicting Bendinsky as a closed airport. This place would fit our purposes if the weather was good enough to find it when the time came.

I stayed in a loft in Brooklyn while waiting for the operation to begin. Some of the participants, the ones who would meet the plane at Bendinsky to unload it, lived there. It wasn't a very long wait and another indication the Feds were involved. Police are on time. A few days after checking out the airport in coal country we got word it was show time. I took a flight to Kingston, Jamaica where Justinic came to my motel room and we met for the first time since the lunch in New York. He asked me if I was armed. I was not and more surprised by the question than curious. I was so naïve.

We met early the following morning in the hotel lobby and went to the airport. While he filed the flight plan, which surprised me, I continued like a lamb on its way to slaughter. There were two other men waiting to file their flight plans, too. These other fellows were in their late twenties, clean cut and fit looking. Justinic finished the paperwork and started toward the exit. I followed him out to the airplane.

I was thrilled getting into a multi-engine aircraft and asked all of the flying questions I could muster. More questions about flying than what we were doing. This guy was straight with me about flying, not patronizing or condescending no matter how wrong my thinking.

We took off from Kingston and went to the airport in Ocho Rios on the north side of the island. The airport was unattended early in the morning and we taxied to the end of the runway where we met Michael. This was a frenzied affair, since we would have all ended up in a Jamaican jail if caught. Michael and his "bimmies" (locals) were running in and out of the bushes with bails of grass while Justinic and I loaded them into the Navajo. There was only room for half a ton and away we went. It was necessary to go around Cuban airspace on the way to Fort Lauderdale Executive Airport. We would get refueled, and then on to Bendinsky, Pennsylvania. Justinic did not know the destination. I had a phone number to call when we were ready to leave for Bendinsky.

From Ocho Rios we flew as normal traffic. We weren't down on the deck so low the windshield picked up the surf spray crossing the beach into Florida. Even with all of these telling displays of a setup I was oblivious. My mind was on airplanes, who cares if we brought some pot in with all the other things in the world needing attention. I was wrong, very wrong.

When we stopped on the fuel ramp in Fort Lauderdale Justinic said he had to go piss and I should wait at the plane. After he crawled over the bales to the back of the plane where the airstair door was, I followed. When I got out the same two fellows who I saw at the airport in Kingston were there, cuffs in hand. In an instant I felt like the biggest fool in the world.

They addressed me by name and arrested me. From then on until I was turned over to the Dade County jailers, they soft talked me for information on the load's destination. "Are the cuffs too tight?" and "If you want to help yourself now is the time, James," from the good cop. "Have you ever been to Atlanta? That's where the max security Federal Prison is," from the bad cop. Back and forth they went. I wasn't going to be the guy who brought the troops to Bendinsky. I would have walked if I had.

The night in the holding tank at Dade County was brightened some when the evening news came on and some of the inmates recognized me on the television from the airport.

"Hey is that you?" said one of the prisoners.

Sure was me and I'm in the shit now.

Morning brought the bail hearing and Justinic's first appearance since, "I have to take a piss." He came to the holding cell where I was waiting my turn and he continued with the government's position of seeking cooperation from me. It was a soft sell with enough of the real possibilities they could hammer me with. Making sure the FAA never let me fly again got my attention like a slap in the face.

He wanted Michael's last name and a statement from me. Michael wouldn't have cared if it got me out but I just couldn't. I told him the name of a detective in the township where Michael and I grew up. Justinic left the cell and worked the detective connection. There was no bail bondsman anywhere on my behalf, so I was on my own. The statement wasn't so hard to give up since loyalty seemed in short supply from the others involved.

The detective, Marty DeLeo, was like family. He babysat my brother and me when we were toddlers. Two years before this Florida incident I was arrested for use of marijuana at my home in Martinsville. Marty refused to participate in the arrest or take credit in the press. The anger in his face was evident when I was brought into the police station, though. A year earlier he had arrested Michael for possession resulting in a jail sentence.

When Justinic came back to my holding cell with Michael's name he told me I would be released but I had to give a complete statement. So it went. The statement had an attachment, which required my testifying in future proceedings related to this case.

I was released and made my way back to Truckee. Chris and I moved to Palo Alto where I found a lawyer in Menlo Park, Doug Sorensen. He told me how to go about obtaining the best results possible. I was to get a meaningful job, matriculate into college, or otherwise infuse myself into society, so putting me in jail was ripping me from a positive lifestyle. He also wanted the best letters of reference I could gather. I followed his advice and judge shopping commenced.

There were three possible venues for my case in the Federal Court system. The offense happened in the Southern District of Florida; I lived in the Eastern District of California at the time of the offense, my present address was the Northern District of California. The latter would mean a San Francisco judge, which my attorney was pressing for to give me the best possible chance to avoid jail time. The opposition was doing their own research of sentences handed down from these districts. The compromise was the Eastern District of California in Sacramento and Judge McBride, but I had to show up in the Fort Lauderdale court for arraignment to make this happen. The formal written indictment was sent out. The letter began with The United States of America V. James Gannone and made my heart feel heavy.

After traveling to Florida, I went to New York to meet with Michael before returning to California. He had buried the last of his money near a house he rented in the Catskills. He picked me up at the airport and we went to where the money was and split his last ten grand. At one point I started to talk about the statement and he stopped me to say he didn't care what I told them. "Anything to get out of there," he said. Not taking the Feds to Bendinsky was what counted.

Chris had gone home to care for her mother. I went back to California where I had friends in Santa Cruz who helped me. They were attending the University of California at Santa Cruz and I soon became a student there as well. I was living in a dorm when the parole officer came to do her presentence report. I answered the door and she identified herself badge and all. She asked if I knew why she was there. "You want to see if I'm of any worth," I said. She chuckled a bit and agreed. We talked for at least a half an hour and I must have been charming because she wrote the best report my lawyer had ever seen. It included her statement of how this was "atypical behavior for Mr. Gannone."

The letters of reference were more painful to get. Some of them were obtained without the wrath of the individual relative or friend I reached out to. But some were ass-chewing. I deserved it all. Of the fifteen letters, my lawyer trimmed it down to ten. He assembled them in order of the most impressive letterhead down to the most common. They all, of course, pleaded for leniency and said what a good fellow I really was. Some blamed Vietnam.

When it was time for sentencing, my lawyer and I went to Judge Thomas McBride's courtroom in Sacramento. I stood up and he said, "I sentence you to five years," he paused to let it sink in. It shook me to my bones. "To serve six months at the Federal Youth Correction Facility at Pleasanton, then five years' probation." I was hoping for Pleasanton and not Lompoc so it sounded pretty good after the initial scare. My lawyer wasn't so happy, though. He said it had been a long time since he had a client sent away. The judge postponed the sentence until the end of the school quarter. I was to report to the Sacramento County jail the day after.

Again, I was fortunate in the big things life brought me. I could have been sent to Lompoc (a real prison), but instead I went to the place where Patty Hearst was an alumna. I spent my free time with a small group. Two were bank robbers and one was in for some petty crime. The four of us played cards whenever we could. If we weren't playing cards, we were reading. I started playing bridge at Pleasanton with Gary Miller (our teacher and a bank robber), Charlie Weeks (bank robber), and John Leon (drugs). We were just one of the many groups comprising the population of this penal experiment where medium security prisoners were mixed with minimum security inmates in a minimum security, co-ed environment.

Pleasanton was a much more genteel atmosphere than Sacramento County jail where I sat for a month awaiting the U.S. Marshalls to transport me to Pleasanton. While in the Pleasanton facility I took advantage of every program I could. They had a few college courses in the humanities and I went to them all. They also offered a welding class and I signed up for it, too.

I finished my sentence including the probation and haven't been at odds with the law since. There was the matter of my annual FAA physical though and it caught me off guard the first time I renewed it. At the bottom of a list of things needing the answer "no" or an explanation, was the crucial question. It wanted to know if there were any changes in the application since the last time. This is where arrests, DUIs, psychiatric treatments, and other miscellaneous maladies would require explanations. I choked. Then I lied. Subsequent applications were answered more truthfully.

Chris and I were married two years after we met and I have no regrets. On the contrary, I was lucky once again in the big things. Chris was the bright spot in this bump in the road, though. She stuck by me while having troubles of her own. Springtime and preparation for sentencing brought us to Palo Alto from Truckee, but Chris had to leave to go home and care for her dying mother. I had the easier task over those months by far. When her mother passed she came back to California to visit me while I was finishing my time out at Pleasanton.

After my release we went to New Jersey and were married in the summer of 1975. Then, I returned to the Bay Area to finish the flight training where it started in 1973. I went to a school in San Jose with several tail wheel Citabrias. They are fully aerobatic airplanes. The school was VA approved and I had enough left in my entitlement to cover the courses needed. Chris and I were again living in Palo Alto. She worked at a translation company as an office manager and I tended bar at a nightclub.

I bought a small radio with an aviation frequency so I could hear the instrument clearances given to the airplanes about to depart the local airport. Listening to other pilots' responses was a way of practicing my clearance shorthand. Combining this with the aviation courses given at Foothill Junior College, including meteorology and courses for airframes and power plants, allowed me to do it all on the cheap. I had to.

When I finished with the gathering of licenses and ratings I was soon facing a bleak job market. I was woefully lacking in the experience required to be competitive. Perhaps more schooling would help. I found an aerial application school and with help from my mother I was able to afford its tuition. The school was in the northern part of the Mississippi Delta and that was the only thing northern about it.

Chapter 7
Commercial Pilot

The agricultural aerial application school I went to was at the northern end of the Mississippi delta. This was William Faulkner country, even if he was from Oxford, Mississippi, farther to the east. I thought this place was as southern as possible. The whites acted as if they took care of the blacks because they needed to be cared for. When I was young my family went on vacation to Williamsburg, Virginia and passing through Richmond we saw the "Whites Only" and "Colored" signs at public drinking fountains and other places. Now I was down here where cotton is king and didn't know what to think of segregation while surrounded by white people who thought little more of me because I was Yankee than they did of "their" blacks.

Merigold Flying Service was in Merigold, Mississippi, the home of the one-time famous Johnny Doer and his wife, Miss Dot. The technique they used to sell their training school was to challenge the prospective student by questioning his ability to make the grade in the ag flying business. "Mister Johnny can tell if a pilot is going to make it just by hearing him take three steps across the floor," said Miss Dot. Mister Johnny wasn't telling you any of this himself because his speech was compromised by his drooling and by the rest of his crippled body. He had eaten so much pesticide in all those years he was left in a wheelchair, or, on a good day, a golf cart with Miss Dot.

"The chemical trucks waited in line on that highway (pointing outside) to load the airplanes when Mr. Johnny was flying," said Miss Dot. They had their day in the sun and now were in the twilight. He didn't make an appearance until she had shaken us down for the tuition money. Lionel Cartier, the other student, was from Ontario, Canada. Two students and one instructor in this class sold as the "best ag aviation school" ever. I was getting the feeling Miss Dot and Mr. Johnny were the king and queen of bullshit the more I saw of their low overhead operation.

They used old military trainers from the 1930s and followed the Army Air Corps' methods of training, for which Johnny Dorr instructed. The next day we met the freshly painted equipment. The fleet consisted of the famous J-3 Piper Cubs and PT-13 Boeing Stearmans. The PT in the case of the Stearman means primary trainer. All U.S. military pilots in the 1930s trained in them before moving on to other aircraft. These were the perfect airplanes in which to learn the basics of flying. Basics were what we were here to fine tune.

Maintenance was suspect in this fleet, too. The second day in the J-3 with an instructor, when we were over the field at four hundred feet, the engine blew. I mean not partial power loss—the damn thing seized. The propeller stopped and everything was quiet. I wasn't concerned and rather welcomed it because there was enough altitude to make an abbreviated landing pattern, short base then turn to final. Could have happened to anybody, right?

Then there was the instructor's rationale for the leaking prop seal putting an oil mist across the windshield. "It simulates what the chemical from the spraying will do and you'll have to deal with it." Sounded weak but turned out to be true in real life.

The training started at four hundred feet with the most basic of ground reference maneuvers to humble us into believing they knew more about flying than anyone else and we should be duly impressed. The S-turns across a road and the crossroad-8s were flown in a pilot's first hours of private pilot flight training—but at a thousand feet. At four hundred feet there is an accuracy required that is not needed at one thousand feet. This was a theatrical ploy on the part of the school. It guaranteed humiliating most of the students, including the occasional high-time pilots who came, by setting them up to fail the most basic examples of airmanship. This established the school's superiority in spite of its very humble facilities.

In addition to the J-3 Cubs and the other Stearmans, their queen of the fleet was a 300hp Franklin-powered Stearman spray plane. Graduates were permitted to fly it the last day, spraying water on an open field. The antique spray plane's control stick was solid hickory.

We did those S-turns and crossroad-8s ad nausea at Merigold Flying Service. They are both started in the same position, which is on the downwind side of the road two hundred feet from and parallel to it. The airplane is banked towards the road and the wings are rolled level just as the leading edge of the wing comes even with the road, without gaining or losing any altitude. Then the pilot turns back towards the road in the other direction with less bank angle—otherwise the wind's influence will cause the airplane to come back over the road before you get the chance to roll the wings level. The more wind you are dealing with, the shallower the upwind bank and steeper the downwind bank must be if you are to maintain the two hundred feet radius. It takes practice, hour upon hour of practice, to become second nature.

The crossroad-8 puts it together by finishing an S-turn back in the direction of the starting point. We did them over and over again, like the scout bees that return to the hive with the message dance of where to find the flowers. Then on to chandelles, which are maximum performance climbs finished in a 180 degree turn from the original heading. This is where a lazy-8 joins the maneuver and the airplane continues the turn and is flown to the beginning altitude of the chandelle, arriving with the same speed as the entry.

These maneuvers are really the sum total of what is necessary to spray any field. The airplane begins spraying the downwind side of it, like spreading fertilizer on a lawn. At the end of the field, after the spray handle is shut off, you pull up just before taking any of the trees with you. When clear of obstacles, you execute a small turn downwind and start a chandelle back into the wind. At the top of the climb, you complete a lazy-8 back down, just over the trees, into the field completing the turnaround and then the money handle is opened once again. Done properly, it is a short aria leading you into the proper alignment for the next swath so as not to have skips or overlapping in the material application. This kind of flying requires skill with a heavily loaded airplane. I knew a pilot who had a tune he hummed in his turnarounds. Another said, "If you've never hit anything you're just not getting close enough."

I came back to New Jersey after the Mississippi experience and sent out a hundred of my meager resumes, getting three responses. There were two polite "Thanks but no thanks," and one offer from Action Aerial to tow banners in Ocean City, New Jersey for the coming season. It was time to push forward and I accepted the banner job. All that ag training, just to tow banners—how underwhelming.

When I got to Action Aerial early in the summer of 1977, I was the last of four pilots hired. Two of us had no experience, one had a previous season, and one was much older, at the final stage of his career. By the time the season ended there were three bent up airplanes, two others demolished and one dead pilot. Chip, the pilot who died, was the one who was overconfident from a previous season of experience.

Banner towing is fun in the beginning but by the end of the summer becomes monotonous and boring. One thing never became tiresome: the pick-up of the sign. Two six-foot-tall poles with small flags on top are spread about eight feet apart on the ground. The loop end of a hundred-foot tow rope, attached to the sign, rests on top and stretches across the poles. The airplane flies over the poles, beginning the rotation before getting to them, and attempts to capture the loop with the grappling hook dangling at the end of a ten-foot rope. There is a pilot-controlled mechanism to release the attached hook. The pilot climbs the airplane as steeply as possible trading speed for altitude and pushes the nose over before the impending stall. This peels the banner off the ground without damaging it with excessive speed.

That is how it should happen. Not only are there plenty of misses in the beginning of the season but there are times when the tow rope gets caught in a part of the airplane and won't release. This often happens following a number of misses on a windy day when the pilot is pressing to get the hook through the gate.

Landing with a sign requires a little technique to prevent it from pulling the airplane out of the air when the sign comes in contact with the ground. The trick is to get the airplane down to a couple of feet off the deck before the sign settles onto the surface of a hard runway. Company procedure was to go to Woodbine airport, a fifteen-minute flight, where the sign slides more easily on the surface.

The pilot who was at the end of his career had lost his airline job and turned to banners for the summer. He brought a six-pack to work, daily, and had to be reminded to throw the empties out over the bay and not in the field where we worked. One morning he missed the banner with the tail hook, picking it up on his main gear. Instead of going to Woodbine, he landed in the sod field we were using, which flipped him over when the sign caught in the grass. The tail of the airplane was damaged and John, the boss, fired him on the spot. The incident was not a result of equipment failure, just good old fashioned pilot error.

He was flying so hung over he might as well have been drunk.

I was shaken by the fatal accident. The other pilot and I were supposed to pull two signs in formation with me in the lead. I came into the pickup area and hooked my sign with him not far behind. After getting some altitude, I turned back towards the field to find his whereabouts and saw his airplane's tail sticking out of the ground at an angle, with some smoke rising out of where the nose was buried. I dropped my sign, made an abbreviated landing pattern and got to the wreck as fast as I could. As I was landing I could see the two banner boys just standing, frozen in fear, around Chip's wreck. These were adolescent teenagers who were lucky they weren't under the plane.

I pulled the dying pilot out of his cockpit. I laid him on his side so the blood wouldn't drown him. He hung on for another week in the hospital. The doctors put a nose on him for the sake of his parents and anyone else who looked at what was left of his face.

After the ambulance left, I flew another banner to do the get-back-on-the-horse-that-threw-you exercise, pulled it around Ocean City, dropped it back in the field and parked the airplane. I wasn't sure about what to do next.

Listening to my boss, yet another Marine, carry on about what the accident had cost him and did I know I had left signs in the field, I wasn't sure I wanted to work for him. My not flying those signs represented money lost. I told John I was taking tomorrow off to go see my brother.

"Are you coming back?" he asked.

"I don't know." I said.

My brother remains the most descent and level headed person I know. We didn't dwell on what happened but just being in his company had a calming effect on me.

The next day I returned to Ocean City to finish the season. I learned numerous lessons flying those corroded airplanes. What makes flying banners a particularly dangerous affair is the lack of experience most pilots bring to it. Every once in a while you will see an older pilot doing it, but not often. It's an entry level job into grass roots aviation. However, on the positive side I found out that most women looked good from two hundred feet as I was pulling the banners across the waves breaking onto the beach.

I wrecked an airplane during that summer—a Super Cub John had just bought. It had flaps, unlike the other planes we were using. This company didn't fix things until they were broken. The boss bent up one airplane by trying to use it when one wheel had no brakes, which he already knew about.

I borrowed the Super Cub so Chris and I could fly up to Manville. We came back to Ocean City after a cold front went through but it was still too windy for my talents and I lost it on the runway. We ended up in a tidal ditch upside down. My dry rotted seatbelt broke on impact and I rolled out of the airplane into the marsh grass. I turned around to look for Chris and she was hanging upside down attached to her seat. I released her seatbelt and eased her out while she was still holding a bag of tomatoes we brought with us. Wrecked the airplane but didn't break a tomato skin.

"Ah, John, I busted up your airplane." It's not a fun call to make. He told me, "You have to live with it." And I have, unashamedly. Turned out I fit right in with the insurance statistic spikes, where accidents accumulate. This one was at four hundred hours total time. The next potential pitfall would be six hundred and then twelve hundred. When John got to the site of the wreck, I tried to continue the apology but he stopped me with, "No one gets on a good man like a good man." Nothing more was ever said.

One of the better pieces of flying advice I ever received came in a banner field from a fellow pilot. "If you don't know what the airplane will do, take it to altitude, not close to the deck, and try it." Once again, good sense—and good sense cannot be bought.

New pilots often become flight instructors to build time and experience. This is a slow process and I was not patient. I wanted to work and build time, now. Being in the right place at the right time with experience in the right airplane means more on a resume than three lunar landings. It was my understanding at least half of young pilots looking for entry level jobs lie about their experience to get a foot in the door.

There is a reason the Airline Transport License requires twelve hundred hours of total flying time. In addition to the time requirements, the new pilot must undergo a demanding check ride. The candidate must pass a rigorous written exam. A commercially licensed pilot can sometimes get into a crewed airplane with a good captain and be brought through the learning progression properly. More often the case, one has to cut his teeth alone flying canceled checks at night or charters down in the islands. At some point, though, you are going to be all alone up there, at night, in horseshit weather and the plane will be making sounds you hadn't heard before. I have never lost the fear of something going wrong beyond my ability to handle it. Bad things can and do happen to good pilots.

Chapter 8
Flying Freight

The VA put a time limit on the availability of entitlement funds—ten years from date of discharge. That date was approaching for me and I found a flight school at Love Field in Dallas with a policy of extending credit for training to G.I. Bill entitled students. The school had a VA-approved Cessna Citation program that would allow me to be type-rated and I had the prerequisites. Citations were Cessna's attempt to get into the business jet market. It is a very simple jet and if I could complete the course in minimum time there was enough VA money remaining to pay for it. This would require some real effort on my part though.

By this time I had added the necessary multi-engine rating to my license. I just spent the summer in grass roots aviation and not a radio in sight. The world of jets is one of technology and complexity, next to which I was a country bumpkin. Regardless, I had to give it a go. I would just study hard and slug my way through it.

The airplane rented for nine dollars a minute. I could not afford to bust a check ride because a do over would be a thousand dollars or more. Passing the course and check ride was nip and tuck but I left Dallas with my first type rating—CE-500—in a jet with only six hundred and fifty hours Total Time. It was the eyebrow raiser on my meager resume.

My flying time was still low but the type rating indicated I was trainable. Submitting a resume can be tricky if you don't know the company's requirements and are not above bending the truth. There is no second chance to add another hundred hours here or there. I embellished my resume with "P-51 time." In the trade that means adding hours with a Parker T-ball jotter pen and not actual time in the famous fighter plane of late World War Two vintage.

I doubled my total time and multiplied my meager twelve hours of multi-engine time by ten. With the type rating and the legitimate tailwheel time from banners, I hoped I had enough to get in the door of an operation based in Cargo City, the cargo area of Philadelphia International Airport. Flight Express Cargo operated Beech-18s and I couldn't have asked for a better time-building opportunity. I was hungry to fly one of their airplanes. They left Philadelphia International (PHL) and Baltimore–Washington International (BWI) to points west five nights a week.

The first night I went to Flight Express one of their airplanes was idling, loaded, on the ramp in the light, cool rain. There were nine cylinders on each of the Pratt & Whitney 985 engines slowly ticking over with occasional plumes of yellow flames bellowing out of the exhaust stacks. Oil leaks streaked the nacelles and undercarriage of the airplane. The sound of the radial engines pulsated through me. They were the roots of the adventure, all very *Casablanca* like; Bogart and Claude Rains could have been standing in front of that airplane in trench coats and not looked a bit out of place.

Inside the Flight Express office I met Chuck Weldon, flamboyant but still a nice chap. We stepped into the cargo bay for him to have a smoke. He skimmed over my resume and said he would try me out as an air crew member. My big chance arrived in the form of a sixty-hour workweek loading and unloading the airplane at every stop. Chuck said the pay was four hundred dollars for the first month, five hundred for the second and six for the third. Captain's pay started at twelve hundred a month if I made it. I had to earn this experience.

Crawling through the cockpit window of the old freighter as an air crew member was exciting. The thrill I felt was from the airplane—a Beech-18 with all of its mileage and scars. This was my chance to advance as a pilot and I was motivated. Flying one of these airplanes said something about you. I wanted this on my resume. Flight time here was night, multi-engine, and mostly instrument simultaneously. If I survived a year here I would have enough time to pursue most pilot entry-level positions and be competitive.

The "Beech" is a twin engine, conventional gear airplane—some say a pilot's airplane. This airplane is "flown" from the chocks to the chocks. Chocks are triangular blocks that wedge between the wheels and ground preventing their movement when the airplane is parked. Airplanes with tricycle landing gear are driven to the point of takeoff and after landing driven back to the chocks.

Taxiing this airplane properly requires technique. To make a turn the pilot must advance the throttle of the engine opposite the direction of the desired turn to bring that wing around. Turning to the right is started by advancing the throttle of the left engine. Asymmetrical thrust in the reverse order is required to stop the turn. This is where one displays the quality called "touch." Does the pilot use just two hundred RPMs or five hundred? If you don't have to use the brakes at all in this turn/stop-the-turn process, you have a touch. You also probably don't race through the radio dials either.

The rudders are inter-connected to the rudder pedals via cables but at taxi speeds there isn't enough airflow going past those small rudders to affect directional control by themselves. Push the left pedal forward and the right comes aft. Pressing on the top of the respective pedal actuates individually controlled brakes. Using brakes alone for turning is bad form, poor planning and usually unnecessary. While taxiing the tailwheel is unlocked and free to turn in any direction.

On the runway ready for takeoff, the tailwheel is locked in a straight fore and aft position to aid in keeping the airplane straight for take-off and landing. With an aft-loaded center of gravity and gusty winds, landings demand that a pilot remain alert. The transition phase of the wheel landing is when the tail is starting to come down after the mains are on the runway. The tail controls lose their effectiveness as they come down. When the locked tailwheel is on the runway there is some resistance to the side loads from a gusting crosswind. The transition is the tricky part; it's a no man's land, between positive air control to positive ground control.

A crosswind landing in a Beech requires lowering the upwind wing to put that main wheel on the runway first with the corresponding engine set a few hundred RPMs faster than the downwind engine. The airplane is kept straight with the rudder inputs from the pilot's active feet as the pilot levels the wing. As the airplane slows with throttle reduction the tail is carefully brought to the runway and pinned there with the control column fully aft in the pilot's lap. The airplane has to be slow enough or the main wheels will lift off the runway as the tail is lowered. Those are the main ingredients of landing a conventional gear, multi-engine airplane. Once in the air they behave like any other airplane.

Flight Express was my introduction to FAR Part 135 Air Taxi operations. A single pilot 135 captaincy is a significant rite of passage for any aspiring professional pilot. It is a bit like losing one's virginity, full of apprehension and clumsiness. The check ride may be the most challenging in the pilot's career for a number of reasons. Except for the self-induced pressure, everything else is usually minimal, from the company-provided training to the experience the candidate brings to the cockpit. Transport category aircraft are complex, but training provided by the FAR Part 121 regulations is very thorough. If a candidate fails a 121 ride, the company's training department is taken to task by the FAA.

Flying with Captain Zook was not fun. When I think of Bobby Zook a short curmudgeon comes to mind—five-feet-five, with deep, dark crow's feet trailing the sides of eyes that begged for sleep. I wondered if he slept at all. He was slim, barely sociable, and when he laughed he made little heh, heh, heh laughs. Until then my only crew experience had been in the Citation type rating training. I was wrong to expect any crew coordination in his cockpit.

Flight Express was an operation with an imaginary line drawn down the middle of the cockpit between the captain and co-pilot—that side is yours and this side is mine—very old school. In the 1970s there was still an autocratic ambiance (the captain is king) in most crewed airplanes. The old timers had a name for the new procedures being initiated through the airlines—charm school. The formal name, Cockpit Resource Management, resulted in an improvement resolving emergent situations. All available resources are used, not just the captain's.

The first night with Zook, excited as a new bridegroom, I crawled in through the window next to the captain's seat. The challenges started there, the only way in or out of the cockpit. First the right leg, up to the thigh, went in followed by the right arm, shoulder and head. Then I squeezed the rest of myself through while Zook was making remarks about me losing a few pounds. The amount of clothing I wore didn't make it any easier. These were cold weather operations and the cockpit heaters were unreliable. My snowmobile boots, ski pants and parka were not overkill.

Once in, I was witness to the Zook way of doing things. When he started the engines they always backfired and blew long flames out of the exhaust while he kept pumping the throttle. During his unique starting procedure I was trying to get situated in the cramped quarters of the cockpit. I had my little writing pad strapped to my leg with the spare pencils, ready for my chance to copy the instrument flight clearance. I so wanted to do well. After the start he told me not to touch the radios; he would handle everything. I sat on my hands while Zook repeated the clearances from memory (virtually the same every night), worked ground control, tower and departure control.

So I watched and watched, night after night. He seemed to know what he was doing but even at this early point I could tell if someone had a soft touch or not. Twisting a radio dial aggressively to change frequencies and not permitting the mechanism to fall into each detent as the dial goes through the sequence indicates impatience, haste and a lack of sensitivity. That spoke of challenges to come. Off we went, destined for Cleveland with a stop in Harrisburg first.

We unloaded cargo at Sundorf Aviation at Cleveland Hopkins Airport and took on more bound for Detroit Metro. Zook showed me where to get the engine oil and how to put it in the reservoirs. The engines were old, very high time, burning and throwing oil out at a gallon per hour. Two gallons per engine Philadelphia to Cleveland was normal.

The maximum gross weight of a Beech-18 was ten thousand one hundred pounds but this company usually flew them a thousand pounds over gross or more. If one of the engines as much as sneezed on takeoff your immediate future was in doubt. These airplanes were built from 1937-1969 and looked it. Beech-18s came out at night hauling freight all over the Midwest. Flight Express Cargo usually flew three or four Beeches carrying everything from car parts to laboratory animals Monday through Friday nights. All airplanes turned around in Detroit, stopping at Cleveland on the way back to Philadelphia, with one overnighting in Baltimore.

Loading the heaviest freight as far forward as possible moves the center of gravity and helps get the tail up on takeoff. If you have enough runway the Beech would eventually break ground. The climb will be slow though. Sometimes a step climb is necessary for the first half hour until some fuel weight burned off.

The start of this technique begins with landing gear retraction. Once the wheels are in the wheel wells the airplane is in a cleaner configuration and will gain speed. The best rate of climb speed (Vy) will yield the greatest altitude for a given time and is the target speed. A shallow climb is initiated until the speed starts to bleed off, then the climb is relaxed to recoup the speed. The little engine that could. When the speed builds back up to Vy the climb is begun again and the step process is repeated as necessary until the airplane can maintain Vy. Airspeed increases with the thinner air in higher altitudes where less fuel is burned.

In the aviation community local pilots called this company "Fright Express Cargo." It was owned by two pilots, the one who gave me the job, Chuck, a former Air Force fighter pilot, and Ron, a crop duster from Kansas. The company got the name because of their policy of flying overloaded airplanes, questionable maintenance practices or suspected lack thereof, and an aggressive, hard-nosed approach to weather. Some said they did maintenance inspections from the cockpit with a pen while en route to the next stop. There was also a matter of the number of airplanes they had wrecked the previous winter. The blemished safety record was enough for the FAA to revoke Chuck's check airman status. As a result, all company pilot equipment and six-month instrument proficiency check rides were done with FAA inspectors. The equipment check approved a pilot for a year of flying by visual flight rules and the six-month was an approval for instrument flying. If this was done in-house, it was less expensive for the company, especially with no ferry time to the General Aviation District Office at North Philadelphia airport and back.

Zook had the unofficial company record for flying the heaviest Beech. He demolished one on takeoff at Harrisburg International one snowy night ending in a ditch upside down. Another new captain ran out of gas and flew into a farmhouse in Pittsburgh while he was looking for an airport with VFR conditions. Chuck took off into a snowstorm from Harrisburg with no flight plan trying to get the plane back to the maintenance base at Wilmington, DE. He received an instrument clearance en route but iced up and lost all power, crashing into a gravel pit south of the airport.

Chuck was a colorful character. He had panache, from his southern drawl to his fine leather boots. His wife Georgia's style and looks gave the office an air of credibility. They were a smart looking couple. I saw Chuck's FAA folder of accidents and violations—almost an inch thick. He told me there were nine accidents, "Not just bent props." He needed only a white scarf and goggles to go with the leather gloves he wore for takeoff and landing. When I flew with him he slept every leg and I had to wake him up for the landing. He yawned and shook some, lit a cigarette, put his gloves on, and painted the Beech onto the runway, never a bounce. I was desperate to land that aircraft as well as he did.

Ron, the other partner, took me on an introductory flight of his own that I loved. On the way back to Philadelphia from Baltimore just after dawn he canceled radar flight-following and flew up the Chesapeake at a few feet off the water. I was thrilled to be there and glad to be alive when it was over.

Ron had me flying with Zook from the night I started with the company. It took Zook a week before he let me talk on the radio and finally let me fly some en route. Zook started giving me a little instruction and let me try to land the Beech. His teaching style involved allowing me to get to the point where I was in real need of help and then making a big deal of his rescue. Patience was not in his makeup as evidenced by his landings. No finesse, just get the plane down close to the runway and push the wheels on after a couple of bounces.

En route, he did amaze me though. I hated him for going to sleep during his leg and I wasn't comfortable dozing off myself since he wasn't minding the store. But he was the captain and I didn't have much say so. After a while I felt foolish being so concerned. At cruising altitude, he trimmed the airplane to straight and level, established the course to the next fix and did not lose or gain more than two hundred feet while he slept lightly. As the airplane slowly started descending or climbing, the propellers went out of sync, causing an audible harmonic imbalance, which woke him up. He eased the plane back to altitude, trimmed, and returned to sleep. He often woke up to switch fuel tanks before they ran dry but not always. In keeping with his rough ways he just switched tanks without retarding the throttle first and easing the power in as the engine came alive with fuel. This caused a violent power surge, not good for the engine or airframe.

I asked Ron if being paired with Zook was some kind of punishment or initiation. He said no, laughed, and started assigning me to other captains. Flying with those other pilots was a relief, even some fun. A little conversation was a breath of fresh air. They actually talked me through approaches and landings as necessary. I grew. Taking the tension out of the process enhanced my learning.

One of the other captains was Tommy Leonzi, from Delaware. He came with a heavily-scarred face from burns received trying to get his passengers out of a wreck he had some months earlier. Leonzi was a Vietnam army veteran, cool as could be. We no sooner broke ground in Philadelphia to start the slow, lumbering climb process when he poured a cup of coffee. I would have been gritting my teeth afraid to let my attention wander this close to the ground to pick up a thermos from the deck of the airplane. He told me, "The gooks didn't get me and this Beech won't either."

My first captaincy was with Flight Express. During a landing at Detroit Metro one cold night Zook forgot to pump up the brakes while on final approach. Making sure the brakes work is a precautionary procedure. There was gusting wind at DTW when he got the main wheels on the runway and went for the brakes for some reason. One side didn't have any and the plane started to get away from him into a ground loop. Ground loop is a euphemism to describe an uncontrolled 360 degree turn on the ground, pivoting on one main landing wheel. The ground loop happens in any conventional gear airplane without much help from the pilot. Just a little inattention or misalignment and the center of gravity behind the main wheels will bring the small tailwheel around to be with the big ones all by itself and the pilot looks foolish.

The procedure in a Beech when such a maneuver becomes imminent is to pull back on the yoke pinning the tail down and "go for the ride." Trying to save it with asymmetrical thrust and braking will often overstress the main landing gear with excessive side loads. Unlocking the tailwheel needs to be done so it "free casters" (free to turn in any direction) and doesn't break off due to excessive side loads. When I saw he had forgotten that part, I unlocked the wheel. The right seat makes you seem smarter because your mind is uncluttered. After doing a couple of 360s across the median separating the runway and taxiway the plane finally came to a stop. We ended up next to the huge propellers of an idling Convair 580 whose crew no doubt saw the whole show.

My presence of mind to unlock the tail wheel and my improved abilities handling the airplane convinced Zook I was ready for the left seat. Zook and I did not have a great relationship and strangely this made his recommendation more weighted. He was a brother Marine who had been discharged out of the Corps before a chance to go to Vietnam. I always felt he resented my having served there. Putting me up for a check ride with the feds was a conundrum. Lying about my time to Ron and Chuck to get the job was one thing. Lying to the FAA, who still had me intimidated, quite another.

When I told Ron the story of my inflated resume he told me to bring my log book into work Monday night and, "We'll have a look see." I spent the weekend thinking I was going to be fired. Chuck checked my log and saw the six hundred plus hours (Flight Express time) written in as aircrew member time. The wording in the company manual, aircrew member as opposed to pilot, does not require the company to flight train someone in the right seat. Training costs are virtually eliminated this way. Chuck laughed as he figured out the solution, which was to have all the captains who flew with me sign off the time as dual instruction since they all had instructor licenses. His plan worked. I took the ride, passed and had what is called an equipment check in the Beech-18. This means I was good to go by visual flight rules but not by instrument flight rules.

The night I took my first flight as Captain, Chuck told me not to run out of gas looking for visual conditions. "We already had a Captain do that." Picking up an instrument clearance in flight was a simple matter of calling air traffic control and asking for a vector to the final approach fix. All the freight stops we used had an ILS, which stands for Instrument Landing System. The ILS gives the pilot guidance information down to two hundred feet above the landing zone. As with other rule-breaking maneuvers, no one asks questions until after an accident.

Flight Express had no radar in their airplanes to help avoid thunderstorms and if the weather looked bad, you knew that you were going anyhow. Punching through squall lines was de rigueur. The Allegheny Mountains, especially around Johnstown and Pittsburgh, were always the worst at two in the morning. At times it rained so hard water came streaming into the cockpit around the windshield and ran down to the electrical switches at the bottom of the dashboard. I wondered what kept them from starting to smoke and popping circuit breakers.

Once I built my time up to the twelve hundred hours necessary total time, I took and passed my first six-month instrument proficiency check ride. That made me a viable commodity in the pilot market. As the title suggests, renewal is required every six months and is needed by those who are doing any kind of air taxi or airline flying. It's not a big deal if you are flying a lot because you are current. However, get rusty from being out of work and once again the proficiency required to demonstrate competency will require some training. Since those days I have failed a couple of rides on my way back into the game after periods of flying unemployment.

After flying as a "line pilot," I started to become concerned about the value of my license and risking it, as well as my ass, with this company. Winter was coming and I knew this hard-nosed bunch would fly right into the ice with the same abandon as they did with thunderstorms. One night Chuck said, "You can usually find an altitude between 4000' and 8000' you can live with," meaning not picking up too much ice. "Live with"—I thought his wording a bit ominous. I had never experienced structural ice and the prospect scared me. One of the keys with ice is to stay out of altitudes with visible moisture (clouds) where the temperature is between plus and minus ten degrees centigrade. In other words, mind the outside air temperature.

Propeller ice striking the side of the fuselage is an alert to start paying closer attention. By then the wing leading edges and engine nacelles already have ice building up. As soon as the airframe picks up an inch of ice it loses ten knots of airspeed. Asking the controller for a different altitude is usually all that is required. "I have to get out of here. Is 8000' available?" There are anti-icing and de-icing systems on airplanes certified for flight into known icing conditions and they are a big help but ice is still a killer. The weight increases, center-of-gravity becomes an unknown and drag also becomes an issue.

Flight Express's Beeches used alcohol for propeller de-icing. A mechanism dispersed the fluid at the leading edge of the propeller blade to dislodge accumulating ice. It flew off the blades and made a racket when hitting the side of the fuselage. I probably should have leveled with Ron and Chuck about my concerns and gotten some advice. A babysitter might have been in order. Some old co-pilot who was well experienced would have been perfect for me, but there were none of those at Flight Express. People didn't stay long at this company, except guys like Zook.

While doing the preflight one evening I found there was alcohol only coming out of one propeller blade, which leads to an imbalance with the buildup of ice on one blade and not the other. This would be worse than no alcohol at all. I complained to Ron and he fired me. His response was probably related to my also having asked a few nights previous for load manifests that stated I was under maximum gross weight. He might have told me how to sling the ice off by rapidly changing the propeller RPM setting instead of using the alcohol but didn't. I couldn't have been the first green captain to become difficult. I went home and told Chris what had happened and she said, "Great, you got fired for having good sense."

I never regretted my time there, quite the contrary. I built time in a compound manner and was a Twin-Beech captain. Having accrued the magical five hundred hours of Pilot in Command multi-engine time made my resume respectable enough to send out. Most of my time was night instrument time in a well-respected, multi-engine aircraft. The key to time-building is to stay employed, not easy in a business that only thrives on the leading edge of a prosperous economy.

Chapter 9
Opening Door To Ag Work

After Flight Express Cargo, I worked for Gelsi Lease Air. These were both Part 135 Air-taxi operations but used opposite techniques to deal with FAA inspectors. Flight Express argued and fought the FAA at every turn when they came to examine records and maintenance paperwork, driving them out with a headache. Gelsi's operation was so squeaky clean they needed to leave a "fish"—a small intentional infraction—for the inspectors to find.

Gelsi operated four twin engine airplanes and one single engine as an on-demand charter business. The main client was a turbine rebuilding company, Airwork, located at the same airport in Millville, New Jersey. This job gave me some New York air traffic exposure. The usual trip was delivering a rebuilt engine, or taking salesmen on calls. Sometimes we took an engine mechanic to an ailing piece of expensive corporate iron like a Gulfstream or a Lear. I liked the work but the pay was weak.

I was type rated in Cessna's first business jet, the Citation, with some respectable experience from the night freight work. It made me a candidate for a right seat in a corporate jet. Why not look up, instead of ag? I could go there later, as necessary. Rubbing elbows with people in the middle of corporate aviation was new for me. Flying the Airwork sales executives to the prestigious Westchester Aviation Mechanics Association's monthly dinners at the Purchase Country Club in Rye, New York, gave me a broader view of what I could do. I was slowly losing focus on aerial application as my path.

After taking a preparation course for the written part of the Airline Transport Pilot License, I went on to pass the practical part when my next six-month proficiency check ride was due. All of this gave my resume at least a pause before it went into the HR trash. My aviation heart was still with propellers and round engines, but jets? They were cool.

When a food processing corporation, Blue Coach Foods, bought Gelsi they came with a small flight department. Their plan was to keep the 135 certificate active to offset some of the cost of corporate transportation. In the changeover process, Cessna Aircraft Company entered the mix and not only sold Blue Coach a Cessna Conquest, but also a dealership with an inventory to sell. In aviation sometimes things move quickly and this time I had the left seat of a turbo-prop Cessna Conquest in a few months. I felt good about flying an airplane worth almost a million dollars. My pay scale for flying this expensive equipment however was way below what others flying similar airplanes were making. The salary survey done by Professional Pilot Magazine showed me well below the lowest of any geographic area in the country. I wasn't happy and felt taken advantage of.

Altair Airlines was expanding to Philadelphia and a friend was an FAA official attached to their certificate. He helped me to the interview process and I was invited to their next ground school. It excited me and I told people who told other people. One of the people who became part of the new Gelsi was a former policeman named Wes Tessey. He was the chief pilot on the 135 certificate but it was no secret to me he wanted my seat in the Conquest. He cozied up to me with soft conversation one afternoon in the pilot's lounge telling me he heard I might have a chance at Altair. "Would you go if they offered?" I told him I would, knowing he would waste no time in using the information to help his cause.

The CEO of Blue Coach called me into the office and asked me if I was planning to leave. The smart response would have been some kind of rug dance asking for a raise. Groveling is not my style and I said, "I'd be a fool not to go to Altair." That slammed the door on Blue Coach for me. As soon as they put Wes Tessey through ground school and he was insurable, I was paid off. During this period of transition, I received a letter from Altair saying they canceled the ground school I was invited to and went out of business soon thereafter.

I was unemployed for a few weeks feeling the fool when Matt Baczeor called me. He said if I wanted to fly an Ag-Cat to call Dick Nixholm at Downstown. He needed pilots for forest fire work in the New Jersey Pine Barrens. A 400,000-acre forestry contract for spraying gypsy moths followed fire season. Matt was an ag pilot who worked for Dick. I had taken Matt's son with me on an Airwork engine delivery to give him some multi-engine experience. Matt returned the favor in life-changing fashion when he helped me into my first ag seat.

The New Jersey Pine Barrens is a valuable participant in filtering the toxic runoff from the industrial urban part of the state. The threat from fires is greatest in the spring when the deciduous trees have not extended their leaves, providing no shade to hold down the moisture. The sun and wind dry the accumulated fuel on the forest floor and make any fire aggressive. This whole scenario is completed by the "fire ecology" of the native short pine trees that grow there—Pinus rigida, pitch pine. Their propagation requires the heat from a fire to open their cones and release seeds.

Downstown Aero was started in 1945 and became the largest aerial application business on the east coast. They have their own airport and are an icon in the agricultural aviation world. I was about to be given a shot at becoming part of it. I went there fresh out of the ag school in Mississippi, with three hundred hours total flying time, looking for a job and was politely told to come back when I had some experience. A gentleman named Dick was the partner who handled the pilots. I went to see him at Matt's direction and he had one of their thirteen Ag-Cats outside of the hangers waiting for me. "Go fly it."

I did. After considerable taxiing around the airport to get acclimated to the cockpit and the landing picture lodged into my noggin, off I flew. I was thrilled to be in the cockpit of an Ag-Cat sitting behind the 450HP Pratt & Whitney engine. I did have to get it back on the ground though and the view was limited like the Stearmans I flew in Mississippi. Tailwheel airplanes limit the pilot's forward visibility, making the side view the reference for keeping it on the runway. I took it up to altitude with enough recovery room below me and did some full stalls and steep turns. It was time to land. Not my prettiest landing, but I didn't bend anything. The pressure off, I just wanted to park the airplane, get in my car and leave before something spoiled it all.

Crop-dusting is a misnomer since dust is no longer the carrier for aerial application of pesticides. The carrier is the bulk part of the mix that takes the active ingredient to the target. Now aerial applications are done by spraying a liquid pesticide mix using water or oil as the bulk carrier in a dosage with enough volume to make an effective coverage of the crop. One of the advantages of aerial application is using the wake turbulence of the flight path to carry the pesticide to all parts of the crop. It gets quite windy down there with a full mist of pesticide. Not many of the bugs survive when the job is done properly.

Someone with the frame of mind to do this work can be accused of being an adrenaline addict but I think it a cheap description. I do like thrills and this kind of work has plenty, but I don't like being scared. It's the immediate gratification and control I find so satisfying. Looking for thrills everyday makes for a short career. The inherent risks need to be minimized. There are some leathery-faced old ag pilots with over twenty thousand ag hours under four hundred feet above the ground. These are salty old coots with real endurance. Work an ag plane ten hours and you know what tired means.

Airplanes warn you before they fail. It may be subtle, but if you are listening it is talking to you. Sometimes one's inner voice shows up with a warning and tries to be heard. It may be a bolt of cloud to ground lightning you saw as you were parking your car at the airport making you feel goosey right there in your rectum. Most of those feelings just have to be ignored.

There is an old FAA cartoon showing two FAA inspectors looking at a newly-licensed pilot standing next to a runway who has a bag in each hand, one full and one empty. The full one is named luck and the empty one skill. The one inspector says to the other, "I hope the skill bag fills up before the luck bag runs out."

Ag work is flying—low altitude precision flying—on crops, small grains or vegetables. Forestry doesn't count in there because you could do it while smoking a cigarette and talking to someone on a cell phone. In the south, if you ask if someone is a good ag pilot you'll be told, "the bad one's 'r dayead." Personally I attribute my survival to luck and fear. The fear kept me alert and the luck—it's better to be lucky than good. I have gotten away with more stupid mistakes than I care to think about or admit to. Even though, I have yet to really bust up an ag plane.

The first load of the morning, usually at daybreak, is the best. You are fresh, not tired and sweaty yet. The air is still, smooth, and as cool as it is going to be for the rest of the day. There is quietness there, as if the god of euphoria stopped by with a blessing just before someone coaxes one of the radial engines to life on a working plane. Most of the ag planes I have worked had the old radial reciprocating piston-powered engines, with seven or nine cylinders spaced 360 degrees around the crankshaft. Most airplane engines produced since the 1940s arrange the cylinders in a horizontally opposed flat configuration, not round. It reduces the aerodynamic drag of the engine. Virtually all the American radial engines have been rebuilt many times over since they were first introduced to aviation in 1925.

The radial engine sounds glorious when started. As the starter turns the propeller and a cylinder fires it takes a few revolutions for the rest of them to catch. Sometimes there are loud backfires if whoever is starting it doesn't have the touch. It's a light touch, moving the throttle up in between those cylinders that fire and the ones yet to, and pulling it back before too much fuel is introduced. Trying not to accelerate past idle speed before the oil pressure has built up sufficiently is a proper technique and a beautiful thing to hear—a radial engine started by someone with a patient feel. It's almost as if there is a respectful dialog between the two of, "I'll take care of you if you take care of me." Once those engines settle down, their idle is a gentle tick-over like a Harley saying, "potato, potato."

I've brushed a lot of trees, rubbed wires, taken some down and cut some pieces off airplanes but never rolled one up in a ball in the middle of a field like some guys. I met a Canadian fellow in Mississippi nicknamed "rack 'em up, rip 'em up" Rick who claimed he totaled thirteen airplanes. He was not at all bashful telling those stories given a few beers and an audience, especially if they were young wannabes. If he was insurable the premiums must have been huge.

I worked the fire contract for thirteen seasons and gypsy moth for eight. There were other jobs in between, but come February I was always looking towards the end of March, the start of fire season. When I worked for Allegheny Commuter, the USAir affiliate, out of Atlantic City, I took my vacation time during fire season, unbeknownst to the chief pilot. Working for a scheduled 135 operator has a personal limit of 1000 hours of commercial flying per calendar year and this commuter wanted it all.

The holding tank of the airplane is fitted with a large, hinged, bottom-mounted dump gate that will release the contents in two to three seconds.

The placement accuracy improves with dropping right down on the fire before opening the gate. How close you can get depends on the amount of wind and smoke. Placement of nearly a ton of water on target before a fire becomes too wild makes controlling it easier. As the water is releasing the airplane pitches up radically, due to the unloading and aft-shifting center of gravity.

Forest fire suppression was the most fun I had ever had with my pants on. There was the heat of the fire, especially when the trees started crowning as they would when the fire really started to roll. The flames involved the whole tree, causing the pitch in the pine needles to explode due to the intense ambient heat. There was the violent turbulence, especially when the smoke started rolling black with the licking yellow flames in it like napalm. Flying into the black, shying away from the yellow, guaranteed a wild ride. The engine would momentarily die from either the absence of oxygen or the negative Gs' starving the carburetor of fuel.

Doing something positive for the environment felt rewarding, the intense excitement a bonus. This aggressive behavior, as in other parts of life, would mellow with age; the flying into the rolling black didn't go on for long. I sent resumes to operators of the big tankers in Arizona and Montana but struck out for lack of the mechanic's license they required. The big planes in the mountains eluded me and I never made it out of the Pine Barrens.

After the first season of fires, I received more respect from Dick at Downstown in two months than in whole time at Blue Coach Foods. I now knew corporate aviation was not for me. So I hit the road and this Yankee headed south to the land of grits, white bread and pork fat to find my job as an ag pilot. An operator in Clinton, North Carolina took a chance on me. He needed a pilot to fly a Cessna on soybeans for the corn earworm season, usually a month. I met my first wire on my first load in my first field of real ag work. The difference between forestry work and row crops is the precision required. Not as much room for error or inattention and the pine trees are much taller in North Carolina than New Jersey.

The first load was for four small fields. Three were close enough to each other to use a racetrack pattern. It's a very efficient use of air time by laying down a swath in one field, coming out making a small turn and dropping into another followed by another, and back into the first field for the second swath, and so on, until you have covered all of the acreage. Back and forth turning around after each swath, working downwind to upwind so as not to fly into the full drift of the pesticide, is slow and tedious in small fields. This is filthy work, handling poison, but that's offset by the drama you control on every run and the money you can make.

When I took down the wire on my first pass, my mouth went dry instantaneously. It had never happened to me before nor has it since. Incoming rocket fire, the first time in Vietnam, was not the same as the fear a wire in the windshield presented. The wire was connected to two telephone poles positioned on the adjacent sides of a ten-acre rectangular field, cutting across a corner as the hypotenuse of a right triangle. Both poles were hidden in the trees and invisible to the inexperienced eye. I didn't see the wire until it was all I saw and it filled the windshield. I probably should have cut through it with the prop, but I dove under it. Missing with the propeller, the wire struck and broke the corroded deflecting cable attached from the top of the canopy I was sitting under to the vertical stabilizer in the tail. I felt it hold the airplane back a little and then let go. I checked my control responses and all seemed in order. I pulled myself together and finished spraying the fields.

Back at the airport I pulled up to the loading area to get more chemical. I asked Thurston, the swamper—the one who mixed and loaded the chemical— who I should call to tell them about taking down a wire. Thurston told me, with a bit of a chuckle, "No need, they already know, but you should tell Henry," the owner of the airplane about "that," while he pointed to the airplane's tail. Not only had the wire broken the deflecting cable but also it cut the upper six inches off of the vertical stabilizer. It had lodged in the upper hinge attaching the rudder to the vertical part of the tail before breaking. If the hinge had failed I would have had real trouble controlling the airplane.

Spraying in North Carolina has its own special issues with very irregular and often small fields, especially soybeans in a land where tobacco rules. Soybeans are used to fill in small spots around the "bacca" fields and they're considered liquor money. About the only thing that made me, again the Yankee, somewhat okay was having been in the Marine Corps and Vietnam. The southern farmers respected that.

Finding the fields in this strange land was problematic. The procedure was to get a description of where the field was, find it on a county realtor's map and hope the farmer had put an empty pesticide jug on a stick in the middle of the field. That jug was a help in the first half of the season before most of the fields had jugs in them.

One morning the inevitable happened—I sprayed the wrong field. In the afternoon the farmer who was expecting one of his fields to be sprayed came into the office. We talked about where I sprayed thinking it was his field. Once we made sure I knew where his field was so I could spray it in the evening when the wind died, he said, "If that man want to do right, he'll come in and pay for it anyhow." It was a civics lesson. People, rural agrarian folks, do right and expect the same in return. Most are flat honest and descent. Crowded urban environments make all this difficult as principals to hold onto, and then suspicion of others creeps in making the whole mess worse.

I went out to see a farmer so he could show me the fields he wanted sprayed. He lived in a large house with his brothers, father and one sister who had clearly given up trying to keep the place clean. They had a big television room with mounted bear heads and paws on the walls along with a couple of deer heads. He told me they jacked deer (shooting deer at night by shining headlights in their eyes to keep them still) to get meat to feed the dogs they used to hunt the bears. This was some special bunch.

The bear hunt was a ritual of going into the woods and turning the dogs loose while the hunters hung around the pickup trucks drinking corn liquor and waiting for the pitch of the dogs' barking to change, which it did when they drove the bear into a thicket. Then whoever was the evening's honoree took his rifle and stumbled into the thicket to shoot the bear. This is the Bible Belt where the Randy Newman song "Rednecks" claims, "They drink too much and laugh too loud," which no doubt proves the temperance believers right.

At the end of the corn earworm season I could have stayed on with Henry at a much slower work pace but chose to go home instead. The homesick feeling for Chris was difficult to deal with. When I was busy and making some good money there wasn't time to sit and question why I was there. Finding enough successive seasons was the key to making this all work. Fitting in with the southern culture was proving difficult. I had to ask farmers if they minded my spraying their fields on Sundays. Some told me, "That's the Lord's day." The bugs don't know what day it is. A liberal agnostic could have trouble here.

The next year when the gypsy moth season ended in New Jersey I went to the Mississippi delta where I knew someone from New Jersey was working his own plane. I was hoping to establish the beginnings of a network. I still needed to contend with a lack of real experience, but I kept trying. Staying in a cockpit was paramount—I had to keep my hand in the game.

Chapter 10
SJA, House, Lillians

The North Carolina season was brief and I continued looking for ag work until the end of summer with little results. Over the winter I flew canceled checks at night between Federal Reserve banks in New York State, Connecticut and New Jersey. This was a bit of a financial fiddle to use customer deposits for a few days before crediting the individual's account. There were checks worth millions in bags stacked in the back of fast, piston-powered, twin-engine airplanes making a tight schedule, five nights a week. I piloted checks around until fire season in the spring.

Chris wrapped up law school with honors—no surprises there—and, after clerking for a Superior Court judge, took a state job at Central Appellate Research in Trenton. She researched appeals and wrote opinions for the higher courts to utilize in their decisions. Heady stuff it was, just right for her.

The biological clock was ticking and the issue of children needed to be addressed. Selfish (as I felt myself to be), I was never a fan of taking on the awesome responsibilities of parenthood. There were times I left the room when the subject came up. I didn't care if he ever arrived knowing he would take over when he did. In the end, I wasn't prepared to say no, never—and soon we were three. I thought I had a grasp on the magnitude of being a father, but I was way short.

In the operating room the whole package hit me. Chris slugged out twelve hours of labor rather than taking any meds or agreeing to a Caesarean. She didn't relent until the baby began to stress. I felt the role of a guardian—nobody in the operating room was going to sleep or step out for coffee during this procedure. I wouldn't take my eyes off anyone in the crew who worked on her. The depth of my feelings for Chris grew during the experience like concrete hardening. The baby came out with all of the proper appendages, but still didn't take the spotlight. Chris was the star here. When the team was sewing her up, I felt relieved to hear someone counting sponges. Checklists are good things.

From the first moment I saw Michael in the nursery with the little knit cap on his head, he had me. In an instant he defined love for me. Nothing was ever the same again—nothing. There were bumpy periods during infancy, but the richness of the experience did not dwindle in the least, even with time. On the contrary, after a few years we talked of his having a sibling. Fortunately for all, Michael got a sister whom we named Lillian Agnes Gannone—after her grandmothers.

The two children were quite different. Where Michael was careful, she was aggressive. "When she was good, she was very, very good, but when she was bad she was horrid." We all lived in a house that was under renovation for almost ten years—really cramped quarters, and with a dog. Looking back, that time was gold—a struggle, but gold.

We moved to the Jersey Cape chasing another one of my jobs. This time (1986) the position was with an Allegheny Commuter, Southern Jersey Airways (SJA), affiliated with USAir. The job came with excellent travel benefits. Paying an annual fee of $120 entitled my family, including parents, to fly standby for free anywhere USAir had flights. We all went to Aberdeen, Scotland with my mother who couldn't have been prouder. Salary wasn't great, but was offset by the travel perks. Chris and I took a long weekend to England and one to Mexico. I even got her to go to the bullfights with me in Juarez. Caught up in the moment, she got in line with the Mexican women to get a kiss from Eloi Cavazous, the star matador.

Working as a regular line pilot in a passenger operation was my first formal crew experience. I was hired as a captain because I had turbine experience and only needed a hundred hours of time-in-type to move over to the left seat. There was some resentment from the first officers who saw me as someone jumping ahead in the seniority protocol.

Captain on a nineteen-passenger de Havilland (DHC-6) Twin Otter flying a published schedule was a pleasant change from being a freight dawg. The Otter is a short field takeoff and land airplane (STOL). We operated out of Atlantic City to Washington National, Philadelphia, Trenton, LaGuardia, Kennedy, MacArthur on Long Island, and Cape May. When traveling, passengers could check their bags in Cape May through to their destination airport.

For me, this job was fine and I wasn't looking to jump to the majors, which set me apart from the other pilots. There was a layover once a month for one night in Trenton and on the other days I could still get home with enough daylight to lay forty blocks on the house. On days off I spent the whole day working on it.

We bought a house near Cape May—three miles north of the Cape May Point lighthouse and five hundred yards in from the Delaware Bay. Originally called a summer shack by the developer, who built hundreds of them on this southern New Jersey peninsula, the uninsulated bungalow was only five hundred fifty square feet on a scant four inches of concrete. This was a project waiting for someone like me. The wooded corner lot had eighty feet high oak trees and was irregular in shape, measuring one hundred ten by ninety feet. I was forty years old, still strong and a good thing, too, because I needed to be.

My brother drew the plans for the expansion, which called for a twenty-four by thirty-two foot, two-story masonry addition attached to the rear of the existing stick structure. This would quadruple our living space. What I thought would be a few years of building turned into a ten-year sentence. All of our patience and tolerance limits were stretched while living in a construction site.

Because I had cultivated additional masonry skills over the years—watching as a laborer and taking a brick-laying course at a vocational school—the decision to build with masonry materials was academic given the material/labor ratio. In masonry construction labor represents ninety percent of the total cost, and materials only ten percent. While building with wood, the ratio becomes fifty/fifty. By discounting my labor to zero, the decision was simple—besides, my carpentry skills couldn't handle such an undertaking. Without an engineer's seal on the plans, the building inspector required building the first story using twelve-inch block and the second in eight-inch. I laid over two thousand blocks before I was done, in a structure containing two fireplaces with a stone veneer. There are 2300+ square feet of living space as a result.

I took wiring and plumbing courses at the local vocational school enabling me to wire and plumb the house well enough to pass the building inspections. The only parts of the house I couldn't do were the roof and boiler installation. I did everything else. The wiring was the most difficult to get started on but once I got going the fear subsided. The plumbing didn't scare me like the electricity.

Without access to fancy instruments for laying out the footings or establishing elevations, I resorted to basics. I could make a water level and had a tape measure and mason's line. The water level provided the elevation and the tape measure the right triangles. A line pulled between two points is straight and when set at the same elevation provides guidance to level the first course of blocks.

A water level can be as simple as a length of clear flexible tubing with a liquid in it. A line between the positions of the water at the open ends of the tubing will always be equal, due to the presence of the same atmospheric pressure at both ends. Using a long enough piece of water-filled tubing, you can establish a bench mark by attaching one end to a fixed point like a grading stake in the ground. Take the other end of the tube to where you want the corners of a building and mark another grading stake at the level of the water. The flexibility of the tubing makes this vital information easily transferable.

The tape measure lets you check the right angles necessary at the corners of the footing and other places. Start with a three by four by five measured three-sided figure, which according to Pythagoras' theorem is a triangle with a ninety-degree angle opposite the longest side (hypotenuse). Pythagoras proved that three squared, added to four squared equals five squared. The only aspect susceptible to error is in the measuring.

A line stretched from corner to corner at the proper altitude, taken from the bench mark, provides the reference for the first course of blocks. When this process is repeated, the square or rectangle can be verified as true when the distance between the opposite corners is equal. Maintaining these measurements of square and level requires diligence and some skill. The rest will take care of itself if you maintain the square and level (the symbol for Free Masons). All of the data necessary for this type of construction can be obtained from those simple means.

A mark on grading stakes at the other corners provides the elevation information needed to start digging a footing. Once you decide where you want the top of your footing, you add its depth, and then measure down from your benchmark and excavate. Lay the reinforcing iron work, place the concrete and the result is a foundation on which to build.

After finishing the first story of block work, and with the second story floor in place, I put all of the material needed for the second story up on the floor. The material weight would more than verify the weight bearing capabilities.

There was another simple technique I made great use of in this project— the wheel and inclined plane. Moving heavy objects can make for big accidents. The challenge was to get the very heavy masonry lintels up to the second floor by myself. Lintels are single pieces of building block material of various lengths with reinforcement steel rods inside them. They measure three and five eighths inches by seven and five eighths inches and of whatever length is needed to bridge an opening for a window or door. The three-eighths of an inch allows space for the mortar joint.

Getting the lintels up to the second story on my own was difficult but I was able to do all but the ten footers by myself. Moving one end of a lintel at a time to the foot of one section of my wooden extension ladder, I could then lean them up onto the ladder rungs. The ladder was alongside the building at approximately a sixty-degree angle. Once against the ladder, I tied a rope around the top end of the lintel and put small pipes between the lintel and the flat ladder side rails. The small sections of pipe would act as axles to virtually eliminate the friction component of the work equation.

The ladder extended over the edge of the second floor, which became a fulcrum. Using the pipes as rollers and the ladder as the inclined plane, all I had to do was pull the lintels beyond mid-point of the fulcrum. The rope was applying down pressure to the top of the ladder as well as pulling the lintel up. As soon as enough weight was above the edge to offset the ladder's weight below, the whole thing would come down to the surface of the floor like the kid on a seesaw.

The hardest part was getting enough pieces of pipe to stay in place for the lintel's journey up the ladder. Often I had to pull the lintel up a few feet at a time, tie the rope off, climb back down another ladder and slip another pipe into the path.

These are basic Newtonian laws of physics applied to building techniques going back before King Hammurabi of Babylonian times (1770 B.C.). He put in place the first building codes, which have since become quite complex. His original law was simple. If you build something for someone and it falls, killing his son, he can do the same to your son. Derived from the eye-for-an-eye way of thinking, this is a simple but effective means of insuring quality control.

With all this sweat and hard work, comes the immediate gratification of seeing what you have built. This is a double edged sword, though, because you know all too well the mistakes made on the job and always see them when others may not.

The commuter airline had two shifts, called lines, an AM line and a PM line. They were scheduled for one-month periods with different routes and days off. Pilots bid for them according to seniority. At times there were ten different AM lines and ten PM lines. The most senior pilot could make his pick and the number two in seniority had the next choice and so on until all lines were assigned.

Being older set me apart from the other pilots. I wanted AM lines, which were not as attractive to the young pilots. Given the attrition rate of captains, I soon had what I wanted on the AM schedule. I left for work between four and five-thirty in the morning and got home in the early afternoon. At times the house construction seemed never ending. The romanticism of building a house for the family withered in the dust and sweat of the ten-year sentence it became. The house is still not finished, but it is warm and strong, a virtual bunker due to the twelve-inch blocks.

Southern Jersey Airways was a sinking ship. Management and labor were at odds and with the airlines in a hiring mode there was an exodus of captains. I stayed to the bitter end, becoming number one on the seniority list when the company reached Chapter Seven of their bankruptcy process. I was due back pay and received ten cents on the dollar.

There were jobs available to me in other commuters but they required travel. It wasn't the right period in my life to be on the road. This was the only time I would get to see the kids growing up. The house was far from finished and unsellable when SJA closed its doors, but Chris had taken a job in Atlantic City when Lillian was a year old and we were able to get by on her salary. With less money for materials, house construction was slow. I considered commercial fishing but it was the one thing Chris asked me not to do because of the safety considerations. It was a reasonable enough request.

A major challenge of living in a construction site is heating. A masonry structure without an adequate heating system can be very cold in the winter. The first full summer I worked on the house was enough to get the footings, floor, first story walls and second story floor closed in. The kerosene space heater roared like a jet engine but took the chill out of the addition. The wood stove in the kitchen area was sometimes enough to maintain a livable temperature after the space heater was shut down.

One of my British motorcycles spent the winter in the kitchen as well. I couldn't get myself to keep the bike outside in the weather. Finding work in Cape May County in the winter is tricky at best. A plan was needed and the one I came up with was half-baked. It was not the most comfortable winter, but we had a Christmas tree and happy kids.

Early on when I was laying the twelve inch concrete blocks for the first story I set up a place for Michael with some mortar and broken pieces of block. I gave him a small pointing trowel and he was happy to imitate what I was doing. One day, at some other activity, he hurt himself and I tried to talk him out of the crying. I told him to ignore the pain and think about something nice to make the pain go away. As if scripted, within minutes, I hammered my thumb on a block. The blow was hard enough to water my eyes. Michael, of course, was right there to see and promptly explain to me how to deal with the pain. Thank you, Mike.

He was also Johnny on the spot another time. I was trying to get the footings poured with a couple of pilots who were lost outside of a cockpit but game to try and help me. I had to leap across the footing trench and my right foot slid into the concrete. I stretched my left leg to get on the opposite bank and my shorts ripped wide open at the crotch. At the moment I was standing there with my testicles in the breeze, Michael said, "Dad, why did you jump in the concrete?" Thank you, Mike.

Turning a summer shack into a real house may have been what brought about my desire to go back to school and ultimately get in on the smart side of construction—civil engineering. So off I went without having thought the plan through. All of my previous college credits had to be assembled from the four schools I had attended over the years. That came to 112 hours of courses, but with no major.

The challenge was calculus and general physics. Calculus was personal because I had taken it and failed twice already. An engineer told me after those two courses the rest was easy. Atlantic Community College had the necessary calculus and general physics prerequisite courses. Soon I was at the kitchen table at four in the morning before the kids got up and the show started. Hammering through two-hour problems required still air, and zero dark thirty was the only time quiet was available in our house.

My Sri Lankan calculus instructor told the class that in his country they called calculus, mathematics and physics, applied mathematics—made sense to me. My physics instructor told the class that if, after an intersection collision, he had the resting places of two cars, the temperatures of the metals and little else, he could tell you from which direction and how fast they came to try and occupy the same space. This mathematical relationship to everything impressed me more and more. I was no longer looking at algebra as math but rather the language of math, which was calculus.

The real problem was becoming clear to me. There was no engineering school close by to finish a bachelor of science program. I would have to travel to Philadelphia or Newark, and they were just too far. I was essentially doing physics and calculus for my own edification. Yet another course change was coming.

My passion for cooking was kindled by a culinary school that was located at Atlantic Community College in Mays Landing, NJ. There was a lot of European influence from the French, German and Swiss chefs on staff. The school had a strict formal program starting from the basics and building on them. The ag school in Mississippi was the same. Drum the basics in far enough, repeatedly, and they stick. There was no corporal motivation in either school. That was another educational institution I had attended, where the method of motivation was fear and the lessons were learned more quickly, efficiently and indelibly. I began thinking about a commercial restaurant—why not? I jumped through the necessary hoops and was admitted to the program.

Owning my own restaurant was the reason for throwing myself into the cooking school. I wasn't studying to be someone's line cook. My mother was diagnosed with terminal lung cancer in 1996 as I was nearing the end of the culinary program. She was thrilled at the idea of my operating my own restaurant. Her middle name was Lillian. I located a restaurant for sale in West Cape May and thought an appropriate name would be Lillians—no apostrophe. Seemed so very Cape May.

Ramsey's, the operating restaurant property I found, was on its last legs. I hoped it would turn out to be a diamond in the rough. By using our house equity as collateral we were able to raise enough money to get control of it. This rundown, roach-infested restaurant proved to be an uphill battle all the way.

I wasn't interested in seeing any falsified books, so I asked the owner for his last five years of 1040s, figuring they would be the numbers after he had skimmed. What I didn't take into account was that those figures represented the early years of the Cape May renaissance. That had been a growth period, spawning serious restaurants and high-priced B&Bs marketed to wealthy people from New York and Mainline Philadelphia. Initially, the number of restaurants lagged behind the developing hospitality industry, but they caught up and made the numbers I was using outdated and inaccurate.

Using all I could from culinary school and the little bit of practical knowledge I had about the restaurant business from previous commercial kitchen jobs, I gave it a go with Chris's help. In the beginning she still had the attorney's job in Atlantic City and already had a full plate.

The restaurant was a filthy mess. It was hard to believe there was a health inspector within a hundred miles. The landlord helped with some necessary renovations. After a few weeks of cleaning and despite a persistent pest problem requiring an aggressive control program to finally eliminate them, we opened.

My mother had moved into our house during the first season of Lillians' operation. She was under hospice care and was able to see her grandchildren daily. To watch my mother on school days looking out of the living room window while in her wheel-chair waiting for the kids was moving. This was a busy but very good time in our lives. My mother's approach to dying was inspirational and without complaint. Between Chris and the hospice nurse she could not have gotten better care.

There were other family members who came to see her, of course, but when the kids came home her spirits were the highest. My mother was a Scot of the Hay Clan. Her twin sister, Ruth, arrived wearing the clan's kilt and a white blouse with lace collar and cuffs. My mother was nearing the end and Aunt Ruth said with a brogue, "Margret, I've come to see how you're behaving." It was spoken with an uplifting and stern attitude not hiding Aunt Ruth's warm feelings. The night my mother passed away, my father's sister, Aunt Jennie, was next to her bed, rosary beads in hand.

My mother's death was a subtle but strong awakening for me. Now was the time to grow up, plain and simple. My father had been gone for many years. When he died I was thirty years younger, hard and just home from Vietnam. A little numb to death, I barely shed a tear. Just knowing my mother was at the house in Martinsville still cutting the lawn at eighty years old was a solidifying feeling. Now, my younger brother and I were orphans. This was different, and frightening, too. She wouldn't be there to fall back on anymore.

In her will she named my brother and I as co-executors of her estate with explicit instructions to sell everything and split the cash down the middle. That eliminated any possibility of squabbling. She was saving money for us even when she was on Social Security. She loved my brother and me, as I love mine. From their blue collar roots, a postal clerk and auto mechanic, she and my father had put together an estate worth over four hundred thousand dollars. At the house in Martinsville after the burial we had a Piper in full dress playing the pipes while he walked around the lawn. It was proper and fitting. She had to have been smiling.

Lillians turned out to be yet another failed restaurant. It might have worked out differently if I had a few years in the kitchen of a Greek diner where they know something about making things from nothing. Fortunately, aviation's return to my life softened the blow significantly otherwise I would have been crushed.

As good as the Culinary Institute was in teaching food preparation, it came up short in educating its graduates to the limitations of the American palate. I went at this restaurant with a positive attitude believing people would appreciate freshly prepared food—the less processing the better. Fresh comes at a slightly higher labor cost in the kitchen and we did get compliments on our food. However, when I succumbed to trying a frozen product, not one customer seemed to notice. I was crestfallen.

All along we had been buying fresh chicken breasts, trimming them, and pounding them out ourselves. Then after three years comes this frozen, precooked, grill marked and perfectly uniform breast of chicken and no one noticed? I realized the American palate was absolutely comfortable with mediocrity, perhaps even preferring it.

I felt foolish in squandering so much of my inheritance trying to keep the restaurant afloat instead of pulling the plug on the whole thing earlier. The efforts made by those involved, both family and friends didn't make closing the doors of Lillians easy. Using the house I built as a cash machine, by borrowing against it, was a questionable practice in itself but not atypical of my reckless approach to risk taking. It's a wonder I accumulated over eleven thousand hours flying airplanes without killing myself, because I wasn't always the careful and prudent one there, either. I had a friend who was a stone carver who told me his father said, "You can always tell a Lynch, but you can't tell him much." I think it speaks for me as well.

There were periods at Lillians with some consistency, when the help wasn't rotating through the place and there was a rhythm in the day-to-day procedure. Those moments made me look as if I knew what I was doing. I was getting up at five in the morning so I could get a workout at the gym on the way to the restaurant. At the restaurant by six put me in position to prep for breakfast, if the cook didn't show up. When I had a cook named Steve Ranone, there was consistency and no drama. Louis was another matter and a whole story by himself.

Louis appeared answering an ad for a breakfast cook early on when I was beginning to figure out I could not do all and be all. He certainly knew the kitchen but his social acumen came up short of the mark in spite of his personal opinion of himself. The other issues were his inability to tell time and his mercurial temperament. Of course, it took a few weeks for all this to surface but surface it did including his propensity to make waitresses cry.

Louis was in his early twenties and quite full of himself, the Italian from South Philly, a likable fellow, always with the jokes. My teenage son thought he was very cool and they became fast friends. Louis was waiting for the courts to suspend his driver's license, again and for a longer time. He was unfazed with the idea of lending his Grand Cherokee to my unlicensed son to use as prom transportation, double dating with another Catholic school student. A good time was to be had by all except my wife. This occurred when I was trying to sneak back into aviation and was in fact somewhere in south Texas.

The plan fell apart when the lads failed to make the necessary key exchange, which resulted in Louis standing outside of Wildwood Catholic High School, trying to get Michael's attention through the cafeteria windows. Louis needed his key, which was in Michael's pocket. In due course Brother Carson was on the scene, suspecting some sort of a drug transaction given the age and flamboyant appearance of Louis, plus my son's historically cavalier social behavior. Chris was in bed when Brother Carson called the house. Getting up and driving to Wildwood Catholic High School didn't make her happy. My son's asking to be taken to the after-prom party, in spite of it all, didn't smooth any feathers either.

The peak might have been her attempt at a meaningful lecture to these boys with a story of similar circumstances of underage driving. In her story the boy in question kills himself in an automobile accident. My son's companion who was known to be slow on the uptake asked why the boy would commit suicide over that.

When we took over from the previous owner there were some important decisions to be made regarding employees and customers. Employees came with the restaurant, as did customers, for better or for worse. Our concern not to lose any of the existing patrons influenced our menu price. We didn't charge as much as we could have, especially for breakfast, which was where we made our money. In August on Sundays, we turned the tables over three to four times at breakfast. The plan was to stay open all year doing three meals every day and secure the local trade. An ambitious but impractical plan given the seasonal nature of the town we were operating in.

We also tried to keep all of the existing employees. Weeding out the ones who needed to go was the easiest part. The most glaring example was the dishwasher. The bone of contention was his refusal to mop the bathroom floor, about ten square feet. He already had the mop out because he was doing the kitchen floor after lunch.

He said, "No, that's the waitresses' job."

"What?" I said.

"That's the waitress's job. I don't see why I have to do that."

"How about because you have a mop in your hand or how 'bout 'cause I say so?"

"No, I'm not doing it."

"Just go ahead and clock out," I said.

I really couldn't believe how easy he made it for me to be rid of him. From the time I opened the place I wanted a Mexican dishwasher anyhow, and this fellow, whom I was sending a wage garnishment check to the county every week for child support in arrears, was a slow professional dishwasher. I eagerly went on the hunt for a Mexican dishwasher; they are not afraid to work. I had spent enough time in the Rio Grande valley to see them swimming across the river to a land of promise with lots of mean Gringos. Then they travel another thousand miles to take the jobs the gringo doesn't want anyhow. I have been in the fields with migrant workers in August and the insects alone could cause madness.

His name was Dionesio and my wife and I loved him. He didn't talk to us at first because he couldn't speak English, at all. He just worked. He didn't bring any other baggage with him; he just did his job. If you told him to clean the stove, the next time you looked, it was clean! The grease trap filled up one day and cleaning it is the worst job in a restaurant. Everyone else seemed to disappear, but he cleaned it without even being told. Yes, it is a dishwasher's job but I could imagine what would have happened if I had the local fellow from West Cape May still there as a dishwasher.

Dionesio was great in the garden we had behind the restaurant. He felt better out there, almost happy, certainly more contented. Did he have a green card? I didn't know and couldn't have cared less. In him I saw my Italian grandfather walking to work with holes in his shoe soles. In two years Dionesio missed two or three days of work. On one of those days we had a serious storm flooding Wildwood and the buses weren't running. On another day he sent someone in his place. He made more money from Lillians than I did. He was a good man and I was happy to have known him even a little. One of the others in the kitchen said Dionesio was going back to Mexico to buy a coffee farm. I was happy for him when I heard.

It was becoming obvious I had to stay closer to the restaurant and not be running off trying to put an aviation career back together. I had to be at the restaurant daily to prepare for breakfast because Louis just wouldn't show in time, and anyway he would bring his hangover with him when he did come. Every morning I wanted to pay him off and never see him again, but if I did I would be cooking all day.

Our dinner trade never really got going in sufficient numbers to warrant Dionesio giving up his second job. There was a young, local man who came by looking for work washing dishes one evening so I gave him a try at dinner. The first couple of nights he was the best. I sent him home with food for his kids and thought all was well. Then the roof came down. One of the Irish waitresses we had said he was creeping her out with leering looks and suggestive gestures. "Oh shit," I thought. Here comes the sexual harassment quagmire. I told Chris, the attorney, about what had happened. She said no problem, "I'll handle it."

I was delighted with her confidence. She called the dishwasher into the office and before long I heard him crying and whining something terrible, full of denials. This was getting worse. The solution was to fire them both. To my surprise this labor issue was simple.

The behavior of the customers always amazed me. They told me how to run the restaurant, like which dining room I should have made non-smoking. The seniors felt the packages of sugar substitute were theirs to take home. The worst was the American attitude towards buffet eating: a challenge to consume quantity and not to eat what you want. This learning curve was killing me.

When the annual West Cape May Christmas Parade was two months away, customers started calling to make sure they got "their" booth by the window. An eighty-five seat restaurant is only going to have maybe thirty seats at or near the windows. I hadn't even figured out the menu for the big night let alone decided on how I would book the seating. Finally, I put up a sign stating on the Monday before the parade starting at 8:00 AM we would take paid reservations for seating on a first-come first-served basis. I miss Lillians like a toothache.

I bought the business from a man who lost his wife to cancer and then fell victim to gambling in Atlantic City. A local business man bought his building and let him keep the restaurant with a lease. His Chapter Eleven maneuvering wasn't enough to change the course he was on. The restaurant was ripe for someone like me. A used car dealer will tell you there is an ass for every seat. I may sound it at times, but I don't completely regret having had a go at a restaurant. I am in awe, though, of those who have the talent to make one successful.

All of the hard work made it look like a chef's dream if there were only more people in the seats for dinner. We had the breakfast trade but just couldn't get them to risk losing their hard fought parking places or walk the ten blocks from downtown Cape May to have dinner. We had an herb and vegetable garden behind the kitchen and even a small bake shop. A friend painted a beautiful mural in a small two table alcove. One of my mentors from school came down and reviewed a few processes to get me going in the bake shop. Everything seemed to be in place—*mis en place*—as we were taught in cooking school.

It was all there including the rent, which took all of the cream. Perhaps the biggest pitfall was trying to do everything. I don't think a neophyte can do it. Not keep track of the front of the house, back of the house, cook and do the books, too. No. Not for long. Even just an eighty-five seat restaurant will eat you up.

Before the end of my short career as restaurateur, I picked up a Trade-A-Plane newspaper, where an ad for a position in a jet was waiting for me. I had some experience in the jet listed and made a call. Gus answered the phone. He had another fly-by-night outfit with three old raggedy Sabreliner freighters. Yes, this was another Flight Express Cargo only with jets. Some perversion in my makeup prevents me from turning away rather than towards these outfits.

To subsidize his business and in keeping with his style of using people's passions and needs as a carrot on a stick to extract all they could possibly give him, he would tell you he was also a flight school. "You want to fly one of my jets? You have to pay for your own training. Send me a thousand dollars."

"I'll get back to you" was my response.

We were able to sell the restaurant and escape without owing anybody money. Fatigue made that good enough.

PARRIS ISLAND

Front entrance to the depot.

In the old days recruits took a barge to the island.

Practice, practice, practice until we all got it right.

The rifle range was all business.

Manual of Arms

TO USE IT, you've got to know how to hold it, so the recruit learns the Manual of Arms. This instruction teaches all of the movements and positions using the rifle. Learning the Manual of Arms is a challenge to each recruit and is a very important cycle of his education in becoming a Marine.

You will learn how to handle that piece and get up those ropes.

Pugil Stick

Fun with padded sticks and conferring with the Primary Marksmanship Instructor.

Checking Rifle Score

James Gannone, Jr.

Kenneth R. Kreader

Me , Sgt. Vance (our Junior Drill Instructor) and Kreader graduation day at P.I.

Private Kreader and Private Gannone Parris Island graduation.

Kreader and me Parris Island graduation.

My father, brother, me and my mother at Parris Island graduation. April 1966.

The three Gannone men at Parris Island 1966.

Me and Michael, Parris Island graduation 2001

THE NAM

My John Wayne look behind a houch in Dông Hà.

Aboard ship with (l to r) John Clemens (wounded three times) and Timothy Gahan who went on to become an officer and retire as a Colonel. After that he became a Roman Catholic priest.

Dông Hà 1967 with teenage acne.

Me in front of the tank I smoked my first joint in.

Me with attitude.

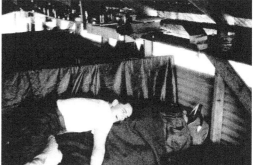

Richard Lisante from Brooklyn who talked me out of extending my tour so I could be in the infantry. Probably owe him my life.

Me on top of a bunker at the edge of our compound's perimeter.

Arturo Cabrara also in the tank giving me that joint.

Sand bag detail.   Xmas 1966 Dông Hà.

Sandbag detail with Connelly.

Houch in compound at Dông Hà 1967. J.B. Smith with George Vail.   Life in the rear, with the gear.

Outside our compound in the dry season.

Dông Hà 1966-67

Edge of trench behind the houches.

Me sitting on a trench, piss tube in the background behind the corrugated metal.

Shower and a tower manned at night for sighting incoming rocket launches. Sighting from another tower yields a cross reference fix for artillery response.

Camp Carrol 1967 wrecker detail to change the tube on an 8" self-propelled howitzer pointed at the DMZ.

Wrecker controls used to change the tube on Howitzer after 10,000 rounds.

Me another sandbag detail.

Arturro with Butch who stood guard with us.

FAMILY

The house my father built in Martinsville, New Jersey.

Last picture of my father at my coming home from Vietnam party.

With my mother at coming home party.

Margaret Gannone, author's mother in her Hay tartan at a Christmas party in Griggstown, New Jersey.

Aunt Jennie (my father's sister), my mother, Michael and Lillian.

July 1975.

Before the kids.

Lillian and I at her first home.

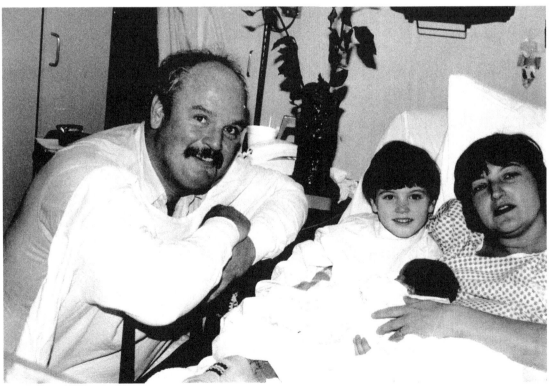

Lillian's arrival.

Chris at her youngest sister's wedding.

Lillian's 3rd birthday.

Chris and Lillian.

Mike and Lillian Xmas.

Halloween costumes by Chris.

Restaurant in West Cape May, New Jersey.

Back of the house at Lillians with Hipolito at
the dishwasher and Steve Ranone cooking.

My plane

Isreali travel team leader in Red and White belt. Michael with Sensi Dave Kawajiri in the fore.

Mike Kelly and I randori at Vineland Judo club.

Lillian HS graduation 2006.

Mike 's P.I. graduation 2001.

Triumph Bonneville that spent the winter in the kitchen.

Hell Gate Bridge, New York City from the prow of a Pearson 26, 2012.

UN, New York City from Pearson 26, 2012

PLANES
Summer 1975 Action Aerial Advertisement

Billy Gowder propping off a Taylorcraft to tow a banner. No electric start on these planes.

Flying through the poles to catch the tow rope.

Banner lifting off the ground.

My handy work in a Super Cub.

Landing definitions are as follows: A great landing is one where the airplane flies again; A good landing is where the pilot and passengers walk away; A bad landing is one where the plane never flies again. These pictures show examples of the last two. It may have been repairable had it not burned after the crash by suspicious means.

The remains with Chris in the foreground.

Flying Freight
Flight Express Cargo

Beech-18 on a ramp awaiting loading.

Tail feathers of the first Sabreliner I flew for
Tim with a pristine DC-3 in the background.

Beech loading
in Cleveland
to return to
Philadelphia.

Beech on ramp
in Detroit.

Another Beech awaiting a dawn takeoff in Cleveland.

Ag Work
Boll weevil contract Humbolt, Tennessee.

Mike Hensel, a colleague who died in an Ag Cat on gypsy moth contract.

Fire plane loaded and waiting.

The Fire Contract

Refueling, and hot loading to
return to an ongoing fire.

AgCat practice for fires dropping water.

Major brush fire in New Jersey pinelands. Going back for more water.

At Downstown on gypsy moth contract.

Mike with me at fire base.

Mike with Chris.

One of Gus' Sabreliners. One of the reasons I got the
job in Africa is that I was current in this airplane.

My last contract: Clifford's operation in Iowa. The
last flying I did. Full circle from where I started.

AFRICA

Tim Roman, Presidential Aviation
My employer

African Gray would sneeze like Chris.

Tennesse Tim's African
Gray on Alée Verte.

Pool at Alée Verte.

Chris poolside at Alée Verte, with lunch served by Papa Joe.

Chris, Papa Joe and Lillian at the pool on Alée Verte.

View from Haute Tensione of Kinshasa and Brazaville. Only place where the capitals of two countries are separated by a river.

Congo River downstream of Kinshasa.

Congo River downstream of Kinshasa.

At New Jeans Kinshasa, DRC.

Maryoth and his father at New Jeans, Kinshasa, DRC.

Me at the house on Avenue Haute Tension, Kinshasa

Me, Jeff and my chauffeur John at the house on
Avenue Haute Tension, Kinshasa, DRC.

At my desk, Wimby Dira Airlines in Kinshasa.

Three Marines at the Corp's birthday ball Kinshasa, DRC. Jeff Litske, Josh McCave and author—the oldest.

Tim's plane: N250EC was shot up in Bunia. Its hulk is resting in Entebbe.

Over Lake Kivu approaching Goma, DRC.

Lava field at the end of the runway in Goma, DRC.

Takeoff view at end of the runway at Goma toward the lake.

Cumulus beginning to blossom in Eastern Congo.

Entebbe after the Bunia incident. Minister of Human Rights, me, Deo and DRC
Protocol officer.

The Sabreliner parked at Kisangani, DRC.

Safari Orchid club Bukavu, DRC.

Volkswagon-size termite hill near Lubumbashi.

A pirogue on Lake Kivu.

Allen Carney: One of the best parts of my four years in Congo was meeting this man. He's a humanitarian and I hold him in highest regards.

Chapter 11
Gus, Guy, and Tim

I took the bait. Gus' ground school, although effective, was unlike any other I had attended. It started after Bob Guin, Gus' instructor and check airman, woke up after a night of flying or standing by and had a leisurely breakfast. The student got ground school as it fit in between the flight schedule. If a charter came up at any time the student would go along and receive training on the non-revenue flights. Bob's breakfast was first though.

Bob was a retired Air Force pilot who flew the military version of the Sabreliner when he trained Naval flight officers. They were being prepared to operate the weaponry of a fighter bomber under the worst conditions. To accomplish this, the back of a Sabreliner was set up with the electronics and radar scopes simulating their future work station. The flight officers were required to operate those electronics while a training pilot did everything possible to shake them loose and make them sick. Bob could fly the airplane flawlessly and I watched while hanging on to his every word.

When Bob thought a Sabreliner trainee could pass an equipment check, which meant being capable of satisfactorily flying the airplane in Visual Flight Rules, Bob would administer the check ride. At the end of my first equipment check ride in a Sabreliner, while on the climb out from Reading, PA, Bob said, "I've got the airplane." As I sat back and relaxed he rolled the airplane three hundred sixty degrees along the longitudinal line of flight so as to constantly maintain one positive "G." I loved it.

He rolled it once, without warning, with a trainee standing between us on the flight deck. Again it was so smooth a glass of water would have remained in place on the dashboard. All this was entirely unannounced; he was captain and not required to get our approval. After my check ride, the first time I flew with him on a revenue flight I got his—one to a student—complete preflight, which was all inclusive. The preflight inspection took two hours. Every instrument, handle, latch, and system was discussed at length and I wanted to have the answers to his questions lest I disappoint him.

He took off inspection plates so we could look inside where mechanics do their work and explained what was happening in there. While going through the cockpit he paused, looked me in the eye and said, "If I ever say, 'I've got the airplane' that is exactly what I mean." This man was a genuine, militarized version of a professional pilot. His attention to detail and method were worthy aspirations. At the end of his shift he did a thorough post-flight inspection as well.

One pilot told me Bob rolled the airplane while on a high right base leg to a landing at Philadelphia. His impromptu rolling of the plane made it seem like he became so overwhelmed with the boredom of flying straight and level that he just had to bust out a little. I never saw him get excited or upset in any way—unflappable. He remains one of the few sterling characters I met in forty years of aviation.

North American Rockwell built the Sabreliner in the early 1960s. Rockwell, a military contractor, built the Sabrejet fighters used by the United States in the Korean War. The Sabreliner was built to military specifications but was also approved as a civilian business jet three months before the first Lear Jet was certified for passengers. Both are close in cruise speeds, 400+ knots, and have large appetites for fuel. These are first generation jets. Fuel was cheap so efficiency was not yet a priority. In the 1990s their market value waned significantly as fuel prices rose.

I took up with Gus' operation before we sold Lillians, hoping to do both. The restaurant started to really fall apart with my absences so I went back to it fulltime. By then I had only accumulated ten hours in the right seat of the Sabre. Over half of the time was en route flying to and from freight stops. No time was spent doing anything from the left seat where I would fly the check ride.

I was home taking a nap one Tuesday between lunch and prepping for dinner when the phone rang and it was Gus. "What are you doing?"—in his flippant, salty way.

"Sleeping," I said.

"Want to take a check ride Saturday?"

"Gus, I haven't even done a steep turn in it yet."

"Come on. I've got a check airman (Designated FAA examiner for type ratings in a Sabreliner) coming out from Chicago. He'll meet you at Atlantic Aviation in Philly. Just give him five hundred dollars and pay for the fuel. He'll sign you off."

"I'll get back to you."

We had located a real estate agent who was certain he could sell Lillians for us. As a result I went ahead with Gus' proposal hoping the restaurant would sell quickly. I ended up getting my second jet type rating from Bob, this self-proclaimed "highest paid flight instructor in the country." Another pilot and I met Bob at Atlantic and went into a back room. Like a prostitute he said, "Let's take care of the money first. I hope you guys brought cash."

A type rating exam consists of two parts, an oral and a practical. The oral is usually one-on-one, with a full life-size picture of at least the cockpit dashboard, if not the circuit breaker panels as well. The examiner starts at one end pointing to each gauge, light bulb and switch, asking in turn what they are and what do they do. There is a telelight panel with forty lights in it. They illuminate for different reasons and all tell their own story. The examiner will spend some real time there wanting to know just why one light might come on and be followed by another in the related system that was failing.

When he finds a weak response in the candidate he will probe deeper. The unseasoned candidate can talk himself into some real trouble by volunteering more information than was asked for and not being able to maintain an in-depth discussion. The oral usually takes an hour or more, depending on how much time it takes to convince the examiner of your complete understanding of the systems. This oral was done in twenty minutes for both of us. Even if fancy teaching aids are not available, a blank piece of paper with a candidate's drawing of the fuel system or electrical system will indicate what he knows about a system and what he doesn't know by what he left out.

The check rides my fellow candidate and I took were done on the way to and from Charleston, West Virginia. I just sat in the back for the thirty-minute flight from Philadelphia while my counterpart flew his check-ride. In Charleston I paid for the fuel and flew back to Philadelphia. Bob, the examiner, told me to do some steep turns in the clouds while on the climb out from Charleston. That was the sum total of the air check part of the ride. When we were working Philadelphia approach control he pulled one engine back and told me to do a single engine approach. I called for the proper checklist and kept him as busy as I could, getting weather updates and verifying navigational aids. I finished the approach and landed. The other candidate and I tied up Gus' airplane and as we drove Bob around to the other side of the airport he did the paperwork.

We dropped him off in front of United Airlines so he could get a jump seat back to Chicago. He was all full of himself. Like a good prostitute he had a grand in his pocket for a couple of hours' work. We both got our type ratings and as long as it was treated as a ticket to learn we would be okay. The fine tuning of the competency would come with more experience. Bob Guin flew with me a few more hours before Gus turned me loose as a Captain.

If I had gone to FlightSafety in St. Louis, the insurance-approved corporate standard, for the rating, it would have been excellent training. The multi-million-dollar simulator with the bells and whistles would have cost twelve to fifteen thousand dollars. I had less than two thousand in this ticket.

I was on the road with Gus' operation for two weeks at a time. I met the same characters as when flying freight in the Beech 18s for Ron and Chuck. At first all of these people seemed a little strange. They were pale and had cigarettes burning in ashtrays on desktops in dark rooms with table lamps. Maybe they were vampires only coming out at night—this being the night shift and all. It was not long before I looked around and realized I was one of them. Freight pilots are called "freight dawgs," in the business. The term has an element of respect to it.

Pulling up at two in the morning to some small hanger on a ramp in the middle of Ohio or Wisconsin in the blowing snow, loading it up and leaving was not the fancy jet job of my dreams. It was pilot-in-command time I was building, though. Sometimes the freight was just a small box of special nuts or bolts needed to keep an assembly line moving in East Jesus, Arkansas. It wasn't often a glamorous destination like Miami, Los Angles, San Juan or even Brownsville, Texas.

After my second six-month instrument-proficiency check ride with Bob I asked him to talk me through the aileron roll. Ailerons control the roll function and rate at which the airplane turns. I had never inquired about these maneuvers of his while I was in the right seat. Any one of them could be worth three or four violations if done in the presence of the wrong person.

Bob visibly perked up and explained what he referred to as confidence builders. He started with, "First you shut off mode C." It is a function of the transponder, sending altitude information along with the position of your airplane to the controller's radar scope. "Next trim it to a two hundred sixty-five knot climb." Trimming the airplane to a certain speed means it will continue that way, hands off the controls. "Then just keep feeding in the aileron until you get to the stops—you will need all of it as the speed bleeds off." As the airplane is finishing the three hundred sixty degrees of roll along the longitudinal axis, the controls need to be neutralized to stop the roll.

Gus kept an apartment near the airport in Philadelphia for the crews to standby in. The usual work day was to standby at UPS's pilot lounge in Philadelphia at eleven o'clock in the evening. There we waited for one of their planes to get delayed and not make the sort. This was our primary responsibility. UPS and FEDEX bring all their freight to regionalized freight hub facilities, arriving at about two o'clock in the morning. They sort the incoming packages for various destinations and reload the airplanes to send them back with the out-going freight.

UPS has well-maintained equipment. Sometimes a week would go by before we were called out. If we got a trip, it would usually be to take a plane full of the overnight letters to West Palm Beach or somewhere else on the East Coast, then wait there for another trip. It could be to anywhere in the United States, Mexico or the Caribbean Islands. If nothing came up, we returned to Philadelphia in the evening to standby again. Gus made out what ever happened given the low overheard of his operation. He would get paid more than a thousand dollars for having an airplane in position and ready at UPS until six o'clock in the morning, when we were relieved, and more if there was a trip.

I got a lot of good experience with Gus' outfit and only one violation. It was luck considering the equipment we operated. These were airplanes with leaking fuel tanks. The best option was to wait for a trip and if possible already be loaded before you fueled it.

The travel, especially to Mexico and the trips to the border at Brownsville and El Paso, helped me tolerate the rest of the operation. This was when NAFTA was just starting. We dropped off parts in the mountains of Mexico and picked them up a day later installed in a bigger part and took them back to Michigan.

Gus was always trying to make a buck off someone else's risk. One night, when I was clearly way over the legal limit for duty time, Gus wanted to add another trip on me. His go-to line was, "Come on. Work with me a little here. I'll give you another hundred."

He had a good side to him reserved for his family. He was also very vain and lonely. He lived in a guarded community in a garishly decorated house with an Aston Martin in the driveway. Word had it he made his fortune transporting drug money. It all ended when he made CNN one night on some airport ramp with all the lights on him. He was getting out of a Sabreliner full of cash and being taken away in cuffs.

The first thing in the training program was making a Commercial Aviation, Gus' company name, identification card. Guin gave me a business card signed by Gus as Director of Operations on the front and on the back I put my name, date of birth and a passport-size photo. The lamination of the picture was the finishing touch. Identification as an employed pilot is a necessary part of the Gus Maestralis employee travel benefits package. This actually worked most of the time.

The jump seat is the captain's seat on an airliner for him to give away to whomever he sees fit. It is a long standing union custom used by pilots getting to and from work or anywhere else they want to go. A flight attendant will tell the captain someone is looking for a jump seat. The captain will usually tell the one looking for a ride, whom he sees as a colleague, to find a seat in first class if there is one.

Gus' work schedule was two weeks on and one week off. The relieving crew had to travel to where the last captain parked the airplane at the completion of his two weeks. Usually this meant some freight hub like Philadelphia, Louisville or Miami. Getting there was the challenging part. Gus was not paying for an airline ticket without kicking and screaming. He referred to his jump seat method as a benefit in his pay package. It was also your means of returning home at the end of the two weeks. He wasn't paying for that either.

Commercial Aviation was a Part 135 operation and jump seat privileges are for Part 121 airline operations. Some schmoozing was required to reach the captain, who makes the ultimate decision as to who hitches a ride on his airplane. There were a couple of steps involved to contact him though. First there is the ticket agent at the gate to get by and they can be the most difficult. "This is not a 121 operation is it?" A smile, with gray hair and "We do it all the time to get to work," often succeeded. Clearly it was an abuse of the system. One captain looked at my identification card, chuckled and said, "Looks like you made this at Staples last night. Get a seat in first class if you can find one." I chuckled, too. "Get off my airplane," is the other response I have heard. Some cared and some didn't.

Gus had more tricks to weasel his way, like for avoiding noise abatement fines. The Sabre is an old jet and quite loud. Some places like West Palm Beach in Florida are particularly testy about noise after dark and they have enforced fines in place to discourage late takeoffs. We were parked in Fort Lauderdale one day after delivering a load of overnight envelopes. Spending the day in a seedy motel there, sitting hot-ready to go on some trip, yields little meaningful sleep. This is not a valid crew rest time for FAA regulations, either. When it was time to reposition to Philadelphia, Gus told me to take the plane back to UPS.

I had the aircraft fueled and was about to file a flight plan when the fuel attendant at the fixed base operation told me of the noise abatement fine. The Sabre would set off the decibel-measuring instruments at the end of the runway—ringing the bell. It was Jim to the rescue, like the threat of the carpenter's picket line. Once again I was naïve and wrong. I called Gus, getting an impatient and bored response, as if I should have known. "Just file as a lifeguard flight, I have a doctor who covers for me." Lifeguard flights are for ambulance work and get priority treatment. They are often called gizzard runs, transporting organs for transplants or toxicology reports after an accident.

"Wheels in the wells in one hour," is what Gus promised the freight agents when he was selling his services. With three Sabres positioned in various airports he usually had one fairly close to a freight hub. Another part of the Commercial Aviation package was booking flights in the worst weather. Other companies were turning down trips and Gus was grabbing them. The onus was on the captain to say no and argue with Gus, or face the FAA music if there was an emergency. Everything was okay until it wasn't.

When Gus heard I was looking into a job in Africa his nasty side really came out. He was mostly upset because he hadn't extracted enough hours of service from me to make back what he thought was minimally acceptable—as if he had paid for my training and not I. He was successful in delaying my getting to Africa, but not stopping it altogether.

Gus knew more about the Africa job than I did. The Sabreliner community is a small one in aviation circles and they're familiar with each other. He asked me about it and I told him I was going. Then he started with stories of not getting paid, HIV/AIDS and on and on. He gave me a disgruntled, former airline pilot's number to call, who of course had nothing good to say about the job. All of this was enough to make me pause, though.

I had already given Gus notice and I'd sent resumes out. One was to a fellow in Tennessee advertising for ag pilots. In the middle of all of this doubt about the Africa job I had thought about ag work. Although it had been some time since I had been in an ag plane wearing a helmet, sweating, breathing pesticides and dealing with the drama every load brings, I needed a job. I was qualified, just not current.

Guy Londe had a federally-subsidized boll weevil contract in Tennessee and called me at the best time possible. I was just off the phone with the pilot who didn't make it in the Congo and into my second Martini. I liked Guy immediately.

The morning after I spoke with him I called the state pesticide office in Memphis and asked about Mr. Guy Londe. He ran an operation in Humboldt, Tennessee and paid his bills. Nobody had anything bad to say about him, not even a pause when answering. Guy had a sense of humor—"a man who refused to grow up"—and someone I came to love. He was another Marine but missed Vietnam when he injured a knee in training. I am still happy I went to work for him.

Guy could tell a joke with a straight face like nobody I had ever met before. He introduced me to Clifford Crowl. He said, "Clifford is the president of the Iowa Gay Ag Pilots Association." It hung in the air for a long moment before someone, who knew Guy's sense of humor, started laughing. This was good ole boy country to be sure.

Another time, as soon as Clifford left to work off another air strip, Guy called there and told the dispatcher he was sending one of his best pilots. "One thing though, I heard he has AIDS but it's in remission. Even though, maybe you shouldn't sit too close to him." Clifford got there and everyone was giving him a wide berth. At first he couldn't understand it and finally smelled a rat. He asked if Guy had called and knew exactly what had happened.

Another Londe prank came when the FAA was on the ramp to check out the airplanes. They were gathered around one plane and Guy was taxiing out for takeoff after having just reloaded. As soon as he got near them and was upwind, he hit the smoker and held it. The smoking device was a requirement of the contract and used to determine the wind direction—by flying down into the field and momentarily pressing a button, which released oil onto the hot exhaust pipe, it made smoke. When you pull up, the wind direction was evident by where the smoke traveled. Guy held the smoker on so long you couldn't see the planes behind him or the inspectors coughing. No one thought it funnier than Guy.

His personal technique in spraying was doing his work low. When the plants were still small and less than a foot high he would do some wheel rolling. His main landing gear would touch the ground from time to time; you couldn't get any lower. I guess he sold the technique to farmers who believed lower was better. The truth of the matter is the best spray pattern is achieved from a height of one-half the wingspan length.

Londe's airplane would always have some of the crop, cotton or beans, hanging off of it. Always from the landing gear, but sometimes also the prop tips and wing leading edges. He once hit a deer when it jumped up in front of him while spraying some corn.

He flew a fine Ag Cat and could "work it." The term is saved for pilots who are bold enough to do "half-ass hammerheads back into the field"—i.e., at the end of the field the airplane is pulled straight up until it almost runs out of speed and then the rudder is pushed all the way over in the direction of the turn you want. From there it is really just falling out of the sky until you get enough airspeed to pull out of the dive. If you don't have enough room, it ruins your whole day. It's a quick way to turn the plane around but leaves no margin for error. "There are old pilots and bold pilots but there are no old, bold pilots." I haven't met many.

Guy turned out to be a stand-up guy who was loyal to his employees. After the season when I was named in a lawsuit for pesticide drift, he told me, "Don't worry about it. I'll take care of it." And he did. They don't make them better than Guy. I took the job and was never sorry for it.

I hadn't been in an ag plane for some time, so getting back to seat-of-the-pants flying took a little time. I had to come up to speed with the new technology taking over the business when I wasn't paying attention. An improved Satlock system had become wide spread during my absence. Now the system was considerably more accurate with a recording disk connected to it showing the airplane's every move. It could burn you or save you at litigation for drifting pesticides.

I knew I had to go easy with the flying at first even though this was an old man's job. Our pay was hourly flight time, not piecework as it usually is. There was no reason to make any tight, raggedy, stall-inducing turns, which kill young ag pilots every year. Those tight turns are done to maximize the acreage sprayed during the time available to fly, by getting back into the field quickly. The usual rate of pay is twenty to twenty-five percent of the operator's fee per acre. Thousand dollar days for ag pilots are not uncommon and, in the case of modern turbine-powered equipment, more than twice that.

Some of the large operators in the west, using the latest in GPS equipment connected through the internet, have the pilots' pay deposited into their bank account as soon as their assigned field has been sprayed. Some pilots check their account via cell phone on their way back to the strip. It might not be such good form, though. I knew of a pilot eating a sandwich on his way back to pick up another load who ran into a tree.

There was another Clifford I became friends with at Londe's: Clifford Ashe, a Vietnam Vet, and an Army pilot. He has forgotten more about ag flying than I ever knew. He helped me figure out the Satlock system the easy way.

"Just spray the field the way you would without it and refer to it to check your alignment." After a while his reasoning sunk in and worked. His Texas humor was always spot-on as well. I came back to the pilot lounge one morning complaining about all of the power lines littering the field I was spraying. Clifford twanged, "Well Jimmy, you know you cain't grow cotton without electricity."

In my opinion, the Boll Weevil Eradication Program had an overconfident title. Bugs are really difficult to eliminate completely. One of the most basic of rules with pesticide use is adherence to the label—what it says, and it says plenty. Chemical companies spend upwards of thirty million dollars in research and testing to get approval of a new pesticide, which is all represented on the label.

Everything from the name of the pest, to the application method, dosage, and content is listed. It is absolutely illegal to use a greater dosage to increase the kill because the survivors will be a species even more resistant. The rule says not adhering to label directions is illegal, period. The time it takes to get approval of a new pesticide makes it a catch-up game, with the bugs in front of the curve. I thought it very ambitious to use the word eradication in the title, but this massive Malathion application was successful in Mississippi a couple of years before. The program requires all cotton in the stipulated area to be sprayed whether the farmer wanted it done or not.

The government did have some protection from the pilots who would take advantage of such a program. The contractor's equipment requirements included a downloadable computer disk showing where the airplane went, how fast and how high. The GPS signals had recently been desensitized to provide civilian equipment an accuracy capability heretofore only available to the military. The Satlock system took care of this requirement by recording an airplane's position within two to three feet of altitude or the same laterally, as well as ground speeds.

The Malathion used on this contract was almost pure and sprayed in ultra-low volume (ULV), one quart to the acre. A field is sprayed from the downwind side to the upwind side so the spray material can move away from the next swath. When there is little or no wind, ULV applications hang in the air and result in flying through the slow-to-settle spray on the second swath. The chemical covers the windshield with an oily blur-inducing film. The first swath of a load was the only one you saw through an unaffected windshield.

The pilots who showed up for Londe's operation were great. At least four of us were Vietnam Vets and we all got along. Like the banner towing operation, almost everyone roughed up an airplane to some degree. Mine was a really stupid move at a small field of four acres with tall trees all around it and a small power line going right across the middle.

I saw the obvious wire and flew over it on my first pass. It may have been the sunbather at the swimming pool during my turn around who made me forget about the wire but forget I did. It wasn't visible through the oil blurred windshield anyhow; even so I should have remembered it. I dove into the field and heard a noise like a bang, followed by loud wind coming at me. As I instinctively pulled up, I looked in my lap and there was a six-inch triangular piece of windshield. I looked further up at the engine instruments on the dashboard and everything was reading what it should—"in the green." Guy was so proud of the brand new prop on this plane, too. The only upside was being able to see clearly straight ahead through the hole in the windshield all the way back to Guy's strip.

Soon after the Tennessee contract finished, there was another ad in Trade-A-Plane for the Africa job. The same man, Tim Roman, was behind the ad and had been ready to hire me when I took the Tennessee job. He was a little miffed when I told him Gus' stories, which made me pull away from going over there. I didn't know just how difficult it was for Tim to find a willing American pilot. His ad read, "Looking for a Sabreliner Captain for one month in Africa to give my man a holiday."

This time I did not hesitate. I had already researched the Democratic Republic of the Congo and was not going to be deterred. The CIA's website was matter of fact about it; the Center for Disease Control said you'll get sick; and corporate aviation guides said, "At all costs don't go. Child soldiers cannot be reasoned with." None of it fazed me. This was an opportunity, a major opportunity. The fellow for whom I would be working was on the winning side of a revolution and living at the top of the food chain.

Tim was not friendly in the least. I think he had been burned too many times by pilots promising anything to get a job in a jet and not being able to cut it. He paid for a pilot's training at FlightSafety who came to Kinshasa and never even flew the airplane before he quit. That helped explain Tim's cold demeanor.

Before I saw Tim in the flesh, and with what few words we exchanged, I was expecting a lean mercenary type with deep set and maybe vacant eyes. I was way off. Tim was more obese than I and, even though five inches shorter, was almost a hundred pounds heavier. In brief conversations prior to our first face-to-face he referred to himself as a warrior. To me obese does not at all suggest warrior. The warriors I had known were all quite lean. He did have some meanness in him, though— quite racist and a "Kurtz" wannabe. (Kurtz is the station manager's character in Joseph Conrad's short story "Heart of Darkness.")

Tim and I met at Philadelphia International Airport where he was waiting to get a flight back to Kinshasa. When he returned to Congo, he was going to take the President to China in the Gulfstream. Tim had been home to Hazleton, PA, to buy some farm and construction equipment he planned on shipping to the Congo for one of his enterprises. We stood outside the Air France baggage check area, smoked a couple of cigarettes and talked about the job I was going to perform. He didn't make any promises or tell any horror stories.

In spite of some haunting questions the idea of going to Africa, where I had never been, was growing on me. This was an appealing adventure and there was a buck to be made. Remuneration was in cash USD, no paperwork.

In a dictatorship, a fancy identification card, like the one I had with Presidential Aviation on it, a Black Diplomatic Passport or a very strong belief in a god—preferably as a member of the clergy—is the way to go. The ability to speak the language is another big help. I didn't know these things before I went, but figured them out quickly. The Democratic Republic of the Congo requires a Presidential invitation to get a visa. Putting a hundred dollar bill in with the passport and visa application when you mail it to the consulate in Washington is advisable. The cash will turn the passport around in one day and prevent the application from being misplaced.

A magazine published an article written by Carl Hoffman, titled "Strange Bird," about Tim and the following is an excerpt from it:

"Need something (or somebody) flown around Africa without a lot of questions? Can you pay with bricks of cash? Then you want old-school bush pilot Tim Roman, a man with Kurtzian ambitions, a deft touch on jungle runways, and a place on every smart dictator's speed dial."

Chapter 12
Flying in the Heart of Black Africa

I arrived in Kinshasa, Democratic Republic of the Congo, in March 2002, to pilot an eight-passenger jet. Flying in Africa proved to be the richest experience of my aviation career. Much more than the new places, sights, and smells, it was the lifestyle swaying me so. Daily living was different from my stateside existence. I had servants. Meals and drinks were served, doors opened, bags carried. I was bowed to and saluted, addressed as Commander, Colonel, Patron, and even Bwana. This was not just in the house but everywhere I went—the market, the airport, the cop on the street as we drove by. It took me no time to get beyond being accustomed to this treatment and enjoying it.

Kinshasa is the third largest urban area in Africa composed of twenty-four municipalities. Its residents are known as Kinois and over half are unemployed. Life there is a daily struggle of survival for most.

During the first few months of my stay in Kinshasa I lived at a company guesthouse on a street called Allée Verte with the mechanics Tom and Tennessee Tim. These were the southeast suburbs of Kinshasa in hills overlooking the Congo River and Brazzaville, capital of the Republic of the Congo (French Congo), which comprises the northeast border of the DRC. It's the only place in the world where country capitals faced each other. The northern border of the DRC met the Central African Republic and the northwest side South Sudan.

Avenue Nguma climbed out of a commercial district called Kitambo Magasin. This was the eastern end of Kinshasa where the commercial docks began and extended four miles to the east along the southern edge of the Congo River. It was where the country's main artery of commerce began and ended.

The hills above Kitambo overlooked the city and river. Avenue Nguma was a well-traveled route into Kinshasa for daily commuter traffic. Cars, trucks, and buses of all sizes traveled into and out of Kinshasa throughout the day. Boss Tim lived just off Avenue Nguma at the edge of Kitambo in an upscale neighborhood. Allée Verte split off to the left from Nguma about a mile up the hill. Deo's house was right on Nguma another half mile up the hill and the Palais de Marbre where Laurent Desiree Kabila's widow lived was further up. She was also the mother of the sitting president Joseph Kabila.

After my stay on Allée Verte, Tim moved me to a three-bedroom house on Avenue Haute Tension. It spurred off Nguma to the left near the top of the hill. This was a district of large homes behind tall masonry walls with other more modest dwellings in between. Many residents in my neighborhood were ambassadors and other big hitters.

Tim liked to keep his employees in the same vicinity in case there was a need to leave for political reasons, *tout de suite*. His house had a sandbagged bunker, which overlooked the large steel gates manned with a small squad of presidential guards. His very comfortable house was laid out for entertaining. Below a terraced lawn there was a swimming pool, separate jacuzzi and brick pizza oven off to one side. His cocktail parties were splendid with excellent food and drink served from trays carried by white-jacketed servants.

Within two weeks I agreed to stay for six more months, not just the original one month. Chris soon arrived to decide whether Lillian should also come in the fall. School was an issue—it would be Lillian's first semester of high school. We agreed to jump into this African gig with both feet and bring Lillian along. It was one of our better decisions to be sure. We didn't know it at the time, but we couldn't have bought an experience like this for her or ourselves.

The house Tim rented for us on Haute Tension was grand. The driveway forked off and descended along the long side of a one hundred by two hundred fifty foot lot containing the compound. The perimeter was encircled by a whitewashed masonry wall with broken glass embedded on the top. Because of the slope of the land the wall was shorter on the highest part. As the driveway descended it turned to the right to enter the enclosed carport via twenty foot high steel doors at the midpoint of the lot.

The house was laid out so the high side of the lot was used as the back yard with a swimming pool and terraced lawn. A covered porch was next to the pool. The rear of the house facing the backyard was glass, making it visible from the dining room and breakfast nook. The other side of the dining room, again all glass, opened onto a terrace facing the river. Inside there was a level that stepped down to the living room and bedrooms. The master bedroom had a bathroom and like the other two bedrooms had a veranda facing the river. A staircase from the carport entered into the living room. The exterior-facing glass had steel-barred, foldable security gates.

The view from the north side of the dining room and from all bedrooms encompassed most of Kinshasa, Brazzaville, and the Congo River between them. The only distraction was the high tension power lines from the tower on the crest of the hill nearby.

Under the living area was the enclosed carport capable of accommodating four cars. There were servant's quarters below, where the staff did the clothes washing and ironing. They went to their homes in the evening and came back to work at seven in the morning. The guards who came at four in the afternoon stayed down there, too. In addition to the winding staircase up to the living room, there were two sets of stairs rising on either side of the carport to the backyard.

The roof over the porch was close enough to the pool that you could jump off and clear the edge of the pool. There was a breadfruit tree on a terrace above, partially shading the pool. The backyard continued uphill another forty feet with palm trees and a flower bed along the bottom of the masonry wall. There was a banana tree along the side of the house as well as coconut palm trees in the backyard.

A staff of three attended to the house and the yard. John was our cook, Jackson took care of the inside of the house and Alexander was the pool and outside man. They were quite happy to be working and proud of whom they worked for. They dressed well when coming to or going from the house. We had cable TV and every room had an air-conditioner. If you turned on all air-conditioners at once you could hang meat in there. As long as we had electricity we were fine. The boss' house had an auxiliary powered diesel generator.

I earned these accommodations by providing a service, often under adverse conditions. During the first three months I averaged one hundred fifty hours of flight time per month—double what airline crews in the States flew. There was also the equivalent in waiting time for passengers to arrive. To my credit, I was easier to work with than my predecessor, Frank, and more pleasant after hours. As I became familiar with the job it seemed to fit well.

This was not a place where FAA regulations could be looked to for protection. Beginning a conversation with the Congolese who represented the President with, "We can't go back to Lubumbashi again tonight. It will put the crew over duty time limits," might not even get answered. They had the option of putting you in jail if they chose, so one had to be careful when taking a stand.

I was concerned about flying over jungles and wilderness at first. The radar- controlled environment I was accustomed to in the states provided a safety net. Any mechanical troubles requiring landing ASAP could be helped by a controller giving you in seconds a direction, called a vector, as a degree heading with distance to the nearest suitable airport from your position. This was not going to happen in Congo.

To my surprise I was soon grateful not to have the FAA tethered to my every move awaiting an error. I took care of my own navigation and soon preferred doing it. I became accustomed to not having alternate places for landing in between the point of departure and destination at night. Lighted runways in Congo were few. I enjoyed the bold feeling of screaming over jungles at night doing four hundred knots to displace the goosey feeling of the void below. Taking off with full fuel meant we were landing, somewhere, in three hours.

Weather was another issue. The access to weather reports was nothing like stateside in availability or accuracy. We usually got printouts of forecasts but they were often hours old. Fortunately, the weather at the equator was not like the northeastern United States, where fast moving cold fronts necessitated critical decisions. Low ceilings were infrequent and didn't linger. We dealt with cumulonimbi—thunderstorms—big ones. Runways could go from dry in light wind to wet with strong winds, quickly. Getting information from tower controllers, even as to the wind's direction and velocity, was inconsistent.

Stateside airport issues were published as Notices to Airmen and automatically come with the weather reports. In Congo, word of mouth was the best way. Deo was my source for most of this information, which he passed on to me as I needed to hear it. En route to an airport I hadn't been to was when he would decide to tell me that the ground navigational aids hadn't worked there for years. We did have two GPSs aboard so the navigational aid on the ground wasn't necessary unless we had to use it for an instrument approach.

N250EC was the nicest Sabreliner I had flown. Tim told me he kept it on a progressive maintenance program. Zekos and Bart kept it clean inside and out. The engine operating temperatures were not high—an indication of good internal health. High temperatures meant their life was running out. This old, pure jet aircraft was strong and perfect for this rugged country. Treat it with a soft touch and it will take care of me, I thought. I didn't concern myself with the health of the airplane, trusting in my mechanics. I didn't even do a preflight check to speak of. Just going with the flow in the beginning was less stressful.

The autopilot became erratic after twenty minutes. My predecessor, Frank used it, though, and made rough manual control corrections as necessary. Stateside operations would not have tolerated those drink-spilling control movements. Operators—the cheap ones—often rationalize not fixing autopilots by saying, "I'm paying two pilots. Why do I need to fix the autopilot?" We hand flew N250EC.

Cell phones were the primary means of communication and I had three of them. In 2002 there weren't any landlines nor would there be any. Everyone had cell phones. Stores sold new ones; people on the street sold stolen ones and everything else related to the phones. As the technology evolved and Vodacom took over in the marketplace, one was enough. I was also given a satellite phone for emergencies. Initially, email was only done via computers wired to a dish, but by the time I left in 2006 I could email from my laptop while sitting in the airplane.

My job was to stand by, 24/7. I was at the beck and call of the government. Sometimes the phone rang at two in the morning for a six o'clock departure. Such calls were rare and the passengers never arrived before ten o'clock anyhow. Still we had to show up and wait.

Deo lived with his wife Jackie and their four kids in a modest house with a limited staff. Domestic help even at the lower economic levels was commonplace. When we had a flight I drove the half mile to his house and he took over from there. The drive took us down the mountain through Kitambo, where the first traffic jams occurred, then into Kinshasa via a street shaded by tall mango trees and onto a traffic circle. Boulevard du 30 Juin, four lanes wide and named after Independence Day from the Belgians, was the main street through Kinshasa. Avenue Justice was a spoke off the same circle, which went by the UN compound and US Embassy.

The foot traffic was always heavy. In the mornings and evenings pedestrians were three and four deep on each side of the road. Fully loaded VW buses, the most popular form of public transportation, had the seats removed and narrow benches installed to increase the capacity. Fifteen or twenty passengers were the normal load, with always room for one more. Potential riders used simple hand signals to indicate what part of the city they were going to. Kinshasa and its surrounding towns were just thick with people. Trucks, always overloaded with goods, were twenty-feet high and had people hanging all over them.

Women carrying items on their heads stood out from the rest. Their gait was so natural they appeared unaware of the load, which often included a baby strapped to their back. They put a small pad on the top of their head and then whatever they were carrying—water jug or anything else. They were skinny with long, bright colored cloth dresses wrapped around themselves, flattering their torsos and derrières. Head-wraps often matched the dress fabric. Visible skin was moist with perspiration, but it was their proud posture that caught my eye.

Many large bulky items like furniture were transported on two-wheeled carts, pushed by someone called a pousse pousseur or chario man. They were always ready at hand to negotiate a delivery fee from where these items were sold. The prudent buyer watched his newly purchased goods through the delivery process to assure arrival at the destination. These carts added to the grand mélange of the street scene in Kinshasa, at times busy as a beehive.

Laced through all this were the shegues, the street children, mostly orphaned. Their numbers have been estimated to be twenty thousand citywide. Witchcraft is serious in Congo. Occasionally the shegues were declared demons and the police from time to time have rounded up groups of them—not to be seen again.

The ride to the airport took us down Nguma, through Kitambo and then Kinshasa via Boulevard du 30 Juin to the other side of the city. The boulevard ended at the thieves' market where business was always brisk. Everything from African Gray parrots in cages to tribal masks and ivory carvings were available. Then it was on through Limete and Masina, the most squalid of municipalities, and finally N'djili Airport.

At N'djili we drove right past the security guards to the airplane in front of the VIP lounge. A mechanic was usually there to make sure we got off. It was Deo's show from there until departure, when I went to work. I did my very brief walk around, which was little more than kicking the tires, and with novel in hand I went to the VIP lounge, waiting on our passengers.

Deo saw to the loading of our bags, fueling the airplane, filing the flight plan and dealing with Colonel Richard. He was a left-over from the Mobutu regime. His English was excellent and the reason he was still there. Most flights started with his calling Deo with the details. He was the one who was supposed to get us clearances into other countries and had a fifty-percent success rate. Only generals were close to punctual. Despite everything that could and did sometimes go wrong, we seemed to own the airport.

Our routine often had us home late at night and leaving early the next morning. The first few months of my tenure were very busy. We were out of town much more than in Kinshasa. My first trip was to Lubumbashi, the copper mining capital of the DRC, in the southeast of the country near Zambia. Lubumbashi was our fuel stop before going to South Africa. It was a much calmer city than Kinshasa with a sub-tropical climate because of its altitude at four thousand feet above sea level. We usually stayed at the Cascade on the edge of town. The hotel was low-key but clean with a bar, pool and restaurant.

The peace talks in Sun City sponsored by the South African government were going on when I got to the DRC. The spring of 2002 was the finalization of the peace accord following the Lusaka Ceasefire of 1999. My first three months were spent going to Johannesburg and back to Kinshasa and sometimes back again the same day. Including the fuel stop in Lubumbashi, the trip was six hours one way. When you added waiting times for the always-tardy passengers, a round trip could be eighteen hours. This constituted a majority of my flying although there were trips to Zimbabwe, Angola and Tanzania as well. It became obvious that the long duty hours were becoming dangerous when I caught myself dozing off in a descent into Kinshasa at two in the morning.

I thought a low profile was the way to go with this whole business but there was no way to be inconspicuous. Kinshasa was no longer awash with white ex-patriots as it had been in the 1960s. I didn't ask questions about my passengers' identities or what they were up to. I didn't even do much talking except to say, "Bienvenue à bord." The less I knew the better.

Turning a blind eye to passengers' bodyguards was a little more difficult given their slovenly military bearing. A number of times one of them had a rifle grenade fall from his ammo pouch onto the tarmac or the deck of the airplane because he hadn't secured it properly. Good thing the centripetal safeties in them were intact. Getting upset about things I could not control would have sent me packing early on, so my policy about such things was, fuck it—they weren't about to change for me. This place was the Wild West and I was rolling the dice.

The scenic images from the flight deck were magnificent. Stunning cloud formations in the wet season were more dramatic than in the States. There was no question about avoiding cumulonimbi over here. They weren't to be toyed with like some in Pennsylvania and New Jersey. At night they were their most brilliant and the lightning show was often the width of the horizon. Seen from two hundred miles away while at thirty-five thousand feet, snowcapped Kilimanjaro, when it protruded through a cloud layer, resembled the pate of a Bald Eagle surveying the rest of the continent. There was no end to the magnificence of this place, which made Texas small by comparison.

There was a rainy season and a shorter dry season in the winter months of June through September. *La saison de pluie* doesn't bring rain daily like Vietnam. A hot day here was followed by vigorous thunderstorms in the evening or the next day. The torrential downpours made for flash floods rushing, sometimes several feet deep, through streets and requiring traffic to reroute for hours.

The heavy rain was dangerous. There were many electrical power wires in the ground that sometimes surfaced when the water came—and come it did. Some of those wires weren't as insulated as they once were, which made barefooted travel treacherous or deadly in places.

Except for the extreme altitudes involved with jet travel, the flying in Africa was what it would have been in the States during the 1930s or 1940s. The electronic navigation aids (nav aids) are rather elementary and in disrepair compared to the technology and maintenance in the States today. In Congo, we didn't receive any publications to notify us when certain nav aids were out of service either; there was no operating Postal Service. GPS was a big help and I couldn't imagine flying over there without it.

Stateside it was the responsibility of the pilot to review all publications related to a pending flight. Anything to make him aware of malfunctioning nav aids, severe weather, Notices to Airmen or any warnings on the intended route of flight are considered his responsibility. Those rules apply here as well but access to information was limited or just unavailable.

Voice communication on the radio was not always intelligible and barely audible at other times. There was rarely any radar control and what existed was limited to the former English colonies. Before I left the states I felt a little concerned about flying in a non-radar-controlled environment with the mountains and rugged terrain in Africa. Virtually all of my work in the States was under the watchful eye of a controller who wouldn't vector me into a mountain on a rainy night. He would be watching me constantly, but the downside was the threat of a violation should I make a mistake. It didn't take long for me to get comfortable without controllers in Congo and taking complete charge of my own navigation.

This place was made for me. The more I learned about Congo the more I liked it. Two months was all I required to enjoy being rid of the radar leash and the rest of the rules. I felt more freedom here than anywhere else in spite of the government's constant presence. My previous flying experiences—the junk airplanes, the rule-breaking operators I had worked for and the dirty conditions—made Congo fit like a pair of old shoes. The stick and rudder flying of ag work even helped. I was, after all, flying a jet in the bush.

The protection of flying for the President gave me a secure feeling. It did take away certain liberties, though. Trying to say no was quite difficult at times. Colonel Richard didn't much care if a piece of equipment was inoperative as long as the airplane started and I took off. If the President said the Minister was going to Luanda this morning, he was going.

In the States instrument flights follow a routine. There can be as many as six frequency changes, with information and responses from the parked airplane until it is airborne. Flights conducted under visual rules don't have the communication component to the same degree. In most countries outside of the United States, flights are conducted under instrument rules, which require filing written flight plans.

N'djile was often a busy airport. We called ground control for permission to start our engines and then once started tuned to the tower frequency, telling him we were ready to taxi. I did the before-takeoff checklist while taxiing to the end of the runway usually skipping the before-start checklist and before-taxi list. As long as there was no incoming traffic, the controller would clear us for takeoff when we were at the end of the runway ready to go. Once we were airborne and on our way out of the tower's area of responsibility, Deo contacted departure. When our direction was established with the controller, Deo said bye-bye and we didn't use the radio again until we were near our destination.

If we were going to Lubumbashi, or anywhere else we called their radio about seventy miles out and told them who we were, where and what we wanted to do. This was by no means proper international protocol but it was ours because of the warlike ambiance and the passengers we were transporting. These fellows didn't want their presence advertised. A missile took down the Rwandan president's airplane one night while attempting to land at Kigali and this still had people sensitive to night flying in eastern Congo. The incident started the Tutsi-Hutu horror in 1990, which cost six hundred thousand lives in a matter of days, mostly by machete.

There were a few times in Africa I became uncomfortable with the radar control in Togo, a country north of the Gulf of Guinea. It was the suddenness of its operation catching me off guard and unprepared. I had become used to flying without the controller's participation. Even when the service was published on the approach chart it couldn't be counted on. I used the standard published approach and suddenly a controller gave me vectors altering my route. This would typically happen after a long fatiguing day in an unfamiliar area of small mountains (no mountain is small when it is a hard spot in a cloud). Waiting for the controller to turn me in towards the final approach course, while keeping me clear of the mountains in the northern part of Togo, was unsettling. I was gritting my teeth because this was a deviation from the approach plate I was using and had briefed myself with. These are fine points but when a pilot was tired and in unfamiliar surroundings at night bad things could happen quickly.

Our night takeoffs from Entebbe were always heavy. They had excellent duty free shops where we loaded up on the wine and liquor unavailable in Kinshasa. Entebbe to Kinshasa was a two-and-a-half-hour flight at least. Sometimes we landed with minimum fuel—twenty minutes' worth, maybe.

There were a couple of nights coming out of there over Lake Victoria, with its crocodiles, when a particular species of insect was swarming. The air was thick with them at dusk when they hovered over the runway. On takeoff roll, in spite of otherwise clear weather, by the time you accelerated to rotation speed you had used up most of a very long runway. Part of this was due to the extra drag on the leading edges of the wings and fuselage due to the paste-like remains of those bugs. We were in instrument conditions because the windshield was covered with them. Three hours of friction caused by four hundred knots at cruise speed didn't clear the windshield. At Kinshasa it was necessary to look out the side window for help in seeing the edge of the runway when landing.

My first flight to Entebbe required that I take three generals there and park at the old terminal. The civilian part was a modern structure up on a hill where we parked if we were transporting politicians. While waiting for the generals to return from their business I noticed small circular marks on the buildings and broken windows. I asked one of the officers what the story was. He told me they were bullet holes from the rescue operation of a hundred and two Israeli hostages by the Israeli Defense Force. The Black September movement took them hostage in a hijacked Lufthansa airliner on July 4, 1972, landing here at Entebbe. The Israelis, with high altitude pictures provided by the CIA, came in commando style and it was over in ninety minutes. They destroyed the Ugandan Air Force consisting of thirty Russian-made jet fighters, shot the place up proper and sent the Ugandans a bill for the operation.

Chapter 13
Deo and Maryoth

Deo was about five feet five inches tall, slim, with a receding hairline and quite dark skinned. He was my babysitter. Without him my time there would have been difficult if not impossible. He knew how to get around Africa like I do the States. The quality I most admired was his quiet, reserved nature. I was curious about Frank's behavior as captain but getting Deo to say anything about him was not going to happen. There were other questions on my mind, too. I was uncomfortable asking him what was expected of me besides flying the airplane. His English was good but there still remained a communication barrier due to cultural differences. Like other Congolese, Deo often told me what he thought I wanted to hear.

He was with Frank when they ran off the runway while landing at Kinshasa one evening, wrecking the previous Sabreliner. I was curious how Frank did it, given the runway is near three miles long. Deo would never say anything about the incident or anyone else. It is a fine trait to have—one to admire, really. The reason for his reticence was Congo itself, its colonial days and more recently a dictatorship. He was not the only educated person I knew who was hesitant to voice an opinion, especially when it came to politics.

When I arrived Tim told me, "You make all landings and takeoffs." Fine with me, I thought. I asked Tim if Deo knew this. He said, "Yes." Sitting on my hands while a green First Officer fought through a challenging landing was not something I did well. In the States the crew alternated the flight duties on each leg of a shift. The captain would usually fly the first leg with the non-flying pilot working the radios and reading the checklists as called for by the captain. Doing all takeoffs and landings myself made me curious to find out if I should expect any rancor because of Tim's edict. It turned out there wasn't any.

Deo and I had clearly defined jobs. He arranged everything on the ground, which made me very lazy and in need of a caretaker. I grew to depend on him but could have learned much more if I had followed him around all of the different airports we flew into. Instead, I sought refuge in the air-conditioned VIP lounges. In self-defense, it was usually hot, not just warm, wherever we went. One could melt at some of those places.

At every airport outside of Congo, immigration forms and flight plans needed to be filed. Cash had to be given to the civil servants at these offices to get permission to start engines when it was time to leave. An enclosed airplane on a one-hundred-degree tarmac without running engines to power the air-conditioning gets warm fast.

Determining if a pilot couldn't make it as a captain was not easy for me. Flying the airplane was not Deo's strength. I figured he never had the chance to get up there alone and be forced to make the decisions coming with the territory of the left seat. In the States it is rare a pilot goes from a flight school to the right seat of a complex airplane without having done considerable time as a single pilot in a twin engine airplane.

Single pilot flight operations under FAR Part 135 Air Taxi rules at night, flying in the clouds in the high traffic of the northeast corridor of the United States, is as busy as a pilot gets. Dropping the pencil just when a controller is about to issue holding instructions, creates pressure. When there is a two-man crew in the cockpit, the flying pilot just flies and the non-flying pilot does the rest of the work.

One of the key elements in making a check ride easier with an examiner as the acting first officer is to keep him busy all of the time. Ask for this, that and the other constantly so he has less time to pick on you.

Deo started in the right seat of a Boeing 737 and never got the chance to develop as a pilot. This was old school protocol for flight crews. The first officer was not groomed to move over. I adjusted to his lack of airmanship. His instrument approaches were not disciplined, which I expect came from the bad examples of other captains.

When he started to deviate from a published approach procedure I was all over him. "Not with me aboard. Get back on course." I didn't want to let even an insignificant breech go unspoken and construed as approval. My own philosophy was always not to "bust minimums" for fear of it becoming a habit. Do it once and get away with it and the second time is easier, which eventually leads to catastrophic results. Descend through a hole in a cloud before reaching the designated point on the approach and the first thing you might see is a tree coming at you at one hundred thirty knots. Whoops.

Deo was great at his job, though. He spoke at least five languages. He got us through the airports and hotels with ease. I never fully appreciated his position until we started dealing with Eastern Congo.

My first year in Congo we didn't go to the war-torn eastern part of the country due to the political unrest—lingering rebel activity. When flying over the east we didn't make position reports or do anything but listen to the radios. Keeping as low a profile as possible was the idea. It was months after the Lusaka Peace Accord was in place before things settled down out there. The rebel strongholds, like Bukavu and Goma, where the action was, were not places our passengers wanted to go. The first time we took cabinet members to Kigali, Rwanda, they brought their own food and water to guard against being poisoned.

They had a sit-down scheduled with rebel leaders and were edgy when they arrived at the airport in Kinshasa for departure.

I was surprised when I got a call from Deo telling me we had a flight to Goma with one of the four vice-presidents, Jean-Pierre Bemba. (He was later put on trial in the Hague at the International Criminal Court and convicted of two counts of crimes against humanity and three counts of war crimes.) At this juncture, Tim was back in the States eating dinner with his friend Barry in an underground Mexican restaurant where cell phones didn't work, so I couldn't call and get his recommendations on how to handle Bemba. Tim had never told me to expect this destination or even let on to a possibility of operating out there.

Historically the Eastern Congo has always been a rebel stronghold and the main reason we didn't go to that part of the country. The condition of the airport at Goma was another reason. In 2002 the nearby volcano dumped lava on the runway making it accessible only to airplanes capable of short-field operations. The runway's altitude of over five thousand feet severely compromised the airplane's performance as well. These things were adding up and not in our favor. It wasn't his decision, but Deo sure didn't want to go and encouraged me to say no.

Bemba, the war criminal turned vice-president, called me wanting to know what the problem was. He had been flying to Goma in the Boeing 737 he owned for some time. I said it just wasn't prudent to go there in the Sabreliner. I didn't tell him our hot running engines were nearly worn out and climbing to altitude took forever. Takeoff from Goma was questionable at best.

The runway was marginal. I was sure the performance charts would back up my decision. In Congo safety margins didn't exist and they flew Boeings out of Goma and Bukavu. The number of airplanes crashing while landing and taking off from Goma would have closed it long ago if it were in the States.

An hour after talking with Bemba I heard from Tim, whose phone was loaded with missed calls from all kinds of ministers wanting to know what was going on with his pilot. He wanted to know what the story was, too. In the end he said, "Go get the charts out of the plane and work the numbers. We'll see how we can lie our way out of this one." After all, the situation I worked in was, as Tim once said, a "lie, cheat and steal environment."

After doing the graph dance with all of the performance charts, the numbers showed us in the lake if an engine whimpered on takeoff. Landing was not so difficult, but leaving always had you with hands full of airplane. With healthy engines, it wouldn't have been the white-knuckle event it always was for me. Age has taken a lot of bravery out of me.

Nobody asked to see my figures from the charts anyhow. If they did, they would get a headache. These charts are put together on a sheet of paper extending from a large loose-leaf binder unfolding to about three feet per page. From the beginning of the first graph, using the appropriate entry data, one follows a series of sloping lines through it to the next graph. Then, you must trace a line from there to the entry point of the next graph through to its end and on to the next graph until finishing the last one. Magnifying glasses help but someone who tries to follow it for the first time has no chance of keeping it all straight enough to understand. The data is all temperatures, winds, altitudes and weights. These charts are based on the best results a test pilot could manage with a new airplane after many attempts. Only a fool would think those figures applied to our plane.

The ugly part of this whole affair was that Deo was fired. Although it turned out to be only for a week it was terrible for him. When it happened, he called me crying, "Why is Tim doing this to me?" Somebody needed to pay and they wanted a white guy flying them. Deo had a family to support and a prestigious job suddenly taken away for no fault of his own and with no hope of getting a comparable position. For a local Congolese pilot, flying Presidential Aviation was as good as it was going to get, right seat or not.

When I flew a couple of trips with another pilot I realized just how valuable Deo had been. Flying smoothly was not Deo's strong suit but he understood what the controllers were saying. I like to think I passed on to him some flying skill but am not sure if I helped.

I tried to get him to give me "callouts" for the takeoff roll but he couldn't get with it. While the flying pilot has his attention on keeping the airplane on the runway the other set of eyes are watching the instrumentation for abnormalities. This relieves some of the workload of the takeoff. The decision to abort a takeoff often starts with clues from small engine instruments. I started letting him do takeoffs when we were empty and emphasized these callouts but they never took root in him. There are a number of callouts helping instrument approaches as well, but I failed to help him appreciate them either. They are common in airline work or anyplace else, but here, in the bushes, they seemed irrelevant.

I also let him do the landings when we were empty and could sense his satisfaction when it went well. I regretted not having given him a chance sooner.

One morning, when we were going to Lubumbashi for a pick up, I was flying and thought I would treat Deo to a roll on climb out. It was unfair to do it unannounced. My roll was not as polished as Guin's either. It scared the shit out of him. That roll was his first ever, in any airplane not just the Sabre. As the wings went past a sixty-degree bank and continued, he began to get the message we were going all the way around. His, "Oh my Gods," started and continued through inverted until we were on our way to right side up. I'm sure he won't forget that incident or some of the others, more thrilling, that occurred over the four years we flew together.

Deo had a wife named Jackie and four well-behaved children. Jackie operated a small pharmacy they owned. Deo lived within his means and had only one wife as far as I could tell. He was a churchgoer as are virtually all Congolese. They have plenty to pray for.

We didn't socialize, but he did come to an occasional party at Tim's house when invited. Ours was a formal relationship with little personal small talk. He never invited me to his house for dinner. I saw him as a good man, nothing more and nothing less. I hope he and his family are well living in that very dangerous country.

Deo knew his job and was comfortable in any of more than a dozen countries we went to in Africa—from Khartoum, Sudan to Freetown, Sierra Leone to Windhoek, Namibia and Durban, South Africa. All I had to do was take us there and he would handle the rest. When we arrived at the hotel, I went directly to the bar. He would check us in, and come to the bar with my key. Sometimes we would have dinner together and sometimes not.

We had a special trip one Friday, which had our handlers, Colonel Richard and Charles, at a higher level of urgency than usual. Deo told me the President's wife was off somewhere and we were to pick up a "reporter" to meet with Joseph. We were going to Cotonou, Benin, which is on the Gulf of Guinea between Nigeria and Togo.

"What about the clearance, Colonel Richard?" I asked.

"I am getting it." Yeah, sure you are. He sent us off with a number written on a piece of paper, which was the request number, not a clearance number. Formalities were a little more stringent on the north side of the Gulf of Guinea and it took Deo's A-game of silver-tonguing controllers and a few hundred dollars to get us in and out quickly.

The reporter and her assistant were waiting for us, although she sure didn't look like a reporter. No pencil in the ear, small notebook or frumpy business suit, not this one. She was a babe—well-coiffed, great makeup and a stunning body. Her dress was a white silk-like material stretching and clinging to every detail of her body due to a minimum of undergarments if not a complete absence. It was difficult not to stare.

The return trip didn't go nearly as smoothly. We were cleared to land after a great deal of talk about a VIP on board and more "Presidential Aviation" thrown about. After landing it was show time though. We were directed to a gate away from the active ones and told to remain in the aircraft until directed otherwise. We didn't have to wait long and a half dozen armed soldiers with a couple of officials came from the terminal and motioned us out onto the tarmac. "Follow me," the chief said.

It was finally in the office of the Chief of Security for the airport the whole story came out. The "reporter" was now being referred to as the Countessa, a very good friend of President Kabila. I was enjoying this comedy, not laughing but not taking it seriously. I never had the fear of ending up in an African jail for days, while Kinshasa and this fellow leading the interrogation worked it all out. This wasn't Rwanda after all.

When the Chief asked Deo a question and his answer referred to our picking her up two days' prior, his whole demeanor changed. He immediately asked about a clearance and it came to light we didn't have one then either.

Now he was making more phone calls in a much more demanding tone. When he got done reprimanding the people who worked for him he tried to start the process for us to leave. Not easy on a Sunday afternoon when the necessary people were off work.

I tried to be helpful and even suggested our spending the night at a local hotel. My plan for a day trip across the Gulf of Guinea didn't work. Kinshasa was on the phone with their apologies and saying they must have the airplane back because we had an important flight in the morning. We spent about seven hours talking and waiting for this whole business to be sorted out. By the time we got home it was about three in the morning and we were back to the airport for a scheduled eight o'clock departure.

I told Deo I wanted to take French lessons and asked if he knew anyone who could teach me. I thought the teacher's English should be good because I spoke virtually no French. If I needed anything Deo was the one to ask. He really came through for me on this one.

The professor's name was Maryoth LaBoya. He and Deo attended the same church. Maryoth came to the house at Haute Tension to teach me French every weekday morning I was in town. He became much more than a tutor to me and I more than a student to him.

Maryoth wasn't tall, five feet six, dark and always cheerful. He walked up the hill from Kitambo to the house every morning and sat with me for an hour trying to get French into my head and out of my mouth. And what a fight it was for the four years I spent in Congo. He arrived on time every morning, thus disproving my theory of Congolais not being able to tell time.

Maryoth was overly cautious in his approach to teaching me. I preempted his lesson plan when I wrote sentences down in English and tried to translate them into French using a dictionary. I pulled out my notes and began my questions regarding a paragraph of what I was sure was French. This is not the way to learn French or any other language. Idioms are the mainstay of conversation. I think he didn't want to risk this job by telling the student who was the teacher. The wages probably fed his family.

Our relationship grew over the years and I came to love him and his whole family. My high regard for him comes mostly from the way he negotiates living in Kinshasa while raising and supporting a beautiful, well-behaved family of seven. So many American families I see in the States seem bent on raising rude brats. They would do well to observe Maryoth and Ester with their children.

Maryoth's education gave him a chance in Kinshasa. The ability to speak English, as well as the national languages of French and Lingala, puts you on top of the labor pool in Congo.

His father, who still lived in the village where Maryoth grew up, was in his seventies—very old for a Congolais. Chris and I took them all to dinner once when his father came to Kinshasa for a visit. We went to my favorite restaurant, New Jeanne's. It was downtown just off of the Blvd and made a duck confit with pomme frites to die for. The kids were delighted to be included. While we ate, Maryoth's father told him, in Lingala or perhaps their tribe's language, this white man must think a lot of him to take them all to dinner at such a place. Spot on.

New Jeanne's was Jeanne's second restaurant while I was in Kinshasa. She was a prostitute before becoming a restaurateur and did well for herself. Both restaurants were very successful. I never saw her wear the same dress twice and she always looked great. Tall with big, bright eyes and a graceful figure as she went table to table schmoozing with the customers every night, sometimes with her Belgian boyfriend in tow.

I went to her first restaurant with Antonio, one of my housemates who introduced me to a "Les Bouquet." It is fish, capitaine (Nile perch (*Lates niloticus*), a freshwater fish, important as food in much of Africa), wrapped and cooked in a banana leaf with a tomato sauce of sorts. Over the years I ate them many times all over Congo. The aroma when the leaf is opened takes you right away. Antonio and I were seated in one of the smaller dining rooms. It had high ceilings with recessed tall windows and ceiling fans. There were six tables of four in various configurations constantly turning-over with new diners.

Antonio was a great dinner companion. He was a long time Africa man from Cape Verde and went to Belgium for University where he earned a bachelor's degree in Agricultural Engineering. He was the station chief for Sabena Airlines in Kinshasa for a number of years with his Belgian wife and daughters living with him. His job ended when the company cut back and stopped serving Kinshasa. Now his family was back in Belgium while Antonio was working for Tim putting the Wimbi Dira Airline together. His prior experience gave him a key role.

Antonio and I spent more than one evening over dinner and wine. It was always good, intelligent conversation from a well-traveled man. I came to know some of his personal history including the story of his father and the string of half-brothers and sisters Antonio had throughout Africa. Antonio was a tall, thin gentleman who could have passed as Italian. He was always pleasant except when he had to deal with Tim.

I met his wife once when she came back to Kinshasa from Belgium to spend a week with Antonio. She was a beauty and intelligent, too. They seemed happy at the time visiting with their friends who still worked in Kinshasa but their marriage would come to an end in the months ahead. Antonio's daughters had friends who were still in the Congo where their parents worked. These friends had heard talk about Antonio and "another woman." Sadly, the divorce followed in due course.

The other woman was quite a package and had me thinking Juju could be real after all. I wasn't wrong in my fear of beautiful women, either. Men are no match for some of them. She had a job at Wimbi Dira and was pursued by the Belgian accountant there as well as having Tim's eye. She went after Antonio and he didn't have a chance.

Antonio seemed to have lost his mind. Seeing her walk, and she knew how, down the rough street leading to the airline's offices in spike heels open at the toe and heel could cause car accidents. There she was navigating her way around and over the rough dirt and rock road of Avenue des Aviateurs, with aplomb. Amidst the small black plastic bags that rolled around Kinshasa like tumbleweeds in Tucson she was clearly a diamond in the rough. Only a parasol could have been added to the package. She had skin the texture of café au lait. A beautiful, but somewhat hard, face atop a five foot six "mince" frame with large young breasts; she was a drop-dead heart stopper. She was not a water bearer.

In this land of hunger, if a family can't afford to keep its girls in school they will become working girls—prostitutes—and support the family. She would have been the one to support her family. Many students use this oldest of professions to pay for an education. Sex in Congo is not considered some big hidden prize awarded for good behavior. It is a much more natural and necessary function, like eating.

An attractive girl in a starving household is going out at night to bring back money for food. If she can speak English, she might get a conventional job but that is more the exception than the rule. A mother would teach her daughter how to please a man. It's a matter of survival and not something to trifle with. Clothing is an investment. These women are very possessive once they latch onto a man who is considered a sponsor. I have seen women fight in bars with beer bottles over a man.

There is desperation at the root of all this behavior. They will use superglue to hold the false nails on their fingers, talcum powder to make their skin lighter. Makeup comes after food on the needs list.

The following is from Maryoth.

Hi mon ami,
Thanks for the question and here is the truth of what we actually experience in Congo. Girls are not born prostitutes but they may end in prostitution when they don't have good conditions of life in their families. First of all, parents' poverty may lead young girls to prostitution. You know if one is not eating well in his family, he may beg food at the neighbor. This is where men take place of sponsors and start abusing. Hunger is

the base of prostitution in my city. There are families where a mother who have grown up girls (you know in Congo, a boy or a girl may stay in his (her) parent's house even after he (she) is 20 years old if he (she) is not married or if he (she) has not got a job) ask her daughters to go out at night so that they get something to eat in the morning. Some girls prostitutes themselves to have money to pay school fees or tuitions. Many of those who are in the streets at night are students at universities. The fact of having many kids with small means is another factors. When one have to pay for all of them at school, it is not an easy task for parents. Can you imagine a congolese office worker who earn less than 50$ a month, he has to pay for renting, electricity, water, feed kids, take them to the hospital when they sick... All these factors make it difficult for people to survive and contribute to girls prostitution.

The DRC is a man's country. Marriage customs begin with precise dowry negotiations ranging from money, to clothes, cooking oil, goats, and chickens.

Hi mon ami,
This one about death is: "L'orgueil de l'homme meurt quelques jours avant sa mort," i.e. Man's pride dies few days before his death.
Hi Jim,
Sorry to respond late. I was very busy all the weekend. Here are some points that may be of some interest for marriage and divorce.
Here is the process. The young man gets in touch with the young lady who accepts to get married. Then he will go to meet the young lady's parents to introduce himself as the candidate who wants to marry their daughter. The girl's family (father, mother, brothers, sisters, uncles, aunts, etc.) will meet to discuss about what they will ask their in law to pay as dowry. They will draw up a list of things which in most of the cases contains: cash, (approximately $US 1.500 to $US 2.500); 4 (super wax: $US 100 each) clothes for the girl's mother, 2 handkerchiefs, 2 pairs of shoes for the mother-in-law, a can of milk, a machete, some cola nuts (for some tribes), 5 living chickens, 2 goats, a bag of salt, a jar of palm oil (25 liters), a big (water) basin, a big pot, at least $US 200 to give to the mother-in-law in order to talk to her because the man cannot talk to his mother-in-law the same way he talks to his father-in-law (this is for the Baluba tribes). For the father-in-law, he will have to give a suit, a pair of shoes, socks, a hat, a tie, and at least 30 racks of beer and soft drink, a radio, a gun if there is a hunter in the girl's family. In some tribe, the man pays the double because the girl's uncles will also ask something on the list. It is only when the man gathers all these things that he can meet his family-in-law and on that day it will be a big ceremony.

Mon ami, please don't hesitate to ask me any question you want for clarification. I am not afraid if you use man name in the book. That will also serve a reference for my kids who will read it in the future.
Thank you

Regarding divorce, many facts enter into account. In most of the cases, it is the man who takes the decision to divorce. A divorce may occur if:
- The man surprises his wife with another man.
- The wife does not bear children. (In this case, the man can divorce or marry another wife)
- But if she only bear girls, a man can marry another wife who if possible can bear boys.
- The wife is not obedient.
- The wife does not respect her (husband's family) family in law.
- The wife is a witch. In this case the man notices that he does not prosper and his wife is the cause.

Chapter 14
Living in Kinshasa

Kinshasa was called Leopoldville when Henry Morton Stanley founded it as a trading post in 1881. Though it has come a long way since then, the nine million people who live there now must deal with an infrastructure in shambles. The only firefighting equipment is at the airport fifteen miles away. It is hard to find the hanging flowerpots that once adorned most of the balconies of the apartment buildings. Small piles of garbage burn on the streets—there is no garbage removal.

During a cocktail party one evening I saw a rugged Belgian security guard begin to weep as he looked at pictures of Kinshasa taken when he was a boy. Kinshasa was called Kin la Belle then and now it is Kin la Poubelle—trashcan.

In the 1960s Kinshasa was like a grand garden and the epicenter of modern medicine in Africa. Today, South Africa is the center of the continent's technology. Mobutu's loss of power in 1991 left behind an eviscerated economy and resulted in the pillage of the city that followed Laurent-Désiré Kabila's takeover.

When Congo's independence came on the thirtieth of June 1960, the Belgians left suddenly before doing anything to ease the transition on their departure. Quite the contrary, the colonialists inhibited the native population's education wherever possible. There were a handful of Congolese with college degrees and the rest with no business sense at all. The takeover of businesses by people who didn't understand something as basic as the fact that inventory needed to be replaced when it was sold, soon made for empty shelves. The Mobutu-influenced way of thinking—steal from the white man or it's a wasted day—didn't work well when all the whites leave.

About the only thing I saw in the DRC truly democratic was the way people drove. The best example of this can be experienced at a railroad crossing on the way into Kinshasa. A long, slow-moving train arrives in the morning overloaded with people hanging out its windows and on the roof. Once the train prevents the road traffic from crossing the tracks to the other side, the cars begin to line up close to the moving train and wait. At first, a couple cue up behind each other and then as more come they spread to the right side of the first car. Soon one fellow will go on the left side of the first car and be followed by another. And so, it goes until the whole street side of the track has cars with not a foot between them. Then more cars accumulate behind the front lines for as long as the train takes to pass. The rub comes when the train passes and the other side reveals the same gathering of cars face to face. Once they close the space between themselves the gridlock can take hours to sort out.

My Friday nights usually started at the Marine House in the US Embassy compound when it was opened to the American expat community. The detachment was comprised of ten Marines with a senior staff NCO in charge. Their primary job was the protection of the paperwork; diplomats came second. The young Marines stationed there all looked quite fit and capable. In order to get into the Marine Security Guard School at Quantico, requires, among other things, height of at least sixty-four inches and first class physical readiness test results. All Marines posted to embassies have security clearances and above average intelligence scores as well.

The Marine Corps birthday ball was held at the Grand Hotel the first year I was in country and as the oldest Marine present I was part of the cake-cutting ceremony. At other birthday balls I attended in the States, the oldest Marine was always someone who had served in the Pacific at places like Guadalcanal or Iwo Jima. So this was an honor and the young Marines at the detachment treated me well. The Gunnery Sergeant in charge told me I was welcome to use their gym anytime. The sign over the gym entrance read *Chez Douleur*—House of Pain—of course.

The ball was formal and well attended by dignitaries from other embassies. There was a band off to one corner of the ballroom playing during the cocktail hour. The leader wore a pith helmet—perfect on him—adding to the atmosphere. His name was Francoise and he was playing an old Les Paul guitar he claimed once belonged to Buddy Guy. When they played "Summertime," Chris and I took to the dance floor and were joined by many others. The British Defense Attaché's wife told us later that our dancing had begun the ball.

The Oasis Club at the British Embassy opened once a month to foreign members and guests. They had a building near the ambassador's residence with a bar and pool table opening to a large outdoor dining area. A lavish dinner buffet was set up next to the swimming pool. I heard a story about one of Tim's mechanics from Hazleton getting drunk and boisterous during one of these events. He was tolerated until he made a disparaging remark about Margaret Thatcher, at which time he was promptly thrown into the pool. The first night I was there I got into a conversation with a fellow named Clive who asked me if I had ever been to the Third World before. I told him I was in Vietnam in the sixties and asked if it counted. He agreed but added, "You know, if you are here, you're not all there." I started feeling like a character in a Graham Green novel.

The local watering hole for my circle of drinking friends and many others from the Embassy was called Supic's, on Avenue Kilo-Moto between Boulevard du 30 Juin and Avenue de la Justice. In the evening, there was a large gathering of humanity on the block-long street, which had six bars similar to Supic's. One of the barbecue places tethered to a tree the live goat that was next on the fire, to indicate the freshness of their product. All manner of street people passed by as the evening progressed.

You can buy anything in the way of carvings, crafts or stolen goods in the thieves' market at the end of the Boulevard. Bargaining was part of the process and the first price offered was at least four times what the item would eventually sell for. One night I bought a herd of small wood-carved elephants with tiny tusks made of bone. After haggling, the price agreed to included a bottle of beer for the vendor.

Most of the nightlife in Kinshasa didn't start until after midnight. Supic's was a staging area for the working girls who used the salon de coiffure across the street to prepare. Many were easy on the eye and if you were seen looking at a particular girl, she would be sitting next to you but quick. Trying to leave alone was not so easy, and just saying no didn't always work. Often they had to be pushed or pulled out of the car.

Supic's was comprised of three steel shipping containers, awnings with tables, chairs and cold beer. A limited food menu was offered as well. The tables were full from ten o'clock with expatriates, merchants and prostitutes. There was live music on weekends. It was my *deuxième bureau,* and very popular with the embassy crowd. Supic's was open all day but really came alive at night. A gatekeeper limited the number of merchants allowed to hawk their wares.

The night clubs all had dance floors with disc jockeys. The girls of Kinshasa know how to dance. When I went in those places I kept my money and phones on one side of my person and against the bar or a wall. Even then, I secured them with my hand when the clubs were crowded. This was prime time for harvesting money from a *mundele.*

The US Embassy had periodic town hall meetings at the ambassador's residence. This was a brief intro course for new American arrivals to educate them on the rules of life in Congo. One of the first rules is not to leave your residence with anything you can't afford to lose. Another, very important rule is to leave the scene of an accident and drive to the embassy where all can be sorted out without the driver becoming a casualty. African justice can be swift but not always accurate, and nobody wants to finish inside a burning tire. With a white man as a target, a fender-bender can escalate into a riot in no time.

The embassy in Kinshasa had been evacuated many times during the transition from Mobutu to Kabila, and in 2002 was just beginning to allow dependents back into the country. Children of American embassy employees were provided free schooling at the American School of Kinshasa (TASOK). The school was in the hills near our house on Haute Tension but the tuition was too expensive for us to send Lillian there.

The embassy had a bunker system and procedures to deal with emergencies. Command decisions could be a weak link in the process, though.

There was an attempted coupe one day and the duty bureaucrat froze trying to decide whether or not to evacuate the school and get the children back to the embassy and their parents. Afraid to make a career-damaging decision, he made none. Finally, one of the mothers took it upon herself to start the transportation system moving and the kids were brought home safely.

Saturday is the day when the police shake down the citizenry, especially white people, for money to augment their meager salary. They stop cars on the street by stepping in front of them. After a vehicle is stopped, the police approach the driver's window and ask for paperwork. The uninitiated give the policeman what he asks for and when all is determined to be in order the driver has to pay to get back whatever he gave to the officer. Those who know the drill do not give up the paperwork, but rather show it through the window in spite of what the police say. Passing a few hundred Francs through a partially opened window usually brings the scene to a conclusion. Even better, just don't stop in the first place. The police are on foot with no motorized means of pursuit.

There was a country club in the center of Kinshasa called Cercle de Kinshasa, an oasis surrounded on three sides by slums. The resident pro at the golf course was a scratch golfer named Kafumpo with a swing to die for— symmetrical from backswing to fore, effortless. I took lessons from him at the driving range near the clubhouse, but golf came too late in my life for me to become anything other than a hacker. I did try though. When I had no morning flights my day often began with a workout at Chez Douleur and breakfast at La Patisserie. From there, I went on to the club. Roger, my caddy, met me in the parking lot and took my clubs to the practice area. After playing a round or hitting a couple of hundred balls, Roger washed my clubs and put them back in the car. Life was good and becoming a member of the club was easy for a Caucasian.

The course itself was fine, certainly challenging enough for me. The water hazards were gray water. They didn't smell but the water was just filthy. Yet there were locals, known as crocodiles, who tried to hustle a buck by retrieving balls from the water and selling them to guys like me who went through a dozen or more balls in a round.

One day, after a good session on the range with my drives going straight, I got out on the course where any suggestion of accuracy vanished. I drove six straight balls into the water hazard on the third hole. Roger never tired of telling me, *"Il est juste une ball."* I never pictured myself on a golf course with my own caddy and being driven there in a Mercedes, no less.

Cercle de Kinshasa was one of the few things the Belgium Kinois had in the way of recreation. The Americans from the State Department and USAID also used the course extensively. As a member I was invited to the most lavish cocktail party I had ever been to. It was at the club's refurbished restaurant where there was no end to the champagne or the hors d'oeuvres served by sweet-smiling Congolese women.

There was also le Cercle Hippique, a French riding school, in the hills behind Kitambo. Lillian and Chris rode there weekly. At lesson time the students go to the paddock where their mounts are all saddled up and held by one of the stable hands awaiting their arrival. The exercises range from walking to trotting, cantering and jumping. A Frenchman named Xavier conducted the classes in the ring where annual international jumping competitions are held. Horses are flown in from Lubumbashi and Zimbabwe for the event. The ring itself had stadium seating for a few hundred on one side leading up to where the bar and the club entrance opened to a parking area. The white Kinois were the majority of the participants at le Cercle Hippique.

People said I had the best job in Kinshasa and, although demanding, I agreed. I got out of town enough to avoid the repetitive drinking cycle, which gripped most of our mechanics who stayed in Kinshasa day in and day out. Many became alcoholic and were gone in six months. One was so bad I thought he was trying to kill me with his shoddy maintenance procedures. Jordan was his name and I was delighted to see him go.

He did fifteen thousand dollars worth of damage to the fuel quantity indication system on the Sabre, which didn't get fixed properly for a year. When I complained to Tim, he said, "You have a watch don't you?" Timing the fuel burn is not a fine enough determination of remaining fuel when working out of high mountain airstrips. Minimum fuel weight is required in those environments because of marginal performance capabilities.

Even with this and other compromises, it was a great job for me. The best I ever had.

Once the Lusaka peace talks were finalized there was a pattern to most of my days. When there were no scheduled flights, I woke at six o'clock in the morning—daybreak this close to the equator no matter what time of the year. I drove myself downtown for a workout, breakfast and golf, followed by a nap. After lounging about the pool with a good novel and if the phone still hadn't rung, I went to Subic's and waited for the embassy crowd to arrive.

When Wimbi Dira started up, I asked Tim if he had a position for me and he made me the manager of the training department. Tim and his partners, Charles and the President, Joseph Kabila—a silent partner—wanted to be the first airline in Congo to get ICAO, the international equivalent of the FAA, approval. My job was to write training manuals for everything except the airplane systems, which were already in place. I took care of all ground personnel and hazardous material handling. The hard part was the language barrier. I suggested Tim hire Maryoth as a translator and he did.

A mechanic for the Gulfstream and the Sabreliner was running amok like so many before him. His poor behavior maxed out one night when he went downtown alone. He was so drunk and disorderly someone had to go fetch him before he got hurt. Word of this came back to the boss. Tim heard this mechanic was doing drugs as well and decided to get rid of him.

Tim made me the Drug Czar for his whole operation, including Wimbi Dira. Soon I had the necessary testing devices to check for alcohol and a service for urine testing. With all this came another class for employees to advise them of what was expected of them regards testing.

Making nice with the street urchins, called shegues, eased getting along in town. They were homeless and much in number. I befriended a few of them in different parts of town, as I did the police. When one recognized my car turning down his street he directed us to a parking spot and cleared the others away as I got out. I tipped him and he watched the car. A partnership was formed with a little eye contact and respect costing pennies.

I had a couple of policemen I took care of on a weekly basis as well. This was a place always only seconds from chaos, so you never knew when a little help might end up to be a big help. I gave them five hundred Franc Congolese a week. They acknowledged the contribution with a salute and "Commander," along with their assistance in traffic and their good will.

You don't expect to end up on the street alone and stinko drunk, presenting an easy mark. When it happened to a nasty Belgian, he received little sympathy from anyone. The accountant at Wimbi Dira was a case in point. He came out of a bar downtown in the small hours one morning falling down drunk and was rolled. Lost his briefcase and whatever money he had on his person. It could have been worse.

When I couldn't sleep and got the urge to go downtown late at night I took along one of our Presidential guards. I parked at a bar, sent the guard a Coca Cola, and nobody messed with the car or me as I walked back to it.

If you have a diplomatic passport or a Presidential Aviation ID card, the police don't have intimidation leverage. This is a country requiring a government invitation to get a visa. When sending your passport to the consulate in Washington, putting a hundred-dollar bill in with the request will help move the process along and prevent delays.

Tim's company usually took care of getting a visa for Chris when she came over. Once, though, she needed a visa quickly. She sent the paperwork overnight to the Congolese consulate in Washington with a prepaid, return overnight letter, a thirty-five-dollar check for the fee, and the hundred-dollar bill tucked in there, too. The visa, her passport and a nice note sending regards to my boss, "Tell Mr. Tim we said hello," arrived a day later. It's the way things work in Congo.

The company ombudsman, a Congolese named Bengilla, was always helpful in tight spots. He was a major in the army and broke out his uniform at times. If we got in a spot with the police, we would just get Bengilla on the phone and he would smooth things out. A tall good looking man with an affable personality and an infectious laugh, Bengilla was about forty-five. His excellent English made him easy to talk to.

He was sent to Texas during the Mobutu era for airplane mechanic training. He told a story of how much he liked being able to make a phone call with a pizza arriving at the door of his hotel room. This wasn't going to happen in Kinshasa, even on a good day. A few weeks after I was there, I asked him if Deo said anything about flying with me. "You are superb, Commander," Bengilla replied. "Deo likes flying with you." The response confirmed my opinion of Frank being a cranky bear in the cockpit.

I had a problem one Friday night at the Marine House. There was a downpour, the kind causing wild flash floods. John, my chauffeur at the time, left the car alone for a while during the rain. The bag I always traveled with was locked in the trunk, along with my laptop, camera, French notebook and cash. The next morning I looked in the trunk, which was void of any jimmy marks or evidence of foul play, but the bag was gone. I got an awful feeling in the bottom of my stomach.

I gave John a hundred dollars and told him to go down town and spread the money around to the cops and shegues who knew me. The money was to look for my bag and whoever found it with the contents would receive two hundred dollars. I could think of little else to do. I knew the cash would not come back but there was hope for the rest. The notebook represented three years of Maryoth's French lessons.

In the morning there were two young men manacled on the floor of our carport. If I was in their position I would have been much more concerned than they appeared to be. One of the men guarding them said they wouldn't give up whom they fenced the bag to. This sounded like a job for Bengilla. I called and he arrived in uniform. John took Bengilla and the two lads to the military base for interrogation. They were persuaded and in the end I got back everything except my French notes and cash.

I am uncertain about the way I handled the situation. My call sent those thieves to electrically enhanced interrogation or other brutal measures. Here I was using their country as a source of revenue and behaving like a colonialist. I once made a remark about Belgian attitudes in the presence of another golf club member who was quick to point out where my own money was coming from.

Chapter 15
Bunia

I was in Africa for a year when I began flying into Bunia with passengers. On one such trip, we brought the Minister of Human Rights on a "humanitarian mission," as his publicist would later call it. The Minister intended to convince the rebels to conform to the Sun City Peace accords, which required that they stop raping and pillaging. He had a small entourage of two men and three women, who were his public relations people. This mission would have been quite a coup if he pulled it off.

In the Eastern Congo, war only pauses occasionally and otherwise remains a way of life. The Uturi rainforest, home of the Mbuti pygmies and teaming with wildlife, is the northern edge of the Great Lakes Region, which includes Lake Victoria (the size of Ireland), Lake Malawi and Lake Tanganyika (the longest lake in the world and second deepest at 4710'). The lakes stretch from Uganda at the north and south through Rwanda, Burundi and Tanzania. This is truly beautiful country where the last of the silverback gorillas live in scenery that rivals the Lake Tahoe part of the Sierras in California, without the snow.

Bunia airport required close fuel planning for our airplane. It is not a long strip for its altitude of 4070' above sea level, and a rather marginal one at best, especially when the temperature rises and density altitude makes the airplane perform as if it were at ten or twelve thousand feet above sea level. Bernoulli's law explains that an airplane virtually leaps off a runway when the air temperature is cold and the air is dense, yet behaves quite the opposite when the temperature goes up and the air thins out. Not only do the wings create much less lift, but the engines that rely on the same principals for their thrust are compromised. It is one of the factors that make mountain flying challenging.

Bunia is one degree north of the equator. The runway is narrow and rough, with no markings to aid identification from the air. It also has numerous old mortar holes in it. Before I first went there, Tim told me, "Put the plane on the end of the runway as slow as you can with the stick shaker going off and bingo fuel." The stick shaker is a system that signals the pilot physically, by shaking the controls and most of the cockpit to indicate that the airplane is getting too slow to fly and about ready to fall out of the air. Not a problem a foot off the deck, but in rough weather at night fighting severe turbulence, and the warning system starts shaking, you are close to some real trouble. Bingo fuel means just enough to return to wherever it is that you want to go, in this case Entebbe.

The takeoff at Bunia was even more of a challenge than the landing. Most airplanes can get into places they can't get out of. Tim also added, "Oh yeah, watch for the two mortar holes near the midpoint of the runway. The gear should fit between them. If you have slowed up enough by then, you might not break a wheel off if you end up in one. Leave an engine running, drop the passengers and get out of there." This was the most information Tim ever gave me regarding anything. This was not a touchy-feely kind of guy, as I would find out, but rather a Kurtz wannabe.

The first time we went into Bunia all went well but this time we never even landed. The minister had a brief meeting with local dignitaries in Kananga while we took on enough fuel for the Bunia stop and the continuation to Entebbe. As usual we sat there burning daylight while these guys talked like they had nothing else in the world to do.

During this time, we could have been in and out of Bunia, on to Entebbe with at least a daylight takeoff for Kinshasa. Instead Entebbe to Kinshasa becomes a night trip with another exciting takeoff over Lake Victoria. Murphy showed up, too. Given this advance notice he had to make an appearance.

As I was starting the takeoff roll from Kananga, I noticed the right wing was heavy with much more fuel than I wanted—another example of my inadequate preflight inspections. I recklessly continued the takeoff, which required some immediate trim once airborne and cross feeding en route to get proper fuel balance.

Most of the exciting moments in Congo were caused by my lackadaisical approach. In the States I would have behaved in a much more professional manner doing the appropriate check lists. One might think that I would be even more careful in Africa where it was considerably more dangerous. No, that's not how it was.

This was my way of coping and avoiding too much stress. The Congolese military personnel I carried, usually as bodyguards for my VIP passengers, were an undisciplined lot and sloppy, too. Rifles were dropped and grenades fell out of improperly fastened pockets onto the tarmac. One night I got out of the airplane and saw one of those grenades lying on the cabin floor. I just resigned myself to whatever was going to happen whether I get upset about it or not.

On to Bunia we went, with time for the drop-off, which would get us to Entebbe with maybe some daylight left. We started the descent for landing out of the overcast and called the radio shack hoping for something like wind direction at least. Finally, a Russian UN helicopter pilot answered and told us to be careful, that one helicopter had some problems earlier in the day. Humph. We came out of ten thousand feet into the clear and couldn't pick up the airport in spite of having ten miles visibility and two GPSs. Tim did say don't fly over the town, just slip in and out from the forest side, which we were doing.

We ended up doing two, three hundred sixty degree turns while descending before we saw the airport. There was a fire a mile from an imaginary extended centerline of the approach end of the runway, which only helped by giving us wind direction. I got the airplane configured for landing, which was to be as "dirty" as possible—meaning full flaps and landing gear down. I lowered the speed break to finish the configuration. We were a mile from the end of the runway and four hundred feet above the ground. I heard "popping sounds" like small arms fire. The airplane began to lose power and yaw to the right.

Deo started screaming, as did the passengers. I pushed the throttles up, retracted the speed brake and managed a positive rate of climb as my world seemed to go into slow motion. I went about the business of cleaning up the rest of the airplane, i.e. flaps and gear.

Deo said, "Land, land there,"

I calmly said, "Fuck no, I'm going to Entebbe." Then the engine fire light came on and a bell started ringing. Determined not to be one of the foolish pilots who shut down the working engine in haste and make an unnecessary crash, I took my time verifying which engine was bad. The working foot was the side of the plane with the working engine. The asymmetrical thrust required heavy rudder input to keep it all going straight ahead and make optimum use of the available power. The engine out identification was then confirmed visually by looking at the engine instruments.

Yes, the right engine had failed and was on fire. I told Deo to, "Get the checklist." His response was, "Where is it?" I was alone. I'd have to fix this myself.

I checked the internal temperature of the working engine and saw that it was in the green which meant we were not killing the good engine by asking more than it could deliver. I pulled the throttle back on the right engine to the fuel shutoff position and then pulled the fire tee handle. That armed the fire extinguishing system making the two bottles of dousing agent available, through cross plumbing, one at a time with the other considered a backup. If both extinguishers failed, the design theory of the airplane allowed the engine to burn off its mountings before losing the tail feathers (the elevator and rudder).

I pushed the appropriate button and the fire went out and the bell stopped ringing. Nice. The airplane was still climbing and I was not abusing the working engine. All was right with the world at this point. The passengers had even settled down some. Deo found the checklist and I told him to check my work and let me know if anything wasn't done. We took care of a couple of details and continued to fly.

We were already going in the direction of Entebbe so if the working engine kept running we would be okay. We cleared the mountains that are the eastern ridge of the valley containing the city of Bunia and got across Lake Edward, still a good half hour from Entebbe. With everything settled down it was time to try the radios and see if we could get Entebbe Approach.

Deo received an answer and I indicated to him that I wanted to talk. This may have been my only time to say, "I'd like equipment standing by," in a calm low-pitch airline captain voice. They cleared us to land immediately with a straight in approach over Lake Victoria to the inactive runway. If the gear came down like it should and the tires weren't flat, we were golden.

While I was talking to Entebbe approach control, I was still busy trying to keep the fuel balanced. Maintaining the weight of the fuel in the wings within the difference limit of four hundred pounds required diligence. In single engine operation you used a high power setting on the working engine, hence high fuel consumption, while the dead engine fuel remained a constant unless some of it was transferred to the working engine.

Sometimes a pilot could get surprised if he wasn't mindful, and just kept trimming that weight off with aileron adjustments, or worse, had the autopilot engaged and it was trimming itself. The imbalance could exceed the control capability when the power was reduced for landing. Then the airplane would roll over and make a smoking hole.

We landed without incident, taxied up to the main ramp, and parked. By the time we got out there were people standing around and pointing under the airplane. When I looked at the underbelly of the airplane it was raining fuel. A dozen ramp personnel appeared to scavenge whatever fuel they could from the bullet holes in the fuel tanks. It sure didn't hurt having taken on that unintended extra fuel in Kananga. Had one of those bullets hit a tire the landing wouldn't have been smooth either.

When I was standing back near the fuel trucks, one of the ramp boys, whom I recognized from previous trips there, said, "God is here, Bwana." It stirred up thoughts of Clark Gable and Ava Gardener in *Mogambo*. No one had called me bwana before. The woman leading the minister's public relations contingent, complimented me in a nervous voice with, "You never say anything, you are always so quiet."

I said, "It just wasn't our day to die." Not to be cute, but it just came out that way.

The airport manager walked over to the airplane and said, "Caribou, Commander." I looked at him quizzically.

"That means welcome in Swahili."

We took pictures and generally calmed down while waiting for transportation to the Sheraton in Kampala. As per the usual procedure, when we got to the hotel Deo busied himself with checking us in, while I went directly to the bar. This night was a bit special and I felt that I had an even better excuse than usual, maybe even a mission, to work on the fine selection of single malt Scotch that the Sheraton offered. Just outside the bar on the other side of the terrace was a large chess board with almost human size pieces. Very cool. There was also a barbecue with a large Indian selection, as well as the usual continental buffet choices and salads. I had been here a number of times before and thought it the best hotel in Kampala—certainly the most modern.

I was edgy and stayed with the Scotch. Not able to get through them all, I went up to my room after Deo came with my key and nine hundred dollars from the minister. Nice tip, but more would not have been out of place.

I was going to try again to get a call through to Kinshasa when the phone rang.

It was Tim and he asked the absolutely appropriate first question, "How are you?" This from the man who was always ever so brief, verbally and in emails.

"I'm okay, thanks."

The funny thing was that I had a satellite phone for just such occasions and, of course, had left it at the house. We talked for a while and Tim said I was to take more pictures of the airplane the next day. Then I got a call through to my friend and French teacher, Maryoth. I wanted to tell him I would not make tomorrow morning's French lesson because I was spending the night in Kampala. I had no idea that word of the incident had already reached Kinshasa—such is this cell phone world. The last any Congolese in Bunia saw was an airplane on fire going out of sight. The radio broadcast in Kinshasa reported that the Minister of Human Rights' airplane had been shot down and all aboard were dead.

Maryoth was crying along with his whole family; I could hear them in the background. I was more than a rice bowl to these people—we were friends. His last son was named James Gannone Luboya. I love and loved these people.

When Chris came from the States she had asked friends for clothing donations to bring with her. She ended up with two tightly packed, large military sea bags full of family clothes. Chris showed them to Maryoth's wife, Ester, who was too moved to speak and visibly choked up. The three girls went crazy until Ester gave them a look.

A friend from the state department passed on a couple of children's bicycles to them during a dinner at my house one Sunday afternoon to similar feelings of emotion. Maryoth's kids, three boys and three girls, were asked by their friends, "Who does your father know?" In the end I think I was able to influence his getting a job at the American Consulate.

In Kampala we spent a couple of nights eating and drinking at the Sheraton on the minister's tab before we returned to Kinshasa. It was three or four nights until I slept well, though. I was still a little tight from the excitement. Truth was, the incident brought some relief. I had been expecting something like this to happen, and I got away with it clean. It was my accrued experience—by this time I was over ten thousand hours total—coupled with the training from Bob Guin in the Sabreliner that got me through this.

In Kinshasa and Kananga I got some flowery press like, "The highly experienced pilot who saved blah, blah, blah." For months thereafter I would occasionally see people in town who recognized me. They always had something to say, mostly in Lingala, which I didn't understand but knew it was approval.

Regards N250EC, it never flew again. When Tim needed Sabreliner parts he took them from wrecks if he could. He had Frank's in a hanger in Kinshasa and now he had one in Entebbe as well. Had N250EC received reasonable attention on the ramp instead of an airliner being backed into its tail feathers, it may have flown again but all was downhill from there. It was moved over to the UN junkyard where it was scavenged twice, once successfully and once not, by mechanics from Tim's company.

When I first left his employ to go back to the States for a hip replacement, Tim hired a Belgian pilot, on the cheap, for the airplane that replaced N250EC. That pilot promptly busted it up in Brazzaville damaging the nose wheel assembly. The hydraulic system was partially at fault so the blame was shared. Tim needed parts to get it back in the air so he sent Andrew Shaw to Entebbe with a mission to scavenge my wreck. Andrew was not afraid to spend Tim's money greasing the palms of officials. He was one of the best mechanics Tim ever had in Congo.

That mission went okay but when Johnnie Tranguoch, the company mechanic, excellent at his trade, went to Entebbe for more parts from N250EC it didn't go as well. Johnnie went by truck from Goma with some Congolese but did not pay the right people sufficiently before he bribed his way into the UN junkyard. On what was to be his final day there, his working party went back to the hotel where they had been staying for one last beer before they hit the road back to Congo.

As they were sitting outside of their hotel a large military truck full of armed soldiers pulled up and the party was over. The military swarmed all over them. The charges were theft of the airplane parts. When I left the airplane after the Bunia incident, I failed to take the registration certificate that had the owner's name on it. It had since been removed by someone unknown, and hence Johnnie had nothing to use as proof of ownership. His Congolese helpers were afraid of the treatment they were about to get in Uganda's custody, fearing death. Johnnie was on his way to a holding tank Africa style.

It was days before Johnnie was brought to a courtroom for arraignment but fortunately someone from the American consulate happened to be there and made inquiries about the white man she saw. That started the release process. In the meantime it was back to the holding tank, an overcrowded cell with a hole in the floor for a toilet. Ask a guard for toilet paper, are you kidding?

The word got back to Kinshasa and Tim started to get Johnnie out. This matter was being discussed at the American Embassy in Kinshasa at the highest levels daily. The end result was bail established and paid, court date set, and

Johnnie booked. He would just have to leave Uganda out of any future travel plans.

Deo and I flew back to Kinshasa via Nairobi with Kenya Air and then I went on to the States to fetch another airplane. These Sabreliners were and are dirt cheap if you consider three to four hundred thousand dollars for a flyable eight-passenger jet reasonable. Retro fitting them with Reduced Vertical Separation Minimums equipment is cost prohibitive. RVSM allows an aircraft to participate in the very desirable airspace above 29,000 feet, where jets go faster and burn less fuel. These regulations are in effect in the United States and Europe for the time being but will spread as the need for airspace increases globally.

Tim found a Sabre in South Carolina that he had put a low-ball bid on a couple of years before. This time they accepted his offer for the same plane, which had not moved. Turns out it was Paul Newman's old airplane for his race team, numbered N33JW. I went there with Barry, one of Tim's friends, and a mechanic, to do what is called a pre-buy inspection. In the horse-trading business of aviation purchasing, this is a procedure where the potential buyer's mechanic inspects the airplane. The mechanic criticizes everything he possibly can and writes up a punch list that the buyer uses to haggle down the price with the seller. In this case Tim chiseled more off the price and declared we would take it as is. Barry put a new battery in it, drained some water out of the fuel sumps and it started.

I was a little concerned about the first flight in an airplane that had spent years on the ramp but sucked it up and off we went. There are eyeball sockets on airplanes allowing the flow of conditioned air as you direct the hole in the ball. On the Sabre next to the captain's seat is a small sliding window with a handle locking it closed in order to seal it. The seal on these tend to dry out after years of sitting in the sun on a hot ramp in South Carolina.

This resulted in a substantial amount of water dripping down the eyeball socket next to the pilot's left knee. The accumulated water made for an intermittent garden hose effect directed at my face from the time we rotated on takeoff. It only lasted a minute but it was a distracting surprise. Barry in the right seat thought it funny, much funnier than I did. It made for an interesting take off to Hazleton, PA, where N33JW would get a once-over before we flew it back to Kinshasa.

Chapter 16
Run Mundele

Mundele is a non-complimentary name for a white man in Africa as Kaffir is for a black man.

I was driving to the Marine House on a Friday afternoon at about five and became involved in a car chase. I was the one being chased, at first by a car full of screaming young men. They were soon joined by many, many, Congolaise all waving their arms and hollering as they chased me through the municipality of Kitambo. They pursued me because I had hit a woman pedestrian not far from my house about one kilometer from town. I was headed in the direction of the Embassy anyhow but this made it imperative.

All Americans are told when they first get in country to go to the Embassy if involved in a motor vehicle accident. Kinshasa is an overcrowded city originally built for three million people but has nine million living there now. There is so much frustration and pain very close to the surface that it takes little to set off an impromptu riot. The city is always just seconds away from chaos and it seemed I started something.

The old woman was either pushed or deliberately walked into the side of the car I was driving to bring on an incident. Walking into the side of a car moving at twenty-five miles per hour requires some motivation. Some State Department people agreed with this setup theory. She made an awful thud when she bounced off the car. I looked up at the inside rearview mirror and saw a body lying motionless in the road. I immediately increased my speed but not as much as I should have. Moments later, in my peripheral vision, I saw something growing larger in my mirror—a car full of angry Congolais men, some hanging outside the car windows shaking their fists and yelling. They were faster than I was and swung around me, cutting me off to a stop. Surprised, I quickly backed up, put it into first gear and started to the right as a fake. They went for it by pulling forward and attempting to cut me off again. Then I turned back to the left, pulled around their rear and was off again, this time as fast as the car could go.

The car I was driving was one of those European model Mercedes, four cylinder with a four speed manual transmission and sporty enough, so I wasn't immediately worried about being able to get away from them. If I had known what I was to be up against, I would have been more concerned. I turned the car loose and went downhill towards Kitambo but the lads were close behind. I took my phone out of my pocket and hit the speed dial for the Embassy. It was answered quickly by "Marine 1."

"This is Jim. I'm being chased. Tell Jeff I'm trying to get there, can't talk now." I said and put the phone down on the console between the front seats.

The vehicle traffic was getting thicker, as well as the foot traffic, and I could hear this unusual yelling all around and even in front of my car. They were passing the word ahead of me. It seemed like the vehicles to my front were trying to block my way now, too. I got through Kitambo and was going down the street lined with tall mango trees leading to the Gombe part of Kinshasa where Blvd du 30 Juin begins. The drama was building with the increased necessity to dodge and go around vehicles and people—not the time to hit another person. I got about three kilometers away from the scene of the incident when they finally closed and boxed me in. I ended up with a sea of people filling up the windows, pounding their fists on the car and screaming.

As the upper right corner of the windshield started to give way I knew I was in trouble. Suddenly, "Mike the cop" showed up with his four colleagues. He came around to the driver's window working out with his billy club on anyone blocking his way. He knew who I was from the car and having seen me in it many times on the way to the airport. Things started looking much better now. He motioned for me to let him in the car and I tried to get the point across it was only to be him getting in. He agreed and again with the help of the billy club went around to the other side of the car, where I cautiously opened the door. Somehow we communicated, with his English as bad as my French. He wanted me to let his men in the back of the car. I agreed and when they were in Mike told me to go, "*Va, Va*, Commander." We pushed on nudging through the crowd, still busy hollering and banging on the car.

By the time we got down to the Boulevard, another kilometer or so, the crowd was gone but still audible. Major Henri was there with a couple of police vehicles. I knew I was okay then. Major Henri spoke more English than Mike improving my position considerably. As I was getting out of the car to his motion I noticed my phone was gone. Loss of my only source of communication now wouldn't help this process at all.

Little did I know what wheels had been set in motion by my call to the Embassy. As it turned out I had more friends there than I realized. My friend Jeff was the Regional Security Officer and a brother Marine. He turned his contacts loose as if on a mission, as did Tom the US Defense Attaché, another drinking buddy. He was a Lieutenant Colonel and Army Ranger who called his connections in the Congolais government. A couple hours later it would prove to be a job getting all these people to stand down. Had my phone not been stolen by one of the cops riding in the back seat of my car, I could have slowed this process with a phone call. Instead it gathered momentum as I stood there talking to the Major.

Major Henri said we should go downtown to Police Headquarters in my car and I was happy to oblige. After I parked I noticed him looking at the sign in the windshield of my car as we walked towards the police building. The sign said in French, "Air Force Let it Pass." Entering the Police building I thought of how many people had been there and subjected to brutal interrogations. Congo is not known for civil rights. As a white, American captain for the president's airlines, I was sure I would not be one of them.

We went into his office with his assistant who, with attitude, started asking me if I had been drinking, "Perhaps at lunch. How much?" While he was doing this, the Major was looking at my most valuable possession, my ID card. As soon as the assistant paused, Major Henri looked at me and said, "We are here for your protection. There is no need for concern." With that the assistant stopped cold. My French professor told me later that if anyone had hurt me, their hands would have been cut off. This can be a tough place. I loved my ID card and still have it.

I was concerned about the old woman and told the Major I would like to find out how she was doing. He said, without great interest, that we could go around to the hospitals and clinics, starting with the morgue, but I would have to drive since his police car had no gas. This is not unusual. The police will help you with their position but you will have to pay. Off we went to the morgue and I was relieved she wasn't there. I could still clearly hear the impact of her body with my car. It's a terrible noise and stayed with me for some time. From there we went to a half a dozen clinics and hospitals where he went in and I waited in the car with one of his men. Finally, we went to Kitambo Hospital and he came out to tell me she was there.

"How is she?" I wanted to know.

"No broken bones. She is okay."

I thought it must have been a setup. She knew how to do it and a few bruises were worth her share of what would be scavenged from me. I would have been lucky to come out of it naked, badly bruised and lying in a ditch

As the Major was standing there talking to me his phone rang. He answered it and his face changed; he handed it to me saying, "It's for you. It's the President." It was boss Tim; Jeff contacted him. He was calling from Belgium where he had flown the President. He asked how I was doing and then added, "Welcome to Congo." As we were talking Ed pulled into the parking area of the hospital where I was standing. Ed was one of Jeff's assistants who had been out looking for me in the last couple of hours. I was still on the phone with Tim at the time and told him of Ed's arrival. He said I didn't need any more white guys there and to let Jeff know.

In the meantime, Tim had arranged for Deo to come with a squad of presidential guards from his house. I was familiar with them from having been at Tim's many times. They all arrived with a party-like disposition, happy to see me. I spoke with Ed who told me he was going to give Major Henri an Embassy-paid

English course at the American school. Nice gesture I thought and I thanked him for coming. Deo said he would take care of the hospital bill and give the woman "some money," and that I should go home. He didn't have to tell me twice.

The idea of doing something so extreme as to walk into a fast-moving car on the chance of getting a piece of whatever could be taken in such a scam suggests just how hungry these people are. They really have nothing. A couple of days later I got a call from the wife of the man in charge of the MFA, a missionary aviation group I had come to know. She said she was sorry for what had happened to me and knew how it felt. She had killed a pedestrian with their car a couple of years before in Congo. I was so touched at the kindness of the gesture my eyes filled up. They are such genuinely good people, maybe even the first real Christians I ever met. They were there "doing God's work," I'd heard someone once say. The woman who hit my car was able to negotiate a week in the hospital by the time all was said and done. I was happy for her. Dirty as those hospitals are they have to be palatial compared to the hovel she probably lived in. Soon after the incident I hired my own chauffeur for one hundred dollars a month and it turned out to be well worth it.

It can be heartbreaking to get close to the Congolese emotionally. If you take in a needy kid to the point of just giving him food on a regular basis it won't be long before the family shows up wanting to be paid for the child. And, yes, depending on the judge you could be on the hook for your act of kindness. A similar situation occurs to men who hookup with a "girlfriend" and then want to move on. There will have to be a settlement for services given, which could go to court. You don't want to be looked at as "Uncle Belge"—hard to avoid if you are Caucasian.

The standard garden variety "manifestation" begins mid-morning on the day after some incident that resulted in one or more deaths. The day following is called "ville morte," dead city, no work. Don't be the white man caught driving around. One such manifestation occurred when I was my transporting someone to Kinshasa from Bukavu one day.

My friend Allen teased me saying I had caused these riots and almost started another war. He based it on my trip to Bukavu the previous day where I had picked up a prisoner who had been sentenced to death as a result of the assassination of Laurent Kabila. I flew this small scrawny looking rebel to Kinshasa to be executed. There had been problems in Bukavu earlier in the week focusing on the UN mandate, which called for non-intervention in military conflicts and only to get involved when civilians were the targets. Peacekeepers not peacemakers were the UN's job. It really was a no win situation for them with all parties involved lying about everything as was their way. Apparently the man I brought back was the center of the conflict.

The students didn't like it, for their own reasons and in the evening, with the street kids, always looking for some action, and the tacit support of the police, they went at the UN compound. They burned some vehicles including an armored personnel carrier, threw sticks and stones and lit up a few tires. The next morning was a much more planned "manifestation," which more than anything meant it would wait for the participants to get up. The police countered their efforts this time and at least one old woman was killed with a rubber bullet.

At six that morning I had driven myself down to the office where I had a second job as the Manager of the Training Department of Wimbi Dira Airlines. I wasn't aware of the riot the previous evening. A friend of mine, who worked in the hi-rise USAID building and lived further downtown from my office, called me and asked, "Are you at work already?"

"Yes, why?"

"They're rolling the tires down the hill and have some burning already. You should stay put."

Setting fire to tires is necessary to any real demonstration. They are often started by the students from what is left of the University up on a hill overlooking the town. My office was in the airline warehouse and not a bad place to be stuck for the day. I had just stepped out of the office when my French professor and chauffeur arrived, both telling me not to go outside today. I got the picture and stayed there. There were phone calls from embassy friends with similar warnings and situation reports from different parts of the city.

Late afternoon the same friend from USAID called to say he was going to his house and I was welcome to join him and his friend Jack Daniels for the night. He said things had settled down in the streets pretty much. I told John, my chauffeur, the plan and he said he would drive around a bit to see if everything was okay. He came back with large banana leaves on the windshield and rear window. I found out they were a message to the rioters the car was okay. It was the white UN people who were the targets, but any mundele would do. When we left for Joe's we called ahead to alert his door guard to hasten the entrance. It was a short drive John made even quicker; he didn't want any trouble either. It wasn't long before I was sipping bourbon with Joe in his air-conditioned living room with a large emergency generator standing by. Occasional shots could be heard, but all was well there.

After the evening at Joe's house, John drove me back to the office while the situation in town calmed somewhat. That afternoon I got a call from Tim asking me to stay at his house. He didn't want it left empty with just the guards and domestics. This meant going up the hill towards my house but I was assured the rock throwing and the rest had tapered off. Before I went I emailed Chris at home to tell her I was fine and was about to leave for Tim's. She told me to drink his best wine and I did not hold back at all. He had a cook and a houseboy just for himself with a little electric buzzer to call them. The house was complete with heated outside pool, jacuzzi and wood fired brick pizza oven. Too bad my stay only lasted a couple of days.

Chapter 17
Vignettes

Returning to Kinshasa in N33JW with Barry became a longer than anticipated journey. The company's maintenance department shaped up the newly acquired Sabreliner, both mechanically and cosmetically, in Hazleton. The cabin was filled with the boss' favorite foods and other goods not available in Kinshasa. With Barry in the right seat, I took off on my first trans-oceanic flight. Barry said he would take the right seat all the way and deal with the radio—fine with me, since the autopilot worked in this one. He was also in charge of the cash and communication with all the ground contacts previously arranged through a company from Houston that specialized in international flights.

From Hazleton, north to Gander, Newfoundland and on to Narsarsuaq, Greenland, where I saw my first iceberg on final approach to runway zero seven. The water was so clear I could see the how much of the ice was below the surface. We topped off the fuel for the next leg to Shannon, Ireland. Once we were all strapped into the airplane, I pushed the start button—nothing but a whine. The starter shaft had sheared and was spinning without driving the engine's turbine.

We weren't going anywhere except to the local hotel. Barry called Hazleton and we began the vigil. Johnnie Tranguch located a starter and began his journey to Narsarsuaq, a Danish possession. First he flew from JFK airport in New York to Stockholm. Then he flew back to Narsarsuaq. Meanwhile Barry and I ate, drank and slept for days. Cultural attractions were limited there.

The day before Johnnie's arrival I got a phone call from the airline station chief asking if I was the captain of N33JW. I said, "Yes I am, but this isn't a happy call, is it?"

"Sir, can you come to the airport now?"

A baggage handler parked a conveyor belt apparatus for unloading bags from the airliners on the ramp uphill from our airplane. He set the brake but failed to chock the wheels. As if the machine had eyes, it rolled and made a one-hundred-eighty-degree descending left turn into the side of N33JW, rupturing the skin. This compromised the pressure vessel and further delayed our journey back to Africa. Then a serious field patching procedure was undertaken, which included special aerospace-approved CherryMAX ® rivets, which the FAA required.

After Johnnie worked his magic, we ferried the airplane to an FAA repair facility in Missouri for proper factory repairs. To his credit and my appreciation, Tim continued to pay me throughout this comedy of errors and even had me transported between my house and airports in a Lincoln Town Car. It was nice to feel appreciated.

Weeks after the incident, Barry and I flew to Kinshasa retracing the route to Shannon. From there we went on to Barcelona, Spain; Algiers, Algeria; Tamanrasset, Algeria; Abuja, Nigeria; and then Kinshasa. Exhausted as I was, being back in the DRC felt good. The only bedtime we had was five hours at the Intercontinental in Barcelona. I needed a good night's sleep before going to Bangui the next day.

Mbandaka

This flight was a drop off in Bangui of the Central African Republic (French Congo). The passenger was a diplomat, for whom we would come back the next day. Bangui always gave me the creeps. The intense hungry eyes of half a dozen soldiers who hung around the airplane where I waited for Deo to file the flight plan was all it took to set me off. I sat on the air stair doorsteps and smoked, went in the plane where it was warmer yet to have some water until I started sweating and then back out for another smoke. I didn't want soldiers in the airplane or asking me for anything.

Fuel was expensive in Bangui, so this time our marching orders included stopping for fuel at Mbandaka in the DRC where the President had credit. A round trip back to Kinshasa was just out of reach. The weather deviations around thunderstorms on the way to Bangui made even trying a return impossible without additional fuel. Normally, fuel in Mbandaka was convenient, but not this time.

"They don't have money for fuel," Tim said. "They" was Presidential Aviation. "Stop at Mbandaka on your way back. Charles will have fuel arranged for you." Charles was Tim's Congolese partner and a menace in this Presidential Aviation operation. He could lie to your face more easily—fluently—than any Congolese I had ever met. There was no telling what kind of fiddle he was running on the fuel.

Our route of flight took us right by Mbandaka on the way to Bangui so we called on the radio while passing to check on the availability of our fuel. They said arrangements had not been made yet—not encouraging news. From the ground in Bangui I called Tim and was told Charles was on it. Hard to say just how many times I had heard similar replies during my time in the DRC, only to find out otherwise.

We landed at Mbandaka, on the way back to Kinshasa and parked on the ramp off the runway next to a small building. There was periodic commuter airline service, on an "if-it-didn't-come-today-maybe-tomorrow" less than punctual schedule, as in most places in Congo. As I suspected, nobody knew what Deo was talking about when he asked them about fuel, about Charles calling to arrange for it or about anything else.

Next to the ramp were little grass huts complete with people, cooking fires and children playing. I saw one of the kids come to the edge of the tarmac, sneaking a peak at the airplane. How far from that hut will he ever get in the course of his life? Not far, I suspected.

Phone calls back and forth from us to Charles and Tim filled the airwaves with more lies and promises while we burned daylight. This was not a well-lit airport, making a night takeoff dicey. There were very few runway edge lights and the runway itself was not very wide, but it did have a centerline—a small help because I didn't have any landing or taxi lights. The last time they worked was in Barcelona. Maintenance was not the highest priority in Africa.

Darkness arrived before the fuel, but I had already decided we were going. Sleeping in the plane, sweating all night and getting maybe two hours of sleep by the end of the ordeal was not for me. This was no Gulfstream where you could close up the hatch and run the air conditioner with the auxiliary power unit while you drank the night away. Even if there was a hotel, we had no ground transportation. This night would likely be my introduction to malaria. I had what people in the aviation world call "get-home-itis."

A successful takeoff required keeping the plane close enough to the centerline to avoid wreck-inducing tall grass bordering the runway during the takeoff roll. Once the wing started hitting that grass, drag would start turning the airplane in the same direction—not good. The grass also made the lights marking the edge difficult to see. No taxiway meant back-taxiing down the runway tarmac via flashlight, a slow process.

"Deo, get the flashlight out." This was going to be a coordinated crew effort of the first officer trying to look out the cockpit window by the light of his flashlight and telling me what he could see. Down the runway we crawled with him saying I was too close or to go closer. I had my flashlight, too, trying to see the centerline but more importantly looking for the end, not wanting to run out of room for turning around before ending up in the bushes. We managed to find the end of the tarmac and then it was show time.

We turned around, pointing pretty much down the center. There were a few edge lights visible but not many. I would need the ones further down, anyhow. This grand taxi procedure built up to a takeoff crescendo and brought my pulse along for the ride. Time to let her rip—throttles up and we accelerated down the tarmac. This would have been a great time for those callouts I tried to instill in Deo.

With the increasing speed, there were a few moments when I had to recover from nose wheel course corrections. The faster we went the smaller the correction inputs on the rudder pedals needed to be or directional control would be lost. Over-correcting would start uncontrollable oscillations from one side of the runway to the other.

The occasional edge light allowed for gauging the center of the runway by appearing larger or smaller than the previous one. There were also peripheral clues from the shadows of the trees opening to the lighter sky above, along the length and width of the runway. Those few seconds before we got to rotation speed were an eternity. I pulled the yolk back and we got to "positive rate gear up" and were clear of the trees surrounding the tall grass. Now I was feeling my pulse and my hands were shaking. Maybe Russell West was right when he told me, "This is a young man's game."

Tom and Allen

I met Tom Gowen at a Christmas cocktail party in the 1990s while we were grazing a groaning board. A conversation ensued and airplanes came up. I said, "Oh, you fly?"

"No, but I've jumped out of a bunch of them."

We continued to chat a bit and the conversation turned to Vietnam. He was Special Forces. Later in the conversation he said, "You know as soon as I saw you I knew you were a Nam Vet." Then it came out that he had gone back on a second tour. I said, looking him up and down, "You got away with it."

"I didn't get back clean on the second one."

I later found out he was medevacked home to convalesce for months in a hospital. He also revealed that he has been running with the bulls at Pamplona ever since. I loved hearing that.

A few years later I bought an airplane; the only toy worse is a boat. He needed a way of getting to Long Island one evening and asked me if I could help. There was a small airport near where he wanted to go or else he faced an eight-hour drive. He offered to pay for the fuel and weather wasn't an issue, so off we went with my son in the back seat. Tom thought it great. "This is better than first class, I can smoke," as he opened the ashtray. We climbed out of Cape May Airport and were cruising at 4500' over Atlantic City International Airport (ACY) when the electrical system on the airplane died. All lighting went dim. Shit. I could create a real ruckus at ACY if I landed there with no radio communication and no lights so I decided to go back to Cape May. That airport has a radio transmitter activated lighting system on a special frequency to turn all the airport lights on by pressing the microphone transmitting button. I just might get the runway lights to come on if any juice remained in the battery at all.

It was not to be. We got to Cape May and it looked like a big black hole. Keying the microphone did nothing. I started to circle the field thinking it all through. After a couple of three-sixties I noticed two red lights, one at each end of runway 19/35. It's the runway with a localizer approach. We were in business. I saw the rotating beacon on the old military tower and with the two other lights I could work this out. On the north side of the airport near the approach end of runway 19 was Fulling Mill Road. Just a matter of waiting for a car's headlights on the road, which would provide a fix about four hundred feet from the threshold of 19.

I flew an elongated and wide pattern to give myself plenty of room to adjust while hoping for a car to use the road to provide fresh reference as I descended. Time to go to work and I lowered the gear with the manually operated emergency pump. No three green lights to indicate the three legs were locked in position—because of the electrical failure—but hearing them fall into place satisfied me that they were down. On my second pattern—I was being patient—a car came along and I managed to coordinate his travel with my pattern. This would be a piece of cake now. All I had to do was get to a couple hundred feet off the deck, line up on the two red lights and gently descend onto the runway without hitting one of the deer, which were so prolific on the airport property.

While in the pattern I had some visible reference from house lights near the airport. The descent continued towards the runway and we flew below the tops of the surrounding trees. Darkness prevailed leaving me only the red light 5,000' at the other end of the runway. I chopped the power and gently dropped onto a wide runway sans deer. The reflective white centerline became visible during the last few feet and the drama ended. Taxiing in was not simple at first but suddenly all the airport lights came on. Someone had keyed their microphone preparing to taxi out for takeoff. He couldn't have come a half hour sooner?

Tom and I stayed in touch and after I had been in Congo for a year I got an email from him. He heard I had gone to Kinshasa and said he had a friend that he runs the bulls with traveling there. He went on to ask if I could meet his friend at the airport and maybe help him get settled. The man's name was Allen Carney and he had worked in Kinshasa before. I said sure and gave him my phone number.

The following week I heard from Allen and picked him, his wife (Masha), dog (Tuks) and their luggage up right on the ramp at N'djili airport. I had them back at my house drinking gin and tonics straight away—delightful. He was looking for a humanitarian job with a non-governmental organization. I had to insist to get them to stay at my mostly empty house beyond the three days where fish and guests go bad. I enjoyed their company immensely. He found a position in Kinshasa with Air Serv International, a humanitarian relief organization. We have been friends since.

Allen usually works for a State Department group that brings aid to human disasters outside the U.S.—like an international FEMA effort. He was in Darfur, Sudan when it was at its worst, coordinating the relief effort there. That is a humanitarian.

The last time we were in Europe, Chris and I visited Allen and Masha at their home at Villeraze in the South of France near Spain. The view from their house looks over a vineyard and the whole ambiance will take your breath. They brought us to a restaurant at a farm on top of a nearby mountain where all the food served was raised on the property. Course after course kept coming with matching wines. On another evening, we had dinner at the home of one of their friend's. All of us were in costume as players in a murder mystery, with a script to read and questions to respond to in character. This visit was a once in a lifetime experience.

There was another remarkable afternoon while we were with the Carneys. I had always wanted to go to an airy café on the Mediterranean and slurp down a few oysters with some nice white wine. I never mentioned it to Allen but after a beautiful ride in the country, the road emerged out of the hills and we were looking at the sea. Soon he pulled up to the kind of restaurant I had imagined but never knew existed. We all consumed trays of fresh oysters with the salt air wafting around us.

Recently, Allen and Masha surprised Chris and me with a visit at our home in New Jersey. Tom was in the neighborhood so he came by as well with a friend. We beat up my wine supply something terrible that night. Tom gave his version of the aborted night flight. He said he wasn't worried a bit because he had a hostage. My son was in the back seat and Tom was sure I wouldn't do anything foolish with Michael aboard.

General Tango Tango

We picked him up in Kisangani on our way back from a drop off in Bukavu. At five feet eight inches he wasn't a tall fellow. His uniform, not much in the way of badges or accoutrement but neat and pressed, was topped off with a clean red beret. Seemed to be a nice chap, not too taken with himself. He and his aides were going to Kinshasa.

Kisangani has an airport just west of the war-torn Great Lakes region of Eastern Congo, about an hour and fifty-minute flight from Kinshasa. This very active airport, especially for the UN's humanitarian efforts, was also a stepping off point for the military. Kisangani was the primary logistical hub for operations in Eastern Congo. We used the airport on our way to and from Goma or Bukavu. Full fuel in the wings of our airplane would be enough to fly to either place and return. Those flights were an hour each way but included two fuel-guzzling takeoffs, which left little reserve by the time we got back. The airport is right on the Congo River, upstream from the city about ten miles via a rough road. The mouth of the Congo River is sixteen hundred miles downstream at the Atlantic Ocean.

Kisangani is where John Houston filmed *The African Queen*. Remnants of intensive commercial operations on the river remain in the form of rusty riverboat skeletons and unserviceable docking facilities. We rode by all of this on the way to the city from the airport. Conrad's character "Marley" always came to mind at the sight of this and thoughts of days gone by. There were fish traps as well in the water but not many fish to be caught anymore. Hunger lead to the consumption of even the small fish—the hungry eating the seed corn. These people do suffer.

Right after takeoff, Tango Tango left his seat and stood in the opening of the cockpit bulkhead between Deo and me. The general chatted with Deo and moved back in the cabin, where he remained standing.

As we climbed through twenty-seven thousand feet, we experienced a rapid decompression. The external lavatory-servicing plug worked its way loose and blew out, which compromised the pressure vessel. Humans require an oxygen mixture in the air they breathe that is found at sea level and up to fifteen thousand feet. Higher, and the air is too thin and doesn't contain enough oxygen to sustain human life.

Cabin altitude in high performance airplanes is maintained by pressurizing a sealed passenger compartment as the airplane climbs through the atmosphere surrounding it. The airplane can be flying in the very thin air near the top of the troposphere, while maintaining a cabin pressure of six thousand feet. The passengers are as comfortable as if they were at Lake Tahoe. The higher altitudes yield a faster airspeed and lower fuel consumption, which translates to increased range.

The attention-demanding master caution light in the center of the cockpit illuminated as it does whenever a system failure light in the telelight panel comes on. The only red light on in the panel indicated cabin pressure over ten thousand feet. There was a loud thump when the service plug blew out just like an instructor banging his fist on the side of the simulator at FlightSafety. That simulated pressurization failure also included the loud hissing sound of air escaping, which we were now hearing in the airplane.

I did what my training had taught me: pulled the power back, switched on the constant ignition to avoid an engine flame-out, extended the speed brake, rolled the wings over at least sixty degrees to dump the vertical lift, then let the nose come down through the horizon gently, minimizing the unsettling feeling of any negative gravity. We hadn't put our oxygen masks on when we climbed through eighteen-thousand feet as we should have, so I was reaching over my shoulder to grasp it during all this flying.

Our situation wasn't nearly the drama it could have been had the failure occurred at a much higher altitude where decompression empties the lungs quickly and the mucous is flying about, adding to the distraction of a life-threatening environment. I put my mask on and got one breath before it stopped giving me oxygen. The mask harness, the apparatus holding it on my head, also failed. Again, if this happened at a higher altitude I may have passed out before the plane descended to breathable air

FAA regulations demand that when an aircraft is at an altitude over thirty-five thousand feet both pilots have oxygen masks around their necks and if only one is at the controls he must be wearing and using it. The regulations are there because little time exists to be looking for an oxygen mask at those altitudes should one be needed.

When I got down to fifteen thousand feet I looked around to the back of the airplane and there was Tango Tango still standing in the cabin unruffled. I knew I liked this guy.

The Second and Third Emergency Descent

Late one evening (17 Oct 05) we were called out for a pick-up in Lubumbashi with a return to Kinshasa. We were cruising at Flight Level 350 (35,000 feet), fifteen minutes from where we normally started our descent into Lubumbashi and the "Master Caution" light came on. I looked to the telelight panel where the smaller red emergency cabin pressure light was on.

I went through the procedure taking us down to breathable air and this time all went without a hitch. During the first rapid descent, the oxygen system only yielded one breath because Deo had not opened the system's valve completely during the preflight check. After the incident with Tango Tango onboard, I scavenged working oxygen masks from other aircraft and installed them. No point in pushing my luck too much. This time my oxygen mask worked properly and did not fall apart when I put it on.

Not having to fumble around with a mask gave me more time to consider the elevations below us while screaming down at thirty-five hundred feet per minute. Lubumbashi is at 4,295 feet above sea level with irregular surrounding terrain. This was nothing like the mountains near Bukavu, exceeding fifteen thousand feet, but still worthy of consideration. The pressurization failure happened at a convenient place in our flight. We were close to the airport so the increase in fuel burn at the lower altitude was not going to make range an issue. If the failure happened at the halfway point of this trip, an hour earlier, we might have been in real trouble managing the fuel burn and figuring our maximum range. There were no reliably lit runways on our route between Kinshasa and Lubumbashi.

When we landed, I called Tim. He would send a mechanic on the first scheduled flight from Kinshasa in the morning. In the meantime, we were off to the Park Hotel downtown where we had stayed many times.

The next day the mechanic opened the unpressurized compartment housing the air cycle machine that provides the passenger compartment with conditioned air under pressure. He found the flexible pipe between the machine and the compartment had separated.

Our third rapid decompression happened with a presidential candidate aboard (8 Nov 05). We had taken him to Kamina Base southwest of Kinshasa. This is a military base where the CIA poured millions of dollars of 1960's technology into the middle of the jungle when Mobutu was an ally. The huge hangers and satellite dishes are being consumed by rust now. This was one big example of inactivity and neglect. In 2004 the United States wanted to refurbish Kamina for use as a B-52 base, supporting Middle East operations, but the DRC officials wanted too much money. The US Defense Attaché told me these fellows looking to line their pockets needed to learn there was more to skim in the long run and to stop going for the short money.

The candidate Deo and I brought to Kamina had returned to Congo from his dental practice in Boston. He must have paid for this flight and was no threat to Kabila's reelection or he wouldn't have been using this airplane. He was six feet tall and husky. His excellent English accompanied a pleasant demeanor. He also had a good tailor.

The flight from Kinshasa was uneventful, followed by hours of waiting in the airplane on the hot, sunny concrete ramp. There was no other place for us at Kamina Base and no fuel for us either. We started the day with full fuel, which should have left us a forty-five-minute reserve for the return trip.

We left for home and the dentist appeared quite comfortable in a business jet, enjoying the Scotch like he was used to such amenities. We climbed to flight level 330 (33,000') and were proceeding along fat, dumb and happy when, yet again, a "pop" was heard and the cabin pressure dropped rapidly. My emergency descent procedure was improving and didn't even spill the candidate's drink while getting us down quickly to breathable air. I was initially concerned about fuel burn rates and quantity, but after minimal computations it was obvious we could make Kinshasa.

When we parked at our spot on the ramp in front of the VIP lounge in Kinshasa, Deo got out first and stood at the base of the stairway as the passengers deplaned. I stayed in my seat and straightened up my workspace. As the candidate exited he stuck his head in the cockpit, simply said, "Thank you," and put a hundred-dollar bill on the right seat. I thanked him and felt appreciated.

A week later I was at Tim's house for one of his cocktail parties. The usual crowd of big shots from business and government were there. Many I recognized as passengers on the Sabreliner. I was working on my second Martini when the dentist entered. He saw me and after he got himself a drink from one of the trays carried by a servant, he came over to me.

"Good evening, Captain."

"Good evening, sir."

"What happened the other day?"

"We lost pressurization."

"Has that ever happened before?"

"Yes sir, as a matter of fact, it has," I said, while suppressing a chuckle.

"That's the last time I'll ever get on that airplane."

Windhoek, Namibia

I had been in the DRC a little more than six months when a morning departure to Windhoek, Namibia, came up. This trip was for the military and punctuality was expected. I was delighted, never having been to Namibia, and was looking forward to a dinner at Joe's Beer House. A South African gave me an enthusiastic recommendation: "You must go there." The word "must" being nearly as common to them as "ay" to the Canadians.

We spent a refreshing two days in Windhoek. The city was clean as could be, a German influence, I thought. We stayed at a hotel with a casino in the downtown part of the city. The suggested restaurant was a necessary stop for first timers there and lived up to its reputation. Joe's Beer House served man-size meals for carnivores. If you wanted Zebra or other herbivore game meat like Springbok, this was the place to go. The portion size was befitting a robust young man in his thirties, though. Joe's had both inside and outside dining areas and left me with a good memory.

Most of Namibia is a desert. The capital, Windhoek, is the largest city and centrally located. This trip took us to the absolute range limit of our airplane—just a little further than Kinshasa to Entebbe. The twenty-minute reserve fuel could be eliminated by unexpected headwinds or higher than standard temperatures at cruising altitude. The course of flight took us south over the length of Angola.

Namibia's western boundary is the Atlantic Ocean, to the south is South Africa, and to the east Botswana. The trip from Kinshasa to an airport called Eros in the city of Windhoek was twelve hundred fifty miles. The generals wanted to go to the downtown airport so they could be closer to the hotel and the women. The main airport serving Windhoek is Hosea Kutako International, forty miles to the east.

General Nkunda was aboard, the kind of guy who can be a gentleman until he has been drinking. He and I saw each other at a market in Kinshasa one Saturday afternoon and had a very cordial exchange. The first time I saw him drunk was a different story, though. He was in Lubumbashi and we were there to take him back to Kinshasa. Deo and I arrived two hours later than expected because another Presidential flight had run late and not through any fault of ours.

The general was agitated and getting more worked up by the minute. Fortunately, Charles was there to greet the dignitaries we transported. Nkunda was pulling a pistol out of his pocket when Charles stepped up to calm him down. Charles kept his hand on the pocket and talked to him before he pulled it out and did who knows what with it.

This is the general who became persona non grata at the American Embassy as a result of his pistol-whipping an American reporter outside of the Grand Hotel in Kinshasa. He tried to apologize to the US Ambassador via the US Defense Attaché to no avail. The same night he had the streetwalkers rounded up and turned over to his soldiers for whatever they chose to do with them. They didn't deserve it. The Ambassador refused to accept the apology and said the general was a bully and not to be reinstated on the preferred guest list of the embassy's social calendar.

The Eros airport was for smaller airplanes, and certainly not first generation jets requiring longer runways like ours. This departure was another of the exciting learning experiences I was having with too much frequency. I needed to start looking out for myself. Windhoek is on a plateau six thousand feet above sea level, which means aircraft performance is severely compromised. The plan was to stay here a couple of days and then take them home to Kinshasa from Hosea Kutako International Airport. It had a two-mile-long runway to get heavy airliners airborne in this thin air but was a forty-mile drive from the city.

According to Tim, he got the Sabreliner out of the downtown airport, so I could take off safely as long as I didn't have any passengers or put any extra fuel on board than was needed to fly to Hosea airport. Repositioning the plane in the morning, while the air was still cool enough, was also advisable. Even though the south-pointing runway was more than seven thousand feet long the altitude and potential for high temperatures made it very short and marginal for our Sabreliner.

The takeoff from Eros Airport was much more thrilling than I expected. Long, high-speed takeoff rolls were always risky. Airplanes fly by airspeed but tires have limiting ground speeds. Blow a main tire at a hundred and twenty knots and there will be directional control problems. The density of the air at high altitudes makes it possible to exceed ground-speed tire limits before gaining enough airspeed from thin air to fly. The generals had to take ground transportation to the international airport where we fueled for the long trip back to Kinshasa. I'd have put a few liters in my pockets if possible. Delays for weather in Kinshasa and we would become fuel-critical.

The immediate adventure was at the smaller airport, though. We put a few hundred pounds of fuel in the Sabre, just enough to reach Hosea, and were taxiing out by ten in the morning. The air was still cool so we hadn't made matters worse by leaving later in warmer air. The clearest flight path with the least obstructions was to the south over a golf course. I taxied to the edge of the north end of the runway and stood on the brakes while the engines spooled up until the brakes would no longer hold us and released them. The roll out was slow, as expected, and the acceleration weak.

The end of the runway was approaching and the airspeed was low. Extending approach flaps late in the takeoff roll would have helped but I hadn't prepared Deo for such a desperate move. The pre-takeoff crew briefing I didn't do was the place for that. Approach flaps make more drag during the takeoff roll but more lift. Extending them once there is sufficient airspeed helps the airplane become airborne. This was "bush technique," only used in the field when desperation calls. I have never used it.

The last couple of seconds had me gritting my teeth as we neared the end of the runway. I pulled back on the control column just as we crossed the runway numbers at the end. As soon as I saw the rate of climb indicator rise, we had positive rate of climb. I selected the gear up position and we slowly gained altitude. I know we woke up every golfer out there on the course with this very loud, slow, and shallow climbing, jet-powered antique. We made it, just. The controls were very sluggish but we were climbing. We had the other airport in sight quickly and after a ten-minute flight over the desert-like terrain, we touched down.

The D CAB

The D CAB (Director of the President's Cabinet) was a cut above all of the other feared politicians in Congo. Many are said to have gone into his office and not heard from again. He was known to be fond of the machete for taking care of business. The D CAB had a menacing face. Just before I first met him there was an internal drum roll. I felt safer and more comfortable as an American to be sure.

D CAB wielded the same or more power than the prime minister, which was a position not always occupied in Congo. He was the president's senior advisor whom you had to deal with before you got to the president. The first time I saw the D CAB was when he got into the back of the airplane. I was at my usual position, in the cockpit, ready to push a starter button for one of the engines as soon as his foot stepped on the stairway hatch. We were taking him to Kananga, which was near diamond country where Louis Armstrong had done a concert during Mubuto times.

This time we were scheduled to take the D CAB to Kananga during the dry season—*la saison sèche*. The airport we used was dusty but cool. Not cool like in temperate climates but cool for the tropics, as opposed to sweltering hot. The smoke from burning trash hung in the air adding to the haze. The diminishing visibility was particularly evident in Kananga's surrounding valley and decreased as the day went on. There was no precision approach and by three in the afternoon the airport was below minimums.

To land in Kananga in the dry season requires leaving Kinshasa by 1400, at the latest. If not we would likely fly there, go right by the missed approach point, the place where the runway must be seen to land successfully, and return to Kinshasa. This information was supposed to be passed along to the D CAB. I told Deo to make sure the advance people knew. I also informed them when they first showed at the airport at ten that morning.

As 1400 came and went with no D CAB, I told his people we weren't going. They looked somewhat stressed. He showed a little after three. They started carrying his bags to the airplane and I stopped them. Deo said I had better go confront him myself. He was right because I don't think the D CAB had been given any of the time parameters from the people around him. His dark reputation suggested he just might have killed a messenger or two.

I went to the VIP lounge with his people and Deo in trail. I looked at the D CAB's face, the mean one with the large mustache, knowing what fear it must broadcast to the locals. I mustered my best, but very limited French, to explain the story of the weather constraints and how a flight at this time would be futile. He looked as grateful as his visage would permit without a toothy grin. I thought this was the first time he had heard the truth all day. He wasn't grinning but told Deo it was fine and we would go earlier tomorrow.

When we arrived in Kananga the next day an excited small crowd of close to a hundred greeted him. This is where he came from—homeboy made good. They were dressed in their best, brightly colored clothes, shouting and cheering for him. He spent the night there and we returned to Kinshasa.

There was even a brighter show the next day. On the ramp was a witch doctor with his own entourage, straight out of a 1950s TV show like *Ramar of the Jungle*. He was there to do his dance around the airplane, headdress on and spear in hand, blessing the voyage. Another, smaller crowd of well-wishers was there as well. When the D CAB's limousine arrived, a group of women surrounded his limo singing, dancing and following him to the plane. After he got in and seated, one of the women was allowed in the plane. In a raised voice she praised him and only toned down momentarily when he gave her a fist full of money. As she went down the exit stairs she showed off the hand full of cash to the others and ran to them. They all had their hands out and shared in the prize. Their collective cheers were the highest pitch of the past two days.

Bata

There was a day we were taking the Minister of Finance or Banks or whatever his title of the week was to Malabo, Equatorial Guinea (a "petrolocracy" in Western Africa). This flight shouldn't have been a problem. Malabo was on a mountainous island but had an ILS approach. I was there before and had the appropriate charts. The minister kept us waiting at the airport all afternoon and well into the dark.

At last he arrived, but in a hurry to leave. The destination was changed to Bata, the country's largest city, on the coast of the mainland. Deo told me of the change when we were taxiing for takeoff. The weather was not good, but if things got worse I had the fuel to go on to Malabo and listen to the complaining afterward. We discovered, after climbing out of Kinshasa, there were no instrument approaches to Bata.

The only good thing was the proximity to the sea, right on the coast with mountains behind it. Our GPS got us very close but wasn't fancy enough to construct a virtual ILS to latitude and longitude coordinates. It did, however, give us the shoreline. Even though embedded thunderstorms were all over the area to circumnavigate, we caught occasional glimpses of the city. Knowing the orientation of the town to the airport made an approach possible but hairy.

The altitude of the highest mountain was published, but that wasn't enough information for us to maneuver over land searching for the airport. This meant weaving around and under the cumulonimbi that were present and in full bloom over the sea. They created an intermittent, blinding light show. We came in low from the waterside, but got blocked in by clouds and had to turn back toward the sea. The second attempt got us close to the city and we saw a part of the airport. I wouldn't have wanted to be sitting in the back of the Sabre the way I was wracking it around those clouds. There was plenty of turbulence as well. I would have made Bob Guin proud.

I finally found the right hole offering a glimpse of the airport environment and dove for it. We leveled off under a ceiling. There was spotty visibility from showers but the sight of a runway relieved the drama of the previous fifteen minutes. The Minister gave us an excellent tip when we left the airport for the hotel.

Bata is not the best place to spend an evening but preferable to those where you end up bathing while standing up in a bucket pouring water over yourself. However, this was not a place you were going to find twelve-year-old single malt Scotch either. At Malabo, the capitol of the country, there are much better options.

Chapter 18
The East, Bukavu and Goma

We didn't go to Bukavu until 2004 for security reasons. It is in eastern Congo, the most beautiful part of the country, where the silverback gorillas live. Both Bukavu and Goma, also in the Great Lakes region, had airports presenting significant performance challenges for the airplane we operated. Moreover, in the case of Bukavu the runway had deteriorated to the point where the blacktop was becoming gravel in places. This makes it possible and likely for jet engines to ingest these stones and be severely damaged—a real problem on takeoff. It is called foreign object damage, FOD. Bukavu is located in the mountains at the south end of Lake Kivu and Goma at the north. This is where the Second Congo War began, ending the Mubuto regime. Since 1998, 5.4 million people have died there.

It took me a number of flights into Bukavu before I became at all comfortable with it. There was always a question as to whether we could even find the airport due to the clouds so often obscuring it. Takeoffs were no less a drama than landing due to the mountain we had to go around immediately off the end of the short downhill runway. The down sloping runway was used for takeoff and the up sloping for landing regardless of wind direction.

The eastern edge of Lake Kivu borders with Rwanda and, further south, Burundi is on the northern edge of Lake Tanganyika, another of the great lakes. The usual route to Bukavu would have us flying from Kisangani about an hour into the mountains. Kisangani is remote—the very heart of Africa on the Congo River.

Most airports have what is called a published instrument approach. By using the navigation equipment in the airplane and the navaids on the ground, which emit a guidance signal, locating the airport visually often becomes possible. Adhering to the depicted courses and the altitude restrictions of a published instrument approach chart will prevent flight into known terrain. This is really an absolute—fly it as published and you won't hit anything.

The first problem was to find the Bukavu airport visually since there was no published instrument approach procedure. We had GPS equipment in the airplane so we knew where it should be, but clouds over mountainous rain forests near large bodies of water often made for visibility issues. Pilots who fly in mountainous terrain will tell you, "Those clouds have hard spots in them."

The method I used was to climb on the proper course from Kisangani to the published terrain clearance altitude found on en route charts and continue until we were over Lake Kivu. The cloud cover was often broken in spots and the peaks of the mountains could be seen sticking above them. We would look for breaks in the clouds to find Lake Kivu and spiral down with visual reference to the water. The smaller the hole in the cloud covers the tighter the spiral. The altimeter helped by telling us how close to the water we were during the high speed descent with the tight turning needed to stay in clear air. At some point, usually a couple of thousand feet from the water, we could get under the clouds and with the help of the GPS be able to locate the airport. It was then time to deal with the narrow uphill runway. If we couldn't locate the airport we had to climb to the published terrain clearance altitude and go back to Kisangani, get fuel and try again later if we had enough daylight. This was not the place for night operations.

With the airport in sight we would then have to slow the airplane, extend the flaps and landing gear into what is called a standard landing configuration. Since we were dealing with an airport at a high altitude where the air is thin and runway is of minimal length, we needed to reduce the speed even more. This is accomplished with the additional drag of the speed brake, a two foot square door-like structure extending almost vertically from the bottom of the fuselage. A high power setting is used to provide instant acceleration when the airframe is cleaned up by retracting the speed brake, landing gear and flaps. This assures our ability to safely and promptly abort the landing attempt should it become necessary, without waiting for the engines to spool up to a high power setting. Bukavu kept you busy. The airplane needed to land on the end of the runway this way to get it stopped comfortably given its short length. Unless you have everything right it is difficult to make the Sabreliner fit on this runway.

Sometimes we were scheduled to go right from Kinshasa to Bukavu and needed to use Bujumbura, Burundi, for an alternate place to land if we couldn't get into Bukavu. Bujumbura has an Instrument Landing System (ILS) providing heading and altitude information to a fine degree right down to two hundred feet above the runway threshold. It's a big help when needed due to bad weather. We would wait for the clouds to clear in Bukavu, take on fuel and go back or spend the night in Bujumbura. The city is on a hillside overlooking the northern shore of Lake Tanganyika, a beautiful view from town. I heard the Muslim evening prayers for the first time echoing off the hill and buildings late one afternoon there. It was eerie and chilling for me.

Once you get to Bukavu there is a backbreaking two-hour bumpy road trip to town. The only saving grace is the hope of getting a room in the Safari Orchid Club for the night. The Safari is located on the hillside overlooking Lake Kivu with a view not unlike Lake Tahoe in California. Orchids and other flowers are growing all over. There is a comfortable dining room with a stone fireplace and a water buffalo head mounted above it—all of this with a grand view of the lake, a nice menu and good wine list. The contrast between the natural beauty of the countryside and the war-torn city and evidence of poverty you pass on the way to town can be unsettling. There is a roadside stone quarry on the way to the city with people making gravel from bigger rocks by hand. They are not a part of a road gang. It is a means of making a living.

We took a new "general of the army" to Bukavu one day. He was supposed to calm the troops and officers with promises of pay coming soon, but he didn't have it with him. It was a usual Bukavu trip, and we were lucky enough to get a room at the Safari Orchid. When we went back to the airport to wait for the general's arrival by UN helicopter there seemed to be tension in the air. We were on the military ramp, which was located along the side of the runway and north of the civilian ramp. It had a helipad and a headquarters building. Milling around on the ramp where we had the airplane parked were a number of officers and other troops all without smiles. I heard a chanting coming from some distance and getting louder. I realized it was from troops at a double time march coming towards us. They were in unison; they were disciplined; and they were Mai Mai.

The Mai Mai are fierce local militias, originally hired by Laurent Kabila to resist the Rwandans, led primarily by tribal leaders or war lords. Some have since operated for their own benefit becoming bandits, cattle rustlers, poachers and looters. Hearing them, I thought of Michael Caine in *Zulu Dawn*. They were impressive and scary with their automatic weapons and well fitting uniforms. They looked prideful, comfortable and without fear opposite the undisciplined and raggedy Congolese government soldiers for whom I felt sad.

I looked up on the small hill where they came as a column of twos out of the jungle and then split along the corner of a small ridge overlooking the ramp, which was about ten feet high. It was in the form of a classic L-shaped ambush with our position the focal point. I had been told the Mai Mai were the best and most ruthless troops in the country. The Congolese would be no match for these fellows even if they chose to fight, which was highly unlikely.

I looked at Deo and said, "This can't be good."

"No," he agreed.

I hoped the general we brought had his best dancing shoes on, along with a good enough line of bullshit to get us out of there. We would soon be running out of the daylight needed to get to Kisangani before they closed the airport and shut off the lights. I wasn't getting out of the airplane. Trying to read my ever-present novel for a distraction was impossible due to the presence of the Mai Mai. It was twenty minutes later before the general showed up. After his helicopter landed he went into the headquarters building. A few minutes later some officers came out and talked to those outside. Suddenly the Mai Mai got up and left the way they had come. It wasn't long and we were on our way—much to my delight. This was the most relieved I ever felt on a takeoff. Bukavu always raised my pulse, but this time it was especially elevated.

We took General John Numbe to Bukavu and made a very long one-day trip. We had no working fuel quantity indicating system in the airplane and were using the time method to guess at our fuel burn. This had been going on the better part of a year because the test equipment to troubleshoot the system properly was fifteen thousand dollars and Tim was resisting spending that much. Doing without the accuracy of a proper system, which could not be provided by a watch, made this kind of a flight pretty dramatic.

The flight began in Kinshasa with proposed stops in Kindu, Bukavu, Kisangani and Goma the next day, before returning to Kinshasa. The general had five others with him and I explained we could only take three out of Bukavu or Goma. He had no problem with anything else I said. Our relationship was always cordial.

Our jet needed to fuel in Kindu before departing for Bukavu. I had been told earlier in Kinshasa that there was no fuel for us in Bukavu. This meant I needed to leave Kindu with full wing tanks, the same as flying from Kisangani to Bukavu. Kindu looked like the same distance to Bukavu as Kisangani. Should be no problem, but I was feeling tension anyhow.

We left Kindu later than I wanted to but with full wing tanks. I don't like to squeeze daylight limits. The approach into Bukavu was tight and I was feeling goosey about the fuel we didn't have on board, nor able to get on the ground. We spiraled down over the lake, saw the airport, and rushed the approach because I didn't want to use the fuel to circle the field and get the airplane configured properly. As a result I was high and fast. This is not the way to approach the runway at Bukavu. I pushed the plane on, stood on the breaks, and used full reverse thrust, risking FOD. The end of the runway was coming fast but we came to a stop at the very end. Numbe and his entourage were unruffled, used to rough airmanship I believed. I was not pleased.

I taxied into the ramp area and parked. We got into an awaiting car and were off to the Safari Orchid. The next day back at the airport one of the main wheels had a flat tire. Close external inspection showed no damage, so we suspected it was caused by a slow leak. There are two devices on the main wheels of the Sabre accommodating the excessive tire pressure generated by high heat from heavy braking. There are fusible plugs in the wheels that blow out in extreme cases. The other means of dealing with over pressure is the failure of an O-ring sealing the two halves of the wheel itself.

Deo went to work. He not only found a Welshman—who was an engineer on a large Convair transport plane parked nearby—with a bottle of compressed nitrogen, but he got us a barrel of jet fuel as well. The Welshman and I talked and we believed the O-ring was the source of the leak. He did not have a tire pressure gauge capable of measuring the high pressure needed for our application so he made it look like the other tire's profile. The plan was to get back to Kisangani and, if the tire held up, return to Kinshasa from there.

This was not the first time General Numbe had flown with me and had more of a ride than expected. I sensed he appreciated flying with me by the generous tip he sent to me a week later. We had dropped him off in Lubumbashi one evening and spent the night there. The next day we got called back to Kinshasa and before we left the hotel one of his officers came by and handed me an envelope. When I was in the airplane and starting the engines he called my phone and asked if I received it.

"Yes, General and thank you very much." A six hundred dollar tip is always welcome.

Goma, at the northern shore of Lake Kivu, is right next to Rwanda which gives any Congolese the creeps and for good reason. The Rwandans are by far the superior fighters and demonstrated it by killing hundreds of thousands of their neighbors in the first and second Congo wars. Congolese prefer not to fight but rather to dance and drink Primus beer. They dance as well as the Rwandans fight.

One approaches the airport at Goma from the south over Lake Kivu. The volcano Nyiragongo, the active volcano that erupted in 2002, precludes a northern approach. Lava flowed into much of the city and the airport. There is another runway a mile and a half from the Goma airport with the Rwanda frontier in between. The runways are parallel. It is easy to pick the wrong place to land if you are unfamiliar with the area. The Rwanda runway is also more identifiable as a landing strip. As I lined up on the wrong runway, Deo expressed a heartfelt plea from way deep inside not to go there but rather look to the left. After a while the Goma airport came into sight. I played with Deo a bit when I continued toward the Rwandan runway before acknowledging the one at Goma.

The Goma runway is short with a five-foot wall of lava at the end and airplane wrecks littering both sides of the runway. A brake failure could kill you and as usual the pilots are the first at the scene of an accident.

The airport is half of what it was. There is a DC8 embedded in lava on what was the upper ramp area near the original terminal. It will never move again. The runway was a long one, three kilometers, but not anymore. Just enough of the lava is cleared off of the runway to allow short field capable aircraft enough room to operate safely, but being the Congo B727s and DC9s also work it with no safety margins to speak of. They average losing an airplane or two every year, usually into the populated market off the end of the takeoff runway. When walking the streets in Goma now you are on a couple of feet of lava and have to step down into the shops.

The upside of Goma is the lakeside setting and its mineral wealth, the same two commonalities it has with Bukavu. The valuable mineral is coltan, short for columbite–tantalite, and the element tantalum is used in capacitors for cell phones. Goma has a Lake Tahoe kind of beauty, and the mineral riches there support many generals and their armies. The shakedown of the mine operators is one of the reasons a mineral deposit must be far richer here than other places in order to make it worth mining. While waiting for another passenger one evening I met a man from the World Bank named Ono Rule, a Dutchman. He explained how impossible a mining enterprise was in Congo without political insurance due to the staggering costs of supporting an investment here. It made sense given what I had seen thus far in this lawless place. Who would put up a nickel without some real protection from this government?

Goma had a new hotel right on the water complete with stork-like birds walking around the grounds. Their flying feathers were pulled to keep them from leaving. A launch was available for tours of the lake. Nice as it all was, the thoughts of the takeoff were ever present in the back of my mind. I knew I would have to argue at the airplane with the passengers about the weight of the aircraft. Explaining that three passengers was the maximum we could take was never enough. They showed up with cases of the famous Goma cheese as if it didn't weigh a thing. We would have to repeatedly cull out case upon case of cheese before takeoff. As it was we would wobble out over the lake hoping one of these high time engines would not choose that moment to fail.

Usually the return from Goma to Kisangani was a fuel stop en route to Kinshasa unless some general wanted to entertain one of the dignitaries we were transporting. The hotel of choice in Kisangani was the Palm Beach Hotel. It was home to many of the UN contractor pilots, which was always the mark of the best place to stay. Kinshasa had the Memling and the Grande Hotel. Harare, Zimbabwe and Kampala, Uganda had Sheratons. Lome, Togo had the 4Fervier with the restaurant on top with a view of the Gulf of Guinea, good scotch and the worst restaurant service. There is a traffic circle on the way into the 4Fervier where students would gather all night to use the streetlights to study by because there wasn't any electricity where they lived.

Chapter 19
Out of Africa

By 2006 I was growing weary of Congo, perhaps the ever-present siege mentality wore me down. The political climate was the worst it had been since I arrived years earlier. Guards with AK47s patrolled every night at the house. Really. I had a Kalashnikov next to my bed as well. Prior to getting chased through the streets in Kitambo, I drove myself into all parts of the city without fear. I stopped at any outdoor pub I fancied deep in the city. Rather brazen behavior for a white, non-French-speaking American. After the chase, as I mentioned earlier, I hired a chauffeur. The airplane maintenance needed improvement; the list went on. I decided when the first presidential campaign ended, it would be a good time to exit the grandest of my personal adventures.

Deo and I were the exclusive transportation for the President's reelection committee. We flew them to all the major and minor airports where they could get votes. They visited the east often—Bukavu, Goma and Bunia, especially. On July 5, 2006, we went to Gbadolite, where Mobutu had a palace. He once chartered the Concord SST to bring in guests and case upon case of Roederer Cristal Champagne. The grounds of the estate had been stocked with animals and birds. Not the case when we got there. Like the zoo in Kinshasa; the hungry populace ate the animals. The whole city along with the palace had declined to a poor excuse for a presidential residence.

Votes were purchased with T-shirts, bars of soap, a fifty-franc note, something—anything. These people have nothing, so a little goes a long way. A fellow, who looked like a Belgian left behind from the 1960s, told me, "Gbadolite is the New Hampshire of Congo. Whatever way it goes, so will go Congo." Maybe it was true, but he seemed just another burnout I had met many times in Congo bars and hotels. Self-professed successes in the diamond trade or gold, who chose to live in some shit hole like this—come on. This one in particular was touting a caviar hustle from sturgeon in the Congo River. Another Graham Greene character of the many I encountered in Africa.

I stayed at a shabby guesthouse in Gbadolite, arriving after dark, hungry and thirsty. Deo was at another house so I took off on foot to a restaurant a few blocks away. Finding it was easier than getting back. That difficulty stemmed from the time I spent at the adjoining bar. I started walking in what I thought was the right direction and when I made a wrong turn, I heard a voice behind me say, "No, Commander." I looked around and fifty yards behind me was the silhouette of one of the armed Presidential Guards pointing in the other direction. My passengers had someone watching over me when I was on the road. I was their way back to Kinshasa.

The first presidential campaign came to a close. The tally meant a runoff between the incumbent and the runner-up. Joseph Kabila was always referred to by his first name while the other candidates with their surnames. Jean Paul Bemba was the opposition and he was not going peacefully into the night. Blood was going to run in the streets of Kinshasa and paying attention to the cellphone network was advisable. The embassy security staff added me to the list of those provided text messages on a real-time basis regarding hot spots in town.

There was a firefight at Bemba's residence between his security people and Joseph's police one evening. It was a take-no-prisoners type of operation and Joseph's men prevailed, executing the opposition's wounded where they lay. Order was eventually restored and the city calmed but tensions remained.

I enjoyed the campaign because it took me to places I had not been to in Congo; many were backwater towns with an airstrip. It often meant refueling from barrels with a hand pump, a process sometimes taking hours.

Gemena 22 July 2006

There was less here in the way of accommodations than in Gbadolite and we were spending the night. Ugh. I was road weary and needed a night in Kinshasa. Fortunately, the Gulfstream was here. Tim had brought Joseph on the campaign trail and the crews spent the night in "Hotel Gulfstream," with the auxiliary power running all night for air-conditioning. Tim had plenty of good food aboard, of course, and we drank six bottles of wine between us. A much better evening than I had anticipated.

Kinshasa 30 July 2006

We returned from the campaign trail at 1:30 PM from Bukavu and Kisangani. Fortunately, we arrived at the Kinshasa airport before Joseph. Demonstrators were poised for his arrival. Some were pro-Joseph and some were there to stone his convoy. The police were in their riot gear and looked like Star Wars troopers in black armor. We managed to smooth our way back to town without getting caught in the melee.

Some of what I was going to miss about Congo were BBC broadcasts of Formula One racing without commercial interruption as well as the intense World Cup enthusiasm. My friend, Alan Carney, invited me to a French bar in town with wide screen television to watch the French team play the Portuguese. Before the game, they played national anthems and when I heard *La Marseillaise* I felt like I was on the movie set of *Casablanca*.

Kinshasa 5 August 2006

During the last week of the campaign, I had two near misses—midair collisions. One was at Kinshasa and one at Bukavu. In Kinshasa, I was in a holding pattern at night, waiting my turn to land, when another airplane, at my assigned altitude, flew right through the pattern. It happened too quickly to get scared. In Bukavu, a controller, whom I later suggested retire, cleared us for takeoff after clearing a Boeing 727 to land from the opposite direction. This was a recipe for disaster as the controller mixed his poor English with French, confusing me if not everyone else.

On Aug 15, 2006, we took Vice-President Erodia to Kolwezi, French Congo, two hundred sixty-two miles west of Kinshasa on what should have been a routine flight. My flying time in the weeks after the campaign had fallen to almost nil. Deo had quit because he wasn't getting paid. Tim had put our salary through Wimbi Dira Airlines and I was the only pilot being paid on time.

I had Dimitri with me in the right seat. He was someone Tim told me would be fine in Deo's place. His English was terrible and he knew nothing about the airplane. He even struggled changing frequencies on the radios. It was an immediate issue when we were climbing out of Kinshasa and the tower controller handed us off to departure control. I became so frustrated after takeoff that I said, "You don't understand a word I'm saying, do you?" At which point he pulled out a checklist and handed it to me, with a smile.

I decided to leave Congo because the inner voice was telling me, "It's time to go." The internal temperatures of the engines had been increasing because they were worn out. They still started and, this being Congo, that meant they were good enough. There were sufficient signs to suggest problems on the horizon. The fire warning system would light up on the ground at idle temperatures, not through faulty sensors as Tim liked to say, but because the engines were flat run out. Their time was up and either one could fail on the next takeoff.

I had endured plenty of marginal equipment during my time there. I was just looking for another fifty days and would be homeward bound. The right engine's fuel controller had been changed two days earlier by swapping it from another high time engine in hopes it would work. Troubleshooting the engine fire detection system was an ongoing process in order to overlook a hot running engine. The real story was the engine was running hotter than the limits of the system parameters. Our mechanic recently had disconnected the fire loop altogether. Why did I fly it? Of course, it was for the money. The rationale for continuing with this ailment was: how often does one have an engine fire? The answer is: rarely.

Flying without a working fuel quantity indication system for almost a year was still in my head. When I complained about it to Tim he said, "You have a watch, don't you?" I saw the engine temps as the most immediate threat. An overloaded night takeoff from Entebbe and losing an engine at rotation over

Lake Victoria was daunting. This airplane was on its way to being something Gus wouldn't even have in his fly-by-night company.

Too many negative factors were stacking up against the good ones. I came to this job for two reasons. My financial situation in the States in 2002 was not good. I was afraid to go to the mailbox and see all the overdue bills. I was here chasing a buck plain and simple, the story of my life. After four years, the bills were cleaned up and I had a little in an offshore bank. The other reason, the more exciting one, was the adventure of flying in Congo. This was the best job I ever had. Still, I felt it right to leave now, without a scratch, just like Vietnam.

This wasn't the first time I quit Congo without plans for coming back. About a year earlier than the election campaign I went home for a total hip replacement. I also had my heart's mitral valve repaired. Tim replaced me with a Belgian pilot for less money and was happy until he ran the airplane off the runway in Brazzaville and damaged the nose gear. I got my seat in the Sabreliner back after that incident.

I made some friends there in the US State Department. Two of them said goodbye with touching gestures. One had a lavish dinner party for me and invited whomever I wanted. The other had a large outdoor party. Two of the people in my office at the airline gave me parting gifts, also touching. These were firsts for me. My accumulated miles with Air France allowed me to fly home business class. The difference that makes on fifteen hours of flight time as a passenger instead of traveling steerage is almost immeasurable.

Chapter 20
Full Circle

All of the flying was coming to an end. My failure to take better care of myself forced the issue. The body was breaking down and passing the annual FAA physical became more difficult. Technically, possessing a current physical exam document was a legal necessity because I was flying a United States registered airplane. However, being ramp checked by the FAA in Africa was a long shot; they didn't come to Congo even when Tim invited them.

When Tim offered me a chance to fly the Gulfstream for the second presidential campaign, I told him my medical was expired. "This is still Congo," he said. Flying a Gulfstream—the big time—was enticing to be sure, but I turned it down. There would be nothing resembling a serious training program to get me comfortable in the Gulfstream. Tim might have given me an hour in the airplane to do some landings and a couple of approaches before turning me loose to figure out the rest for myself—a recipe for disaster on my first trip to Goma or Bukavu. Tempting, but it was time to stay home.

Not long after the call from Tim, a Gulfstream carrying some ministers, whom I had flown many times, wrecked in Bukavu killing the crew and Mr. Katumba, a former prime minister to Joseph. They went off the end of the runway when attempting a landing.

A local doctor in Kinshasa was the only FAA approved doctor in central western Africa. Deo took him a hundred-dollar bill and came back with the blank form for me to fill out and then returned it for the doctor's signature. Everything could be arranged there. The anarchist in me still misses Congo.

Stateside, I kept in touch with Clifford Crowl whom I had first worked with on Guy Londe's Tennessee boll weevil contract. He had his own aerial application business in Iowa and grew it into a two-airplane operation. I went out there for three seasons on what in the trade is known as "the Iowa corn run." It lasts about seven weeks. A fungicide is sprayed, increasing the yield, and nets the farmer twice the cost of the pesticide application. Airplanes come from surrounding states and fill the air.

The Iowa landscape of corn and soybeans is a deep, skin-chilling, vivid green, as far as the eye can see. Summers are hot there—ninety plus degrees with little wind. Thunderstorms abound rivaling Africa in size. This is where people still help each other in times of need. Their very existence depended on each other back in the days of the first settlers. Religion was a big support as well. Other survival issues compounded the weather-induced hardships.

Today the weather is still mean but technology and crop insurance have taken some of the risk out of its wrath. Air-conditioned tractor cabs and airplane cockpits are used when applying the chemicals used to increase yields to unheard of quantities. American agricultural technology could feed the world with genetic engineering and the use of too many pesticides.

In Iowa, I sprayed my first mile-long cornfield—not found in New Jersey, and not seen by me in Tennessee, North Carolina or Delaware. It was a joy to run the mile-long swath. Waddling the overloaded plane off the runway made for a lot of tension, as did holding takeoff power to stay in the air most of the way to the field. By the time I arrived at the end of the first run, the plane, at least five hundred pounds lighter, allowed a gradual power reduction. The airplane became responsive and the turnaround nimble. After another couple of swaths, I went back for another load. I was making some money now. I had paid my dues years ago in those miserably short fields and now working for and with Clifford made it all even better.

We are poles apart politically but I have never felt it was in the way of our relationship. He is a self-made man with a strong work ethic who is a pleasure to be around. His quick-witted sense of humor and toothy beard-stubbed grin are a great finish to his quips. He would prefer a fried baloney sandwich for breakfast to eggs benedict every time. This is a man whose word is as good as any piece of paper with a dozen signatures.

I am at peace with ending my flying in Iowa. This completed the full circle. Ag flying was what I wanted from the beginning. It may have been the first ride in a Stearman in 1971 at Pittstown Airport in Hunterdon County, New Jersey, that set the hook. Ag work is pure stick and rudder flying at its best and worst.

I haven't felt the painful withdrawal from flying that I feared. I used to be miserable to live with when I was between flying jobs. The contentment of getting out of it alive eased the withdrawal. I managed to eke out a living for over thirty years in general aviation while never making it to the big leagues of flying for a major airline. My career was not a boring bus route of A to B and back, although I wouldn't have complained about the paycheck. I have few regrets.

Chapter 21
Another boat

I knew both of the best moments of owning a boat: the day you buy it and the day you are rid of it. The time in between was more burdensome than pleasurable for me. My maritime experience probably should have ended with the selling of the Pearson 30 I bought in September of 2001. We sold it in 2004 because it wasn't being used enough. I was off in Africa and some minor mechanical issues made it so unreliable the boat towing company dropped our coverage.

Some sailors say the P30 is the perfect sailboat; the only improvement would be if it had an outboard rather than an inboard motor to make it even simpler. When whimsy got me to buy another boat in 2012, I went for a Pearson 26, which uses an outboard motor for auxiliary power. Other sailors say this is the one—the best sailboat—because it will sail in light or heavy wind. Pearson sailboats get high grades from the sailing community in general. Salesmen pitch them as affordable family racing sailboats, as if you can use the word affordable and sailboat in the same sentence.

Finances speak to the root of my discontent. One needs deep pockets to take on this kind of hobby, considerably deeper than mine. The acronym "BOAT" means "bring on another thousand," in dollars, every time the boat has a hiccup. They are worse than an airplane and I owned one of them as well. As Ben Franklin said, "A fool and his money are soon parted."

The first exposure to sailing for Chris and me was twenty-five years before owning a sailboat, when we took our first vacation together. There was a sailing school in the upper Chesapeake using Flying Scots for teaching the primary students. The Scots are nineteen feet six inches in length and seemed the perfect size. They are an open boat with a sloop type rigging. Learning to sail was great fun, so much like flying. Boating ended for us at that school until I bought the Pearson 30.

The Pearson was also a sloop configuration, which means it has a large triangular mainsail with another triangular shaped sail, called a jib, attached to the bow side of a single mast.

There was no auxiliary power on Flying Scots and they needed to be sailed to and from the slip. It really was a perfect way to approach sailing. We learned all of the nomenclature as well as the proper callouts while sailing the boat. Preparing a crew verbally helped avoid being hit in the head by the boom as it swung from one side to the other when coming about to tack in the other direction.

The boom holds the bottom of the mainsail and provides a shape to the sail for catching the wind. When you change the tack of the boat from having the wind come from the port side (left) to the starboard side (right), the boom has to swing across the cockpit and over or through the heads of any crewmen there. To lessen the chances of this occurring, the helmsman will call out before the change, "Ready about!" This alerts the others aboard and is followed by, "Hard a lee." The helmsman then pushes the tiller over smartly to the leeward side, the boom swings across and the sail fills with air from the other side of the boat.

Sailing is like going nowhere in a hurry. It fells like a lot of action to make six knots, and it really is. A serious powerboat doing forty knots has the same level of intensity. The two are so different and so similar, like a dry Martini versus a glass of fine wine.

The second Pearson was one big story of misery. What made it even worse was my being so sure about buying it. All Chris said was we should have a boat— "We are surrounded by water here." She might have been satisfied with a trailered runabout but it wouldn't do for me.

The Corinthian Yacht Club had a sailing program for kids in the summer using small sunfish boats. The club was perfect with all the necessary equipment to go along with bright people to drink with at a great bar overlooking the harbor's sunsets. When Mike and Lillian were young we joined to give them the opportunity to learn. At lunchtime, Mike and Lillian ate in the dining area with the other kids. Lillian, seven at the time, told Mike he could have whatever he wanted because it was free. "Just give them the number G10 when they ask." Of course, it wasn't free.

I shopped extensively for a Pearson26 only to buy impulsively. The extras on the boat I focused on seemed so appropriate for my purposes. Arthritis had me in its grasp and getting around the rigging would be more than I could handle. The roller furling equipment permits reduction of the amount of sail when the wind gets too brisk. One sailor can deal with both sails from the cockpit and with the aid of a locking steering wheel it should have been easy. The boat was in the Bronx, the same Bronx where the Yankees play. The marina where the boat lived bordered the Long Island Sound at its most western edge.

Arriving in City Island was like stepping into another country. I believe if Customs were set up at the bridge separating the island from the mainland it would look like you were going into a foreign country. It was July and just beautiful, but the view towards the South and Manhattan was a bit frightening, knowing it would be my route. Buying a boat here would entail sailing it to Cape May. It would take days of sun poisoning, thrills and long stretches of boredom after clearing Sandy Hook southbound. Hell Gate and the East River were first and anything but boring.

In the 1600's explorers found navigating the tidal strait hazardous. By the late nineteenth century, hundreds of ships had sunk as a result of the rocks obstructing safe passage. In 1851 the U.S. Army Corps of Engineers began to clear the strait, a twenty-year process, and on September 24, 1876, fifty thousand pounds (twenty-three thousand kilograms) of explosives were the initial charges set for the demolitions. Finally the largest charge was used on October 10, 1885, with three hundred thousand pounds (one hundred forty thousand kilograms) of explosives. The blast was felt in Princeton, New Jersey. It was described as "the largest planned explosion before testing began for the atomic bomb."

Getting myself and this boat to Cape May would be considerably more difficult than the price negotiation. An experienced yachtsman from the yacht club in Cape May, a friend and Chris all offered to help me with the task, but fortunately I was able to turn them down gracefully. The P26 is sold as a "sleeps 5" and you better like the other four a lot because it would be damn snug. Sleeping two would be my maximum and not many nights in succession either. It wasn't like I didn't need some help handling the boat. No, I surely could have used someone with sailing experience or outboard motor knowledge, but I did make it by myself in four days.

Living on a slow-moving boat with someone else for four days, in the blistering sun, would have been intolerable. The only thing I was glad about on the trip, after I cleared Hell Gate, the East River and New York Harbor, was being alone. It was scary during those initial hurdles and having an experienced sailor with me to talk me through it all would have made it much easier, perhaps even fun. I just don't do things the easy way though.

The weather was stable and tides were on my side—not unexpected for July. High tide was about 6:00 that morning so leaving at 5:30 against the last of the tide was fine. It would take an hour to get to Rikers Island and the East River anyhow. I cleared the City Island Yacht Club a half an hour late and was on the proverbial morning tide—going out—just where I wanted it.

Any detour in the beginning would have added a day to the trip. I needed everything to go as planned or I could have been in trouble right away. Floating around in Raritan Bay looking for a marina as the sun was going down, not knowing if the running lights on the boat worked, didn't sound attractive at all. Getting through Hell Gate was the immediate drama though.

The tide from the Long Island Sound dumps into the southerly current of the East River, augmenting the velocity of the river. That's a lot of moving water with some conflicting current directions. I was on top of it all and moving past the west side of Manhattan in a dark canyon made from the morning sun shadows.

A part of the wall of that canyon on the right side started to move. I didn't know what to think at first. It was a huge freighter, about a mile ahead blending into the docks and pilings. That massive piece of steel was starting to leave and slip into the flow of the river. I was gaining on her and didn't want to be. I enjoyed the separation we had, but we got closer and closer. I wrestled with the question of which way I would go if the distance tightened, left or right? To the right would have me crossing her wake not knowing how difficult that would be.

Already, my inexperience came into play. I didn't want to slow down if I didn't have to since I did have the time constraints of the tide. I wanted to be at the Verrazano-Narrows before the tide started to come back in. The lettering on the ship's stern was becoming visible. I was a quarter mile from the ship when the distance stabilized and then, to my great relief, started to increase. She was gaining speed and heading out to sea where she belonged. It was late morning when I reached midtown and the morning sun.

With so much tension released I was almost starting to enjoy some of this huge amount of stimulus. I was taking pictures of all the bridges as I passed under them. After the Brooklyn Bridge, I was relaxing some when I heard this loud, loud horn and looked around to see yet another large vessel right behind and to my starboard side. There was white foam spraying up from its bow as it pushed through the water. I was just out of his path by a few boat lengths. It was a tugboat behind a huge barge. I gave him more room and started paying attention to all that was around me, all of the time. No more cruising for me until I was past the Verrazano-Narrows.

The Staten Island ferry lanes needed to be dealt with soon, too. I stayed between Governor's Island and Brooklyn to avoid the ferry and then on towards the Verrazano and the shipping lanes used by the big boys to get into New York Harbor. I decided to transfer fuel, from my five gallon can to the motor's reservoir. I was near Governor's Island and thought it the place to deal with the fuel, rather than be forced into doing it out under the bridge.

Passing under the Verrazano is intimidating. Before I left, my brother made me promise I would tie a line to myself and the boat in case I fell over. Not bad advice, really. It would be a helluva a thing to watch the boat motor away into the horizon while bobbing around in some fancy self-inflating life vest.

Sandy Hook was just on the other side of the shipping lanes. Some kind of fish must have been running because there were hundreds of fishing boats out there between me and the ships coming into the harbor. The question was whether my speed was right to get across the path of the inbound ships or if I should bear off and deal with their wake as they went by. I had never been behind anything like their size and had no idea what kind of a wake they would be leaving. I chose to get across in front of the first one. It was chest tightening but a good decision once accomplished.

Dealing with the fishing boats was small potatoes in comparison. It was afternoon when I got by them and I could have run up the sail but was still so unsteady about the whole operation I didn't want to do anything differently. "Don't fix it if it's not broken." The wind started coming out of the south and the waves were increasing the nearer I was to Manasquan. By the time I reached the inlet, the water was plenty rough enough for me to know I was no match for the ocean in this boat. The ocean makes one feel insignificant as if it is just waiting for a mistake. It had been a long day starting in the Bronx before six that morning and it was around seven that evening by the time I saw the Manasquan inlet as safety.

I tied up to a slip, refueled, and showered as it was getting dark. There was a decent restaurant in the marina area and I took advantage of it. My hands and arms were swollen with the onset of sun poisoning but I was too exhausted to care. A few beers and some nachos were enough to send me back to the boat to read and sleep. The next morning came quickly enough and I was out again. This time there was no New York ambiance to upstage my poor seamanship.

Southbound from Manasquan along the New Jersey coast is not very inviting to sailboats drawing over four feet, looking for a port. The plan was to make Atlantic City. Poor planning, again, and it was not going to happen in one day under the best of conditions. The Barnegat Inlet is between Atlantic City and Manasquan but not a recommended harbor unless absolutely necessary because of the maze of sandbars and shallow water. I had tow insurance, fortunately, and when the motor died I was closer to the Barnegat Bay Inlet than Manasquan. I was towed to Waretown on the western side of Barnegat Bay and not back to Manasquan.

The motor died from fuel starvation but I wasn't out of gas. The connector fitting at the tank had somehow broken its seal and air entered the feed, which caused the engine to stop. I tried to pull the rope starter but it wouldn't move. I thought the engine had seized. I chose not to pull the starter rope on it anymore for fear of doing more damage. I can usually find my way around motors and mechanical systems but was lost on outboard motors. I had a small sense of relief thinking the engine was cooked and I would have to leave the boat and this voyage on hold for a while. I was tired both mentally and physically. "Fatigue makes cowards of us all."

There was someone at docks where I was towed who certainly knew more than I about outboard motors. He asked if I needed help and he had it running in minutes. He found the leaking fitting, told me I should replace it and then showed me how the engine is made with a safety lock so it won't start in gear. I still had it in the forward gear position. I asked if offering him twenty dollars would be insulting. "Not a problem," he said.

By this time my brother, Duke, who lived an hour away, was coming to my rescue. When he got there the first order of business was to replace the fuel line and fittings properly. I was really a mess with the sun poisoning so he brought me home to sleep at his house in the air conditioning. This was the kind of help I needed and I do hate to admit needing help. The boat and the sun were killing me a little more every day.

Duke drove me to the boat early the next morning and I was off again to Atlantic City. I thought I was close but it took all day to get there partly due to the two hours going from Waretown back out to the ocean. Another six hours and I was into the Atlantic City inlet, which gave me familiar, even secure, feelings. I had seen these buildings many times and it felt good knowing I was close to home. I tied up in a marina and dialed a cab to take me to the bus station. I called Chris from the 552 New Jersey Transit bus asking her to pick me up at a stop near our house. I felt such relief at arriving home and having just one more leg to do. The next morning bright and early she chauffeured me to Atlantic City and I was in Cape May by evening.

Perhaps the worst part of the journey was the realization I was unable to physically sail the boat with any ease at all. I was so unsteady on my feet that moving anywhere on the boat, even just going below, was difficult. I thought the reefing systems, coupled with the lockable steering wheel, would allow me to handle the sails by myself. I had visions of sailing single-handed once I got it to Cape May. As it turned out I wasn't even able to board the sailboat from the rowboat I bought to use at the mooring in Cape May Harbor. The aging process snuck up and when my son got on me for being a spendthrift he seemed right and I felt even more the fool.

My thought was to get one of the sailing instructors at the yacht club to give Chris and me some instruction on the boat in exchange for his use of it. What could happen? There was just such a fellow and I hooked up with him. He was a natural. He sailed a little sunfish boat to the Pearson, tied it to the same mooring and walked right onto mine as if he were strolling through a park. No balance issues whatsoever. He motored to the dock and picked us up. To the ocean we went where there was enough wind to heel it over and get the gunnels in the water. Yes!

The mooring I bought was only a couple of years old and made with first rate materials, but there was another mooring next to mine. Nick, our instructor, mistakenly tied the boat to the other one after he had taken the boat out with a friend. Later in the evening a storm came through Cape May. The Vice Commodore of the yacht club called me the next morning. He told me that my boat was lying on the rocks next to the Coast Guard base. The mooring had failed due to corrosion and it cost me nine hundred dollars to get it towed off of the rocks. I was lucky the hull didn't get damaged. I never told Nick about it. What for?

The sad part of this boat story continues from there. Once September arrived it was time to get the boat "on the hard"—dry land. As is often the result of my MO of trying to squeeze a nickel out of a dollar, I burned myself. The jack stands needed to hold a sailboat upright on land cost a thousand dollars. Remember BOAT? I wasn't doing that. I found an internet posting of plans for a cradle someone had made for a P26 that was "stronger" than jack stands and considerably cheaper.

I made my version of this cradle in the boat yard and insisted it would work well in the face of the doubt expressed by the marina owner. I knew the gentleman, whose sailboat—a museum piece—sat next to mine, was nervous about my boat tumbling onto his. I, of course, would hear none of it. Enter Hurricane Sandy—no problem. No problem because the storm missed Cape May, not because my cradle was so strong.

A few weeks later a Nor'easter came through, blowing in a different direction, and off the cradle my P26 did fall. It didn't hit anyone else's boat, but it was another thousand by the time I got it up and the hull patched. Insurance? That's another one of those nickels I squeezed.

Now the boat was up on jack stands, the hull patched and we were approaching the sailing season. My son and I put a tub of water on the back of my pick-up truck and under the outboard motor, a sweet running Yamaha. It started right up and ran as smooth as could be. A week later someone stole it.

It was time to buy insurance so these things stopped happening. The search for a suitable replacement source of power was costly—BOAT. I have insurance now, what can go wrong?

Michael has taken it out a few times and had a good time on it. That alone has alleviated the bad and foolish feelings I was having. I have even stopped hoping it would sink.

Made in the USA
Middletown, DE
04 May 2022